# TEXTBOOK OF FOOD SCIENCE, NUTRITION AND SAFETY

# Textbook of Food Science, Nutrition and Safety

PRASANTA MUKHERJEE

AMAN PUBLICATIONS
NEW DELHI

*Published by*
Rajiv Jain for Aman Publications
LG-4A, Ganpati Bhawan,
4675-B/21, Ansari Road,
Darya Ganj, Delhi-110002
E-mail: sshjbs@yahoo.com



2018

**Reprint 2025**

**ISBN I978-81-8204-101-1**

SOLE DISTRIBUTOR
**JINDAL BOOK SERVICES**
LG-4A, Ganpati Bhawan,
4675-B/21, Ansari Road,
Darya Ganj, Delhi - 110002

*Jacket Designed by* :
Anshu Gupta

*Printed by:*
Balaji Offest, Delhi, India

# Preface

**The TEXTBOOK FOOD SCIENCE, NUTRITION & SAFETY,** has been written to ensure that the IHM students are able to learn each and every chapter of their syllabus as per the National Council of Hotel Management guidelines.

The key features of the book are: —

- It is written as per the syllabus of hotel management laid down by the Nation Council of Hotel Management (NCHMCT), Noida.
- The book also takes care of the needs of the Diploma students.
- The text book does not burden the students with too much information on any topic because they will also have to learn many other subjects in a short frame of time.
- The text book serves complete purposes of the IHM students.
- The text book includes complete syllabus of the Food Science.
- It also includes complete syllabus of the Nutrition.
- This self-sufficient book will also help all the respected faculties of all the IHMs.
- The text book contains chapter-end review questions which are important.
- The text book contains a list of important terms.
- The text contains Glossary at the end which explains difficult and unusual terms and words and expressions related to the subject.
- This **Textbook on Food Science, Nutrition and Safety** is written exclusively for IHM students that help in the dynamic approach to PBL or Project Based Learning wherever possible. The worthy faculty members of IHMs will get ideas about different projects the students can be involved to make the topics more enjoyable as well as to provide an all-round enriching education. The students will be able to sharpen their research skills with long-lasting deeper knowledge of the subject.

- The text book also contains a question bank at the end which will help the students to know exactly the type of questions that can be framed from different chapters.
- Every chapter outlines at the beginning the purpose or the objectives of the chapter. It helps the students to know what they are going to learn from that particular chapter.

Utmost care had been taken by me while writing this text book to provide correct information on every topic. However any suggestions/reviews for the improvement of the book are most welcome as this will benefit my dearest students.

**PRASANTA MUKHERJEE**

# Acknowledgements

I wish to thank my wife, a sincere teacher, **Mrs. Kuheli Mukherjee**, and my beloved son, a budding engineer, **Prodeepto Mukherjee**, for all their sacrifice, constant support and encouragement that make everything seem easy and possible.

I wish to thank the publisher, **Mr. Rajeev Jain and Mr. Sanjeev Jain** for their valuable suggestions and encouragement which helped me to complete this book.

**PRASANTA MUKHERJEE**

# Contents

## PART THREE: FOOD SAFETY AND QUALITY

# PART ONE
# Food Science

Chapter 1

# Food Science

After reading this chapter, the student will be able to: —

- *Define food science*
- *Know the importance of food science*
- *Know the scope of food science*
- *Understand the inter-relationship of food science with the food chemistry, food microbiology and food processing.*

## INTRODUCTION

The Institute of Food Technologists have defined Food Science as "the discipline in which the engineering, biological, and physical sciences are used to study the nature of foods, the causes of deterioration, the principles underlying food processing, and the improvement of foods for the consuming public".

The Textbook of *Food Science*, defines food science in simpler terms as "the application of basic sciences and engineering to study the physical, chemical, and biochemical nature of foods and the principles of food processing."

When defining food science, we can break the definition down into two parts:

1) Food science involves the study of the physical, biological and chemical composition of different foods, and

2) It involves the concepts of food processing

Food science, therefore, is the branch of applied science that creates and maintains a supply of wholesome food for the human beings.

We can, therefore, say that food science is related to biology, chemical engineering, biochemistry as well as microbiology.

Food scientists ensure that the foods developed by them are both nutritious and safe for human consumption. They also ensure that the food is packaged properly.

It is clear from the above discussion that the study of food science involves physical, biological and chemical makeup of food along with analysis of the causes of food spoilage and concept of processing the food.

## THE IMPORTANCE OF FOOD SCIENCE

The importance of food science cannot be over-emphasised because—

1) The knowledge of food science involves all the food items meant for human consumptions. Therefore, it has a great importance in the food industry as a whole.
2) The food science explains all the chemical changes that take place during cooking. This helps us to understand the food preparation and consumption from scientific angle.
3) The knowledge of food science helps us to ensure adequate supply of safe food for human consumption.
4) The knowledge of food science helps us to build a healthier society through the provision of balanced meals. This helps us to eradicate malnutrition and deficiency disease.
5) The study and research in food science involves many different disciplines such as agriculture, biotechnology, chemistry, genetics, microbiology, nutrition etc. Therefore, the knowledge of food science helps us to understand all this disciplines better and vice versa.
6) The processed food manufacturing industry is based on the application of the knowledge of food science.
7) The study of food science has helped us to develop and produce various foods with prolonged shelf life.
8) The study and research of food science has made tremendous progress in storage & preservation, microbial control, inhibiting the growth of pathogens or disease-causing micro-organisms to provide a supply of safe foods and minimise the spoilage of food.
9) The study and research of food science has helped us to create GM or Genetically Modified foods to yield better quality and quantity of food.
10) The food science and food processing thereby has helped to overcome hunger and diseases, improved food safety, nutrition, convenience, affordability and availability of food to the ever-growing world of mankind.
11) It has equipped us with the knowledge of healthy diet, which in turn has improved self-image and self dignity.
12) It has also helped us to determine, understand and analyse various factors to decide the dietary needs for the citizens of different countries, age, gender, food habits, individual activity level, physiological needs etc.

It is therefore clear from the above-mentioned points that the study of food science has an enormous importance.

## SCOPE FOR FOOD SCIENCE AND NUTRITION IN INDIA

The study of Food Science in the modern days presents far better and wider opportunities than there were in the past.

Following are some of the areas where a food science graduate can work:

- **Food processing companies**: — Food scientists get employment in food processing houses in areas e.g. Research dept., Production dept., Quality Control dept. etc.
- **Hospitals**: — Hospitals also employ graduates in food science for developing therapeutic diets for the patients.
- **Free-lance consultation**: — One may start free-lance consultancy after gaining experience to develop diets for weight gain/loss, disease-related diets for individuals as well as for various organizations.
- **Research and developments (R&D)**: —– Research and Developments is yet another area one can explore. Though, the atmosphere of research and developments in foreign countries are more comfortable than in India.
- **Hotels**: — Chain of hotels employs food scientists to ensure, check and develop proper quality and quantity of nutritious food being served to the elite customers.
- **Food safety Officers**: —Food Safety Officers are employed in different organizations including governments to make sure that food safety guidelines are adhered to by both public and private organizations.
- **Food quality control officers**: —The Food Quality Controller is to ensure that the foods being served to general public at large by different catering organizations are as per the food safety norms as laid down by the government.
- **Academia**: — Those who are interested in academics may join the various institutes and universities all over India (and abroad).
- **MNCs (Multi National Companies)**: — All MNCs dealing with food are highly quality conscious and employ food scientists to help follow the guidelines related to food, hygiene and sanitation in particular as per the country's norms.

The other areas where food scientists can get employments are:

- Analytical testing centers,
- Milk and milk product manufacturing organizations,
- Food production and marketing Units,
- Bakeries & confectioneries,
- Poultry farms,
- Nuts and dry fruits processing industry,
- Frozen food units,
- Food processing division in catering units,
- Distilleries and Breweries,
- Packaging industry etc.

## CHALLENGES

Following are the challenges that need to be kept in mind:

1) **Development of a new product**: —One of the challenges is to develop new products with new ingredients to tackle many common diseases such as cardiovascular disease, Diabetes, Cancer etc.
2) **More pleasant and tasty products**: —Consumers are now expecting every food product to have excellent taste and eye-appeal.
3) **Better quality food product**: — Development of more nutritious food products to create a niche market.
4) **Diversity in food products**: — Ever-demanding market is always looking for more and more varieties of food products.
5) **Convenience food items**: — convenience food items are becoming more popular in the busy urban society.
6) **Cost-effective food products**: —One has to be careful to ensure the cost of the product is competitive.
7) **Ensuring a good supply-chain of foods**: — This is yet another big challenge to ensure timely supply of the food items at the point of sale.
8) **Ensuring food safety and Quality**: — Ensuring food safety, hygiene & sanitation and good quality is yet another big challenge.
9) **Global standard food products**: — As the market is flooded with international standard food products, the challenge is to be competitive in quality, taste and cost.

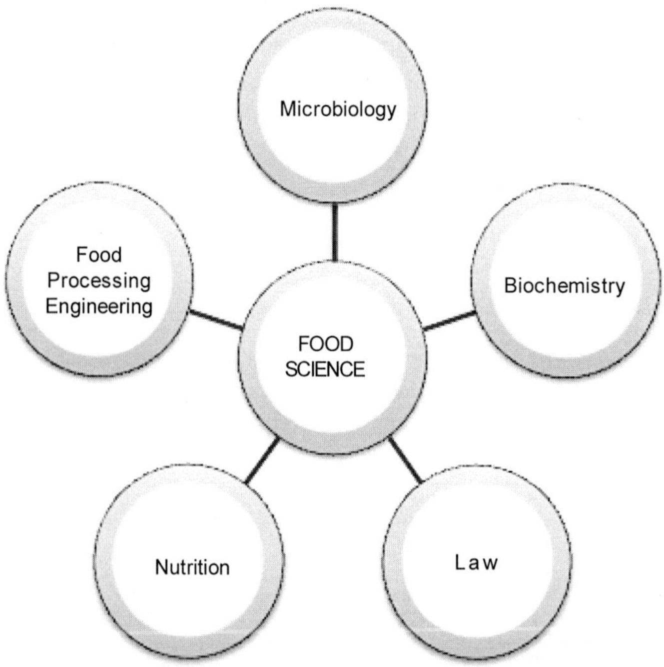


**Diagram: The inter-relationship of food science with other branches of science.**

Overall, food science is a field that is gaining momentum, what with more and more aspirants entering the field, and a wider scope of opportunities available to them. With a fresh lot of companies entering the field, there is a much wider scope for careers and competition together.

## THE INTER-RELATIONSHIP OF FOOD SCIENCE WITH FOOD CHEMISTRY, FOOD MICROBIOLOGY AND FOOD PROCESSING

Food chemistry may be defined as the science that deals with the study of the chemical processes and interactions of all biological and non-biological components of food.

Therefore, this branch of science helps us to understand ——

- The various properties of food items
- The chemical reactions that take place in the food
- The composition of food items
- The structure of the food components.

With the knowledge of all the above aspects of food we can prevent the growth of microorganisms. This will help us to increase the shelf life of food. It will also help us to build a disease free nation.

Food chemistry is the study of both physical and chemical reactions in foods in terms of physical and chemical principles applied to food systems.

Food microbiology may be defined as the branch of science that deals with the study of the various micro-organisms that grow and multiply in the food and contaminates it. It includes the microorganisms responsible for spoilage of food. The beneficial bacteria, such as **probiotics** (the beneficial bacteria and yeasts) are becoming increasingly important in food science. There are micro-organisms which help in the production of various food items such as cheese, curd, bread, wine, beer and many fermented foods and beverages. Therefore, we need to know the various conditions such as temperature, pH level, osmotic pressure etc. in which these microorganisms inhibit and grow. This knowledge will help us to let grow the beneficial microorganisms as well as kill the harmful ones. It is the knowledge of food microbiology that will help us in:

- Food safety,
- Food production,
- Food processing,
- Food preservation, and
- Proper storage of food.

Various microorganisms such as yeasts, moulds, and bacteria are used for the food production. The knowledge of microbiology helps us to improve the flavour of cocoa beans, tea leaves etc. and many alcoholic and fermented drinks.

Food processing may be defined as developing food items in the same or different forms from raw ingredients by employing physical or chemical methods. Thus, food processing develops ready-to-eat or semi-prepared food products. To develop such products various techniques are used. To name a few are Emulsification, Canning, and Pasteurization etc.

Some of the advantages of food processing may be summarised as follows: —

- Preservation
- Removal of toxic component(s)
- Safe and easy distribution of the food product
- Safe and easy marketing of convenience foods
- Proper maintenance of food quality and quantity
- All food items can be made available throughout the year
- The food items can be enriched and fortified to make them more nutritious.
- Ease in transportation to distant areas
- Food quality can be improved by de-activating harmful micro-organisms

## KEY TERMS:

- **Food science** : — The Institute of Food Technologists have defined Food Science as "the discipline in which the engineering, biological, and physical sciences are used to study the nature of foods, the causes of deterioration, the principles underlying food processing, and the improvement of foods for the consuming public".

  The Textbook of *Food Science* , defines food science in simpler terms as "the application of basic sciences and engineering to study the physical, chemical, and biochemical nature of foods and the principles of food processing."

- **Food microbiology**:—— Food microbiology may be defined as the branch of science that deals with the study of the various micro-organisms that grow and multiply in the food and contaminates it. It includes the microorganisms responsible for spoilage of food.
- **Food chemistry**: — Food chemistry may be defined as the science that deals with the study of the chemical processes and interactions of all biological and non-biological components of food.
- **Food processing** : —- Food processing may be defined as developing food items in the same or different forms from raw ingredients by employing physical or chemical methods. Thus, food processing develops ready-to-eat or semi-prepared food products.
- **Probiotics** : — The beneficial bacteria, such as probiotics (the beneficial bacteria and yeasts) are becoming increasingly important in food science. There are micro-organisms which help in the production of various food items such as

cheese, curd, bread, wine, beer and many fermented foods and beverages. Therefore we need to know the various conditions such as temperature, pH level, osmotic pressure etc. in which these microorganisms inhibit and grow. This knowledge will help us to let grow the beneficial microorganisms as well as kill the harmful ones.

## IMPORTANT QUESTIONS

Q. No.1. Define Food Science. Discuss the importance of food science.

Q. No.2. Discuss the scope and challenges of food science.

Q. No.3. Explain the inter-relationship of food science with the food chemistry, food microbiology and food processing.

Chapter 2

# Carbohydrates

After reading this chapter the learner will be able to:

- *Define Carbohydrate*
- *Classify Carbohydrate*
- *Effects of cooking on Carbohydrates*
- *Factors affecting the texture of Carbohydrates*
- *Uses of Carbohydrates in food* preparations

## DEFINITION OF CARBOHYDRATE

Carbohydrates may be defined as a class of chemicals (or Organic Compounds), found in foods, which contain Carbon (hence Carbo), Hydrogen and Oxygen (hence Hydrate). The ratio of Hydrogen and Oxygen in Carbohydrates are always in the proportions found in water i.e. 2:1 or 2H : O

Basic Structure: $C_X(H_2O)_Y$

Important types of Carbohydrates in the foods are: Sugar, Dextrin, Starch, Cellulose, Pectin etc.

## CLASSIFICATION OF CARBOHYDRATES

Carbohydrates

| Monosaccharide | Disaccharides | Oligosaccharides | Polysaccharides |
|---|---|---|---|
| (Glucose, Fructose Galactose) | (Sucrose, Maltose Lactose) | ( Raffinose, Stachyose) | (Starch, Cellulose, Dextrin, Pectin, Gums) |

### Effects of Cooking

**Gelatinization**: When starch is heated with water, it absorbs water, swells, forms a paste and then stiffens forming a gel; this is known as Gelatinization of starch.

As the starch absorbs water and swells forming a paste, this increases the viscosity. Because of this viscosity the starch pastes are used for thickening foods.

The gelatinization process starts vigorously with irreversible changes. The water may be present in the food itself, for example, a baked potato. The gelatinized starch of a dried food item will again absorb water and swell up to the original shape when required. This property of starch is evident in the convenience foods such as Instant Biryani, Instant Rice, Instant Potato, Instant Puddings etc.

The factors that affect the process of Gelatinization are the:

a) **Temperature**—Gelatinization starts at around 55°C. At the waters' boiling point the starch granules may burst and if heated for long the viscosity will reduce.

b) **Proportion of starch to liquid**: With more liquid the viscosity will be reduced.

c) **Types of starch**: The thickening power of starch vary with the foods. The potato having the highest thickening power followed by Corn, rice, wheat etc.

d) **Other added items**: The viscosity is reduced and gel is strengthened by the addition of sugar.

Acid or lime juice thins down the paste.

Addition of fat lowers the gelatinization

Addition of milk lowers the gelatinization temperature.

### Retrogradation

The Amylose (the linear starch) in the cooked starch paste remain in dispersed form and the paste can flow or viscous as long as it is hot. But when the paste cools off the amylose re-bond together and become rigid. This re-crystallization of the gelatinised starch is called Retrogradation.

Wheat and Corn pastes become rigid very fast as the temperature drops. But the rice, potato, tapioca paste becomes rigid slowly and gradually.

## FACTORS AFFECTING THE TEXTURE OF CARBOHYDRATE

Texture of food means those qualities of food that can be felt by the fingers, tongue, palate and teeth. Every food item generally has a particular texture unless there is fault in the quality.

### Stiffness of CHO Gels

The carbohydrate gels become stiff. The Bloom Gelometer is a penetrometer that is used to determine the stiffness of carbohydrate gels. The strength of the gelatine is expressed as degrees Bloom. The properties of Gelatinised potato and gelatinized tapioca starch grains are elastic and cohesive. If however, the starch grains absorb different quantities of water then they will swell also unevenly and form a lumpy texture. The stiffness of the starch gels should be enough, when cooled, that they can be easily unmolded. This is evident in puddings.

### Dextrinization

Dextrins are polysaccharides. The molecular size of dextrins fall in between that of sugar and starch. Dextrins are evident when toast a bread or roast Sevian. Dextrins, therefore, has:

- Colour: Brown
- Flavour: Distinct
- Taste: Sweetish
- Solubility: Soluble in water
- Property: Less thickening power
- Molecular structure: Shorter than Starch but larger than sugar.

When dry heat is applied to starch the starch gets converted into dextrin which is brown in color. This process is known as Dextrinization. This is why the color of the toasts and bread crusts are brown. The flour which has been subjected to dry heat will have less thickening power as some of the starch has got converted into dextrin.

## USES OF CARBOHYDRATES IN FOOD PREPARATION

Following are some of the uses of carbohydrates in the food preparations: -

a) Refined flour or *Maida* is widely used in continental cookery as thickening agent in various sauces and soups,

b) Rice is also used for thickening soups.

c) Corn flour is widely used for thickening soups and sauces in Chinese cooking.

d) Potatoes are used for thickening soups.

e) Tapioca is used for pudding

f) Pre-gelatinised starch is used for Instant Puddings.

g) Pectin is used in Jams and Jellies as setting agent.

h) Caramel is used as colouring and flavouring agent

i) Dextrins are used in coffee extracts.

j) Glucose powder is used in confectionery.

k) Gums are used for thickening, stabilising and gelling agent.

l) Invert sugar is used in preserves.

## DIFFERENCES BETWEEN AMYLOSE AND AMYLOPECTIN

When the glucose units in a molecule exceed a certain number, the resulting high polymer is called "starch". Two types of starch molecules are synthesized by plants:

- When the glucose residues are bonded in a molecule through the alpha-1→4-glycoside linkage, then such a linear starch molecule is called Amylose. But in case of Amylopectin the molecules are branched and has got 1→6-glycoside linkage,. Branching occurs at intervals of 20 to 30 glucose residues.

- This branching in Amylopectin gives it a bushy shrub effect, but the Amylose has a straight line look.
- The Amylopectin are more readily dispersed in water than Amylose.
- The starch grains of most plants consist of approximately one-fourth Amylose molecules and three-fourth Amylopectin molecules.

### What is Syneresis?

The bulk of the water in cooked starch paste is held in the spaces formed by the network of swollen starch grains and precipitated amylase. When a Gel is cut or even as it ages, some of the liquid will seep. This leakage of liquid from a gel is known as Syneresis. The ice crystals present in the network of gel may rapture and cause Syneresis in puddings and pie fillings.

## KEY TERMS

### Organic Compound

- **Starch**: When the glucose units in a molecule exceed a certain number, the resulting high polymer is called "starch".
- **Dextrin**: An important type of carbohydrate found in foods.
- **Gelatinization**: When starch is heated with water, it absorbs water, swells, forms a paste and then stiffens forming a gel; this is known as Gelatinization of starch.
- **Amylose** : The linear starch. When the glucose residues are bonded in a molecule through the 1, 4—linkage, then such a linear starch molecule is called Amylose.
- Amylopectin: In case of Amylopectin the molecules are branched and has got 1, 6—linkage. Branching occurs at intervals of 20 to 30 glucose residues.
- **Retrogradation**: The Amylose (the linear starch) in the cooked starch paste remain in dispersed form and the paste can flow or viscous as long as it is hot. But when the paste cools off the amylose re-bond together and become rigid. This re-crystallization of the gelatinised starch is called Retrogradation.
- **Dextrinization**: When dry heat is applied to starch the starch gets converted into dextrin which is brown in color. This process is known as Dextrinization. This is why the color of the toasts and bread crusts are brown.
- **Syneresis**: The bulk of the water in cooked starch paste is held in the spaces formed by the network of swollen starch grains and precipitated amylase. When a Gel is cut or even as it ages, some of the liquid will seep from the interstices. This leakage of liquid from a gel is known as Syneresis.
- **Viscosity**: The viscosity of a fluid is a measure of its resistance to gradual deformation by shear stress or tensile stress. For liquids it corresponds to the

informal concept of "thickness", e.g. honey has a much higher viscosity than water. Higher viscosity item have higher consistency and lower viscosity product will have lower consistency.

- **Modified Starch**: Modified starch may be defined as starch in which the normal state has been altered either by physical method or chemical method.

## Project Based Learning (PBL)

The students may be directed to visit the nearby grocery store and check the table of nutrient content of mainly Carbohydrate in various

1) Breakfast cereals such as Oats, Porridge, Cornflakes etc.
2) Oats *atta*.
3) Popular brands of biscuits
4) Popular brands of rice
5) Popular brands of infant foods

They should submit the same to their subject teacher within a stipulated period of time.

## IMPORTANT QUESTIONS:

Q.No.1. Define carbohydrate. Classify carbohydrates.

Q.No.2. Explain the effects of cooking on carbohydrates.

Q.No.3. Explain the factors affecting the texture of carbohydrates.

Q.No.4. Explain the uses of carbohydrates in food preparations.

Chapter 3

# Fats and Oils

After reading this chapter, the learner will be able to:

- *Classify fats and oils*
- *Explain Autoxidation, Flavour Reversion, Refining, Hydrogenation and Winterisation.*
- *Understand the effects of heating on fats and oils with respect to smoke point*
- *Know about the Commercial use of fats*

## INTRODUCTION

Fats and oils are organic compounds. They are commonly called Lipids. The fats and oils provide flavour and taste with a greasy touch.

### DIFFERENCE BETWEEN FATS AND OILS:

a) The only difference between fats and oils are that the fats are solid at normal room temperature while oils are liquid. For example, butter, a fat, is solid at room temperature and olive oil is liquid at room temperature.

Similarity between Lipids and Carbohydrates:

a) The lipids and carbohydrates are composed of Carbon, Hydrogen and Oxygen.

b) Carbohydrates and lipids both play the same role of providing energy to the body.

## CLASSIFICATION OF LIPIDS

Lipids can be classified on the basis of their origin as well as the degree of saturation.

### Classification of lipids based on origin

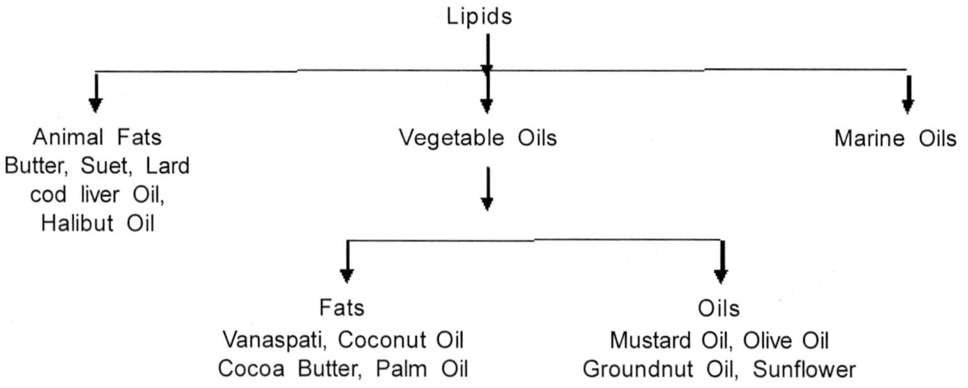


### Classification of Lipids based on degree of Saturation

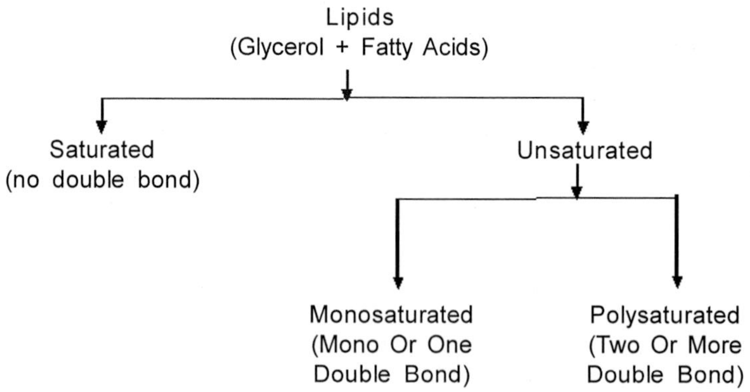


## AUTOXIDATION

Autoxidation may be defined as the oxidation that occurs in the presence of open atmospheric air or in the presence of oxygen and forms Peroxides and Hydroperoxides.

### How to prevent Autoxidation?

Following are the ways to prevent autoxidation:

1. Fats and oils must be stored in dry air-tight containers.
2. Container must not be opened until required.
3. The shape of the container must be narrow to avoid exposure to air and moisture.
4. The container should be stored in a cool and dry place as the fluctuation in temperature or humidity will affect the quality of fats and oils.

While storing food, Lipids may get oxidised due the following factors: -

- Incorrect temperature at which it is stored,
- Contact with Oxygen on the surface area,

- Presence of moisture,
- Presence of light,
- Absence of Antioxidants and
- Presence of Pro-oxidants, etc.

Due to autoxidation or absorption of oxygen present in the atmosphere the properties of fats and oils change and cause Rancidity. The changes that takes place affects the taste of Lipids such as greasy texture, flat taste etc.

## RANCIDITY

Spoilage of fats results in unpleasant flavour and the fat becomes unfit for consumption. These changes are termed as rancidity of fats.

Fats and oils get rancid due to the following factors -

- Air ( Oxidation)
- Water ( Hydrolysis) and
- Enzymes ( Enzymatic Breakdown)
- Temperature.
- Moisture.
- Light.
- Metals.
- Degree of Unsaturation.
- Absence of Antioxidants.

### Types of Rancidity

1) Oxidative Rancidity: Oxidative Rancidity takes place due to oxidation of unsaturated fats and oils. The fats and oils which are unsaturated or having more double bonds are prone to oxidative rancidity in comparison to fats and oils having lesser double bonds. In Oxidative rancidity the oxidation is produces free radicals through chain reactions
2) Hydrolytic Rancidity: Hydrolytic rancidity takes place due to the hydrolysis of Triglyceride molecules producing fatty acids and glycerol, in the presence of moisture. The hydrolytic rancidity may hasten by factors such as Presence of Micro-organism and/or enzymes.

Fats especially polyunsaturated fats may get rancid even at low temperature also.

In wine, autoxidation may take place during aging process due to the presence of Polyphenols, Polysaccharides, and proteins. The Polyphenols form Procyanidin in wines, causing brown colour.

This phenomenon is also observed in carrot puree.

## How to prevent Rancidity?

Rancidity in fats and oils can be prevented. To prevent fats and oils from rancidity one must remember the following points:

- Fats and oils must be stored in a cool and dark place free from moisture.
- Make sure that fat is not kept in a copper or rusted iron container.
- Ensure that the container is air-tight with minimum space left
- No strong smelling food items such as garlic or fish should be around as the smell may be absorbed by the fat.
- Ensure that the opened container has minimum or no exposure to air, moisture, light etc.
- Let only Hydrogenated fats and oils be kept for longer time.
- Commercial fats and oils production units use the following antioxidants to prevent the rancidity---vitamin E, BHT (Butylated Hydroxy Toulene), BHA (Butylated Hydroxy Anisole) or Propyl gallete.

**Differences between Oxidative Rancidity and Hydrolytic Rancidity**

| Oxidative Rancidity | Hydrolytic Rancidity |
|---|---|
| 1. Oxidative rancidity involves oxidation of an unsaturated fatty acid. | 1. Hydrolytic rancidity involves the break-down of fat. |
| 2. In Oxidative rancidity the oxidation of fatty acid produces Hydro peroxide and free radicals. | 2. In Hydrolytic rancidity, glycerol and its component fatty acids are produced. |
| 3. The catalysts for Oxidative rancidity are light and enzymes. (The catalysts increase the speed of reaction.) | 3. The catalysts for Hydrolytic rancidity are heat, moisture and presence of Lipase (enzyme). |

## FLAVOUR REVERSION

It has been noticed that the fats go through changes before it gets rancid. The characteristic flavour of fats is lost just before the onset of rancidity. The taste it turns into can best be described as a flat taste. It also gives a greasy feel. This peculiar change in the fats and oils is termed as Flavour Reversion. This is an indication that the fats and oils are going to get rancid. What happens in the flavour reversion is that an essential fatty acid called Linolenic Acid breaks down through the process of oxidation. This process of oxidation of linolenic acid gives rise to a disagreeable flavour before the onset of rancidity. The Linolenic acid is found in some vegetable oils. Here, we should remember that the cottonseed oil resists this Flavour Reversion

Points to be remembered are:

- Flavour Reversion may take place in both the Hydrolytic Rancidity and Oxidative Rancidity.
- Due to Flavour Reversion change in flavour may start before rancidity.
- Because of FR all types of oils (such as Mustard oils, Groundnut oils, Sunflower oils etc.) may get rancid. A few oils revert such as Fish oils, Soya Bean oils etc.,)
- The flavour change in FR is typical and same for all oils.

- The flavours developed due to FR may be termed as Fishy, Buttery, Greasy, Paint-like etc., primarily depends on the oils which reverts.

The role of different types of fats and oils in cookery:

The role of different types of fats and oils in cookery is mainly based on its composition and properties. For deep frying of foods, liquid fats and oil having higher smoking point is preferred. Whereas, for shortening and tenderizing, solid fats such as butter and margarines are preferred.

Uses of fats in food preparation can be stated as follows:

- It is used as a medium of cooking
- For shortening in cookies, cakes and pastries
- For imparting richness and flavour in foods like *Halwa*, vegetable dishes etc.
- To increase softness or tenderness
- To form emulsions
- Used as spreads

## USES OF FATS AND OILS AS MEDIUM OF COOKING

Due to higher boiling point than water fats and oils are preferred medium as food gets cooked faster. It also imparts a crispy texture and delicate flavor. The higher temperature destroys the disease-causing bacteria, thus making the food safe for consumption as well as the keeping quality also improves. As some fat gets absorbed in the food, the calorific value also increases.

### Uses of fat as a shortening:

Fats and oils help to improve texture as is evident in cookies, gateaux and many Indian fried snacks. The flour do not stick to each other in items such as *Samosas*, *Kachori* and other such items, because of the fat which forms a cover on it. The shortening power will be influenced by the following factors---

- The nature of the fat or oil used,
- The amount of fats or oils used,
- The cooking temperature,
- The other ingredients and their proportions in the product,
- Manipulation and the extent of mixing.

**Differences between Shortening and Leavening agents**

| Shortening Agents | Leavening Agents |
|---|---|
| 1. Shortening Agents are 100% fat derived from vegetable oils. | 1. Leavening agents include yeast, baking soda, baking powder, air, steam etc. |
| 2. Shortening agents are added to make the product softer and flavourful. | 2. This helps to make the product fluffy and causes expansion by the release of gases. |
| 3. There is no gas formation, so the product does not become porous in structure. But makes the product non-elastic. | 3. The product becomes porous in structure. |

The factors that will affect the shortening power of fats are----

- The nature of fat: The fats with higher unsaturation will have higher shortening power. Greatest shortening power means greatest surface area of flour covered in a particular product.
- Concentration of the fat: Higher the concentration of the fat, higher will be the shortening power. This is evident in butter and hydrogenated fat, where the latter has more shortening strength.
- Temperature: Fats tends to become harder at lower temperature. It becomes less plastic at higher temperature. Therefore, the temperature plays a role.
- Other ingredients in the fats:- Presence of other ingredients in the fats will influence the shortening strength of the fats. This is evident in the case of a mixture of oils and fats with the egg yolk. The emulsified mixture has less shortening strength.
- Manipulation of fats: The shortening power of fats alter when it is mixed with flour or beaten or during creaming, rolling etc.
- Uses of fats as a seasoning: Fats and oils are widely used as a seasoning ingredients in many food preparations. Fats and oils are also used in various Indian sweet dishes.

## WINTERISATION

Winterization of oils is done after Steam Deodorisation. Winterization is a process in which oils are quickly cooled, ensuring no movement, so that the crystals of triglycerides fall apart and chilled, viscous oil is obtained. This pre-cooling treatment to remove fat crystals is known as Winterisation. This oil obtained now is termed as Winterised. Such oils are mainly used for salad dressings. Rice bran oil is the most commonly winterised oil since it contains a lot of waxes, lipids and fatty acids. The winterised oils thus obtained remains liquid even when refrigerated. So the winterised oil is more preferred in the cold kitchen for using in salads and Mayonnaise etc. cottonseed oils and Peanut oils may be winterised to retain the typical flavour associated to it.

### Differences between Winterisation and Homogenisation:—

1. Winterisation of oils is done to remove fat crystals

   Homogenisation is a process by which an emulsion of two

   Immiscible liquid is formed.

2. Winterisation is done for oils. Winterised oil remains liquid even when refrigerated e.g. oils used in Mayonnaise.

   Homogenisation is done in milk in which the fat globules are decreased in size so that they remain dispersed in the liquid.

**Differences between Winterisation and Fractionation**

| Winterisation | Fractionation |
|---|---|
| 1. Winterisation is carried out in a pre-cooling, refrigeration temperature. | 1. Fractionation is carried out at a desired temperature. |
| 2. In Winterisation, triglyceride is crystallised and separated by filtration at refrigeration temperature. It is often termed as Dry Fractionation. | 2. In Fractionation, the melting fraction of a mixture of the triglyceride is separated depending on the solubility at a particular temperature. |

## REFINING

The objectives of refining of fats and oils are to prevent degradation, to eliminate undesirable components, elimination of undesirable products, to preserve vitamins, deduce losses etc. The components responsible for the colour and flavor of the fats are the non-glyceride components. Other materials also contribute undesirable characteristics to fats which are meant for human consumptions:

Free fatty acids (FFA), Waxes, Colour pigments, Phospholipids (gums), Carotenoids, Gossypol found only in cottonseed oil).

### Other impurities

#### *Alkali Refining*

Most of the above-mentioned materials are separated by treating fats with solution of soda ash or Caustic Soda at 40 to 80°C. Such treatment, called Refining is carried out in tanks, so, it is also termed as Tank Refining or Batch Refining. The oils refined in this process display following characteristics-

- It is neutral i.e. it is neither acidic nor alkaline,
- It is free from materials e.g. waxes, phospholipids, colour pigments etc.
- It has lighter colour
- Has lesser viscosity
- More chance for rancidity

#### *Water Refining*

Water refining, usually called Degumming, consists of treating the natural oil with a small amount of water, followed by centrifugal separation.

(Degumming is a step in water refining by which natural gums are removed from oils. The fat-protein complexes and Phospholipids are called gums).

## HYDROGENATION

Hydrogenation may be defined as a process by which the oils in the liquid state are converted into solid fats by the addition of Hydrogen. Thus Oleic acid or Linoleic acid or their acid radicals in Glycerides, which are normally liquid at room temperature, can be converted to Stearic acid or the acid radical by the addition of hydrogen. Hydrogenation is done in all countries where margarines and shortenings are produced from liquid oils.

Hydrogenation reactions are carried out, in commercial practice, with vigorous agitation in a steel vessel at a 100-200°C temperature and 42kg/cm$^2$ atmospheric pressure.

### Remember the similar terminologies

**Hydration**: — Hydration is a process in which water molecule or $H_2O$ is added to a compound. The compound combines with water.

$$C_2H_2 + H_2O \longrightarrow CH_3CHO$$

**Hydrolysis**: —Hydrolysis is a process in which water molecule breaks down a compound through chemical reaction.

$$CH_3COOH_3 + H_2O \longrightarrow CH_3COOH + CH_3OH$$

Note that in Hydration there is no breakdown of the compound. But in case of Hydrolysis water breaks down the compound to a smaller molecule.

**Dehydrogenation:** — This is a chemical reaction by which the hydrogen is separated from organic molecules.

### The Effect of Heating on Fats and Oils with respect to Smoke Point

Fats, when heated, gradually reach the melting point and soften.

When heated further, fats first smoke, and this temperature is called smoke point.

Further heating leads to flash and this temperature is called flash point.

After the flash it burns and this temperature is called the fire point.

The smoke point of an oil or fat may be defined as the temperature at which, under defined conditions, enough volatile compounds emerge when a bluish gas or smoke becomes clearly visible from the oil. At this temperature, volatile compounds, such as free fatty acids, and short-chain degradation products of oxidation come up from the oil. The smoke point indicates the temperature limit up to which that cooking oil can be used. It is important for commercial cooking.

The smoke point correlates with the amount of free fatty acid in oil. It varies widely, depending on origin and refinement.

The smoke points of olive oil is 226-242°C

The smoke point of Canola oil is 204-224°C

The smoke point of Vegetable oil is 232°C

The smoke point of Peanut oil is 227-232°C

The smoke point of Butter is 170°C

The smoke point of Vegetable shortening is 180°C

Heating the oil produces free fatty acid and thus heating time increases, more free fatty acids are produced, thereby decreasing smoke point. It is one reason not to use the same oil to deep fry more than twice Intermittent frying has a greater effect on oil deterioration than continuous frying.

### Commercial uses of fats (with emphasis on shortening value)

Shortening is a tenderizer. Shortenings in some recipes are beaten to incorporate air in it. Shortenings, fats and oils of animal or vegetable origin, are used in most dough and batters to impart crisp and crumbly texture to baked products. It is used in dough to increase the plasticity, or workability. Shortenings are not fit for deep fat frying because they have low smoke point.

Important commercial shortenings include

- Butter,
- Lard,
- Vegetable oils,
- Processed shortenings, and
- Margarine.

For most baking purposes, desirable characteristics of lipids include:

- Bland or pleasant flavour;
- Forms emulsion
- No objectionable odour;
- Light or clear colour;
- A high degree of plasticity;
- Long storage life
- Shortening power (or ability to weaken and lubricate the structure of baked products to produce tenderness).

Firm fats produce flaky pastry, oils yield more compact pastry. The proportion of shortening in dough and batters varies according to the product, with breads and rolls containing about 1-2 % and cakes containing 10-20%. Increasing shortening proportions increases tenderness, but very high proportions may cause cakes to fall.

### KEY TERMS

- Lipids: Fats and oils are organic compounds, they are commonly called Lipids.
- Autoxidation: Autoxidation may be defined as the oxidation that takes place in open air or in the presence of oxygen and forms peroxides and hydro-peroxides.
- Rancidity: - Spoilage of fats results in unpleasant flavour and the fat becomes unfit for consumption. These changes are termed as rancidity of fats.

- Oxidative Rancidity: Oxidation of Unsaturated Fats (Oils) leads to oxidative rancidity.
- Hydrolytic Rancidity: It is the hydrolysis of Triglyceride molecules to glycerol and fatty acids in the presence of moisture. The process of hydrolysis may get faster due to the presence of microorganisms and/or enzymes.
- Flavour reversion: -The Fats undergo peculiar changes before it gets rancid. The characteristic flavour associated is lost and the fat and oil has a flat taste and a greasy feel on the tongue. This is known as flavour reversion and precedes rancidity changes.
- Winterization: Winterization is a process in which oils are quickly cooled ensuring no movement so that the crystals of Triglycerides fall apart and chilled, viscous oil is obtained. This pre-cooling treatment to remove fat crystals is known as Winterization. And this oil is said to be winterized.
- Hydrogenation: Hydrogenation may be defined as a process by which the oils in the liquid state are converted into solid fats by the addition of Hydrogen.
- Melting Point: Fats when heated gradually reach the melting point and softens.
- Flash Point: Further heating leads to flash and is called flash point.
- Fire Point: After the flash it burns and is called the fire point.
- The smoke point: The smoke point of an oil or fat is the temperature at which, under defined conditions, enough volatile compounds emerge when a bluish gas or smoke becomes clearly visible from the oil.
- Hydrolysis: Hydrolysis is a process in which the triglycerides in fat splits into their basic components of glycerol and fatty acids in the presence of atmospheric moisture. This is how the fats get degraded. This fatty acid produces bad odours and rancidity.
- Hydrolytic Rancidity: Hydrolysis is a process in which the triglycerides in fat splits into their basic components of glycerol and fatty acids in the presence of atmospheric moisture. This is how the fats get degraded. This fatty acid produces bad odours and rancidity. This type of rancidity is different than the Oxidative Rancidity and is called Hydrolytic Rancidity.
- Hydrogenation: Hydrogenation is a process of adding hydrogen to an oil, by chemical means, to saturate the fatty acids which converts the oil in to a solid. This process is particularly helpful in converting a vegetable oil in to a solid shortening.

## PROJECT BASED LEARNING (PBL):

The students may be instructed to visit the nearby supermarket and note down the names of various

1) Brand names and the name of the manufacturing companies of fats and oils mostly consumed in households.

2) Compare the ingredients
3) Compare the prices
4) Check the brands mostly used in various local hotels and restaurants.
5} Prepare a chart and submit the same to your subject teacher.

**IMPORTANT QUESTIONS:**

Q. No. 1. Classify fats and oils.

Q. No. 2. Explain the following:

a) Autoxidation
b) Flavour Reversion
c) Refining
d) Hydrogenation
e) Winterization
f) Smoke Point

Q. No. 4. Explain the commercial uses of fats.

Chapter 4

# Protein

After reading this chapter, the student will be able to:

- *Learn the basic structure of protein*
- *Learn the properties of protein*
- *Explain types of proteins based on their origin (plant/animal)*
- *Learn the effects of heat on proteins (Denaturation, Coagulation)*
- *Explain various Functional Properties of proteins (Gelation, Emulsification, Foamability, Viscosity)*
- *Know Commercial uses of proteins in food preparations*

## INTRODUCTION

Proteins are made by amino acids. The amino acids are made up mainly of Carbon, Hydrogen, Oxygen and Nitrogen. Though, Sulfur and other elements are also found in some amino acids.

The reason that proteins are very important for our life can easily be understood by the fact that it is essential for formation of skin, nails, cartilage, hair and muscles.

Proteins are primary component of:

- Enzymes
- Antibodies
- Hormones
- Blood

## BASIC STRUCTURE AND PROPERTIES OF PROTEIN

The linear sequence of amino acids in the polypeptide chain is referred as the **primary structure** of a protein. This primary structure is maintained by the covalent bonds such as peptide bonds. The Primary structure and the peptide bond is shown below:

## PRIMARY STRUCTURE

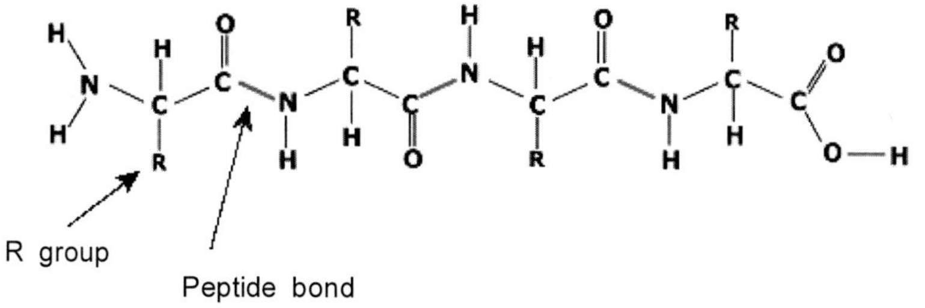


## SECONDARY STRUCTURE

The **secondary structure** consists of 3D arrangements on a localized region of the protein backbone (N-C-C-N-C-C). The secondary protein folding also includes two distinct structures known as:

- Apha helices and
- Beta sheets.

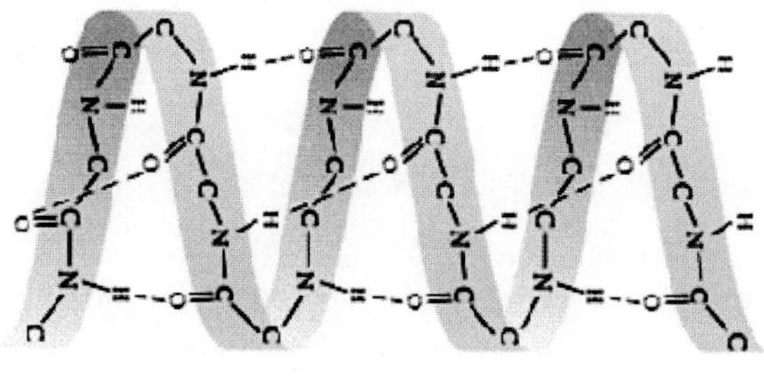

The secondary structure packed into compact globular regions termed as protein domains is the tertiary structure of protein.

## TERTIARY STRUCTURE

The Tertiary structure has only one Polypeptide. More than one will form Quaternary Structure. The tertiary protein domains are formed by Disulfide, Hydrogen, Ionic bonds and Hydrophobic interaction.

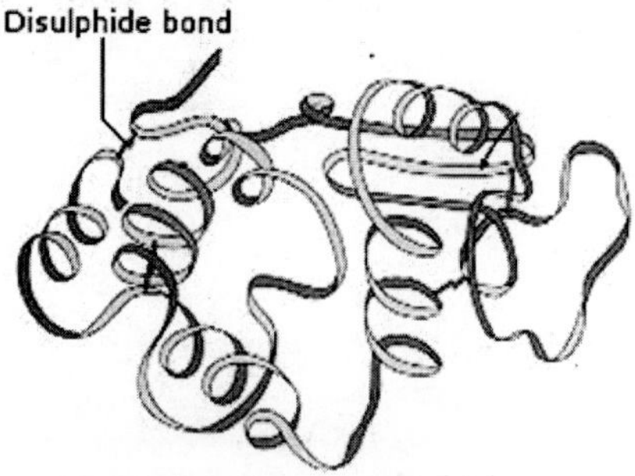


**Tertiary Structure**

## QUATERNARY STRUCTURE

**The Four Lavels of Protein Structure**

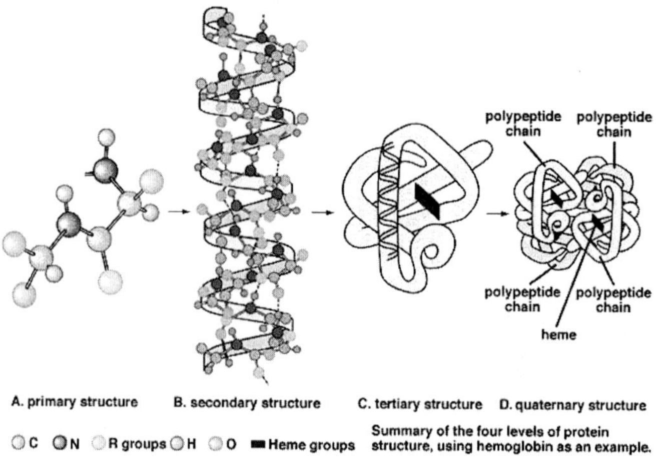


Summary of the four levels of protein structure, using hemoglobin as an example.

## PROPERTIES OF PROTEINS

- Proteins are made of Amino Acids. Amino acids are joined by peptide bonds.
- The amino acids are made up of Carbons, Hydrogen, Oxygen, Nitrogen and Sulphur.
- Proteins are found in enzymes which increase the rate of chemical reactions in our body. Therefore, proteins act as a catalyst.
- Proteins transport various substances to the cell membranes.
- Proteins structure provides support to cells.
- Proteins are main components of antibodies. It provides defence mechanism against the pathogens.
- It is the main component of hormones in our body.
- It responds to chemical stimuli.
- Isoelectric point——The +ve and –ve charged molecular species represent equal concentration or the number of negative and positive charge balance each other. Hence the protein molecule is said to be in "Isoelectric Point".
- Electrophoresis —Electrophoresis is a technique by which the distribution of charged species can be shown by noting the movement of solute molecules in an electric field.
- Denaturation——When the unique spatial arrangements of the helix or the polypeptide chain are altered, a protein molecule is said to be Denatured.

## FUNCTIONAL PROPERTIES OF FOOD PROTEINS

**The functional properties of a protein are:** "Those physical and chemical properties, which affect the behaviour of proteins in food systems during storage, processing, preparation and consumption. It is these characteristics, which influence the 'quality' and organoleptic attributes in food."

The functional properties of a protein are affected by Intrinsic factors e.g. shape, size, amino acid composition and sequence, the distribution of net charges, the ratio between **hydrophobicity (water heating/hydrophilicity (water loving)**, secondary, tertiary and quaternary structures of the protein as well as the protein's capacity to interact with other components in the food system..

The extrinsic factors that affect the functionality of proteins are: pH value, temperature level, moisture level, quantity and types of chemical additives, mechanical processing, enzymes etc.

The three most important functional properties of food proteins in general are solubility, emulsification and foaming.

### Types of proteins based on their origin (plant/animal)

1) **Animal/Complete Proteins**: A Complete protein is the one that contains all of the essential amino acids required for life and growth from this sole source in right amounts and proportions. The Biological Value of these proteins are very high. These proteins are found in animal foods such as poultry, fish, meat, milk and eggs. But gelatine contains limited amounts of Isoleucine, Threonine and Methionine and zero Tryptophan.

2) **Plant Proteins/Incomplete proteins**: Plant proteins are generally not as high in Biological value as the Animal proteins. This is because they have amino acid limitations. For example the wheat, rice, corn lacks the amino acid called Lysine. Legumes have a limited amount of Methionine. Such incomplete proteins may be blended with supplements to fulfil the need of the body. A blend of plant and animal proteins can overcome the limitations also.

## EFFECTS OF HEAT ON PROTEINS

Effects of heat on protein are demonstrated in the form of Denaturation and Coagulation. Both are discussed below.

### Denaturation

**Denaturation** is a process in which proteins or amino acids loose the structure (secondary structure, quaternary structure and tertiary structure) which is present in their Native state, by application of some external stress or compound such as a strong acid or base, radiation or heat etc. When a protein is denatured, secondary and tertiary structures are altered but the Peptide Bond of the primary structure between the amino acids are left intact. Sometimes such a change is required and is initiated in food preparation. But in some cases it is prevented.

These bonds get disrupted in many ways for example:

- Heating a protein dispersed in water
- High concentration of salt
- Acidity
- Spreading in thin film e.g. foaming
- Reducing agents

If proteins in a living cell are denatured, this results in disruption of cell activity and possibly cell death. Protein denaturation is also a consequence of cell death. When an egg is cooked, the white of egg which is Albumin becomes hard and insoluble.

When food is cooked, some of its proteins become denatured. This is why boiled eggs become hard and cooked meat becomes firm.

A classic example of denaturing in proteins comes from egg whites, which are typically largely albumin in water. Egg whites are transparent and liquid. Cooking the white of egg turns them opaque, forming an interconnected solid mass. The same transformation can be effected with a denaturing chemical. Pouring egg whites into a beaker of Acetone will also turn egg whites translucent and solid. When a protein is denatured, secondary and tertiary structures are altered but the Peptide Bond of the primary structure between the amino acids are left intact. Since all structural levels of the protein determine its function, the protein can no longer perform its function once it has been denatured..

How Denaturation occurs at levels of protein structure

- In **quaternary structure** denaturation, protein is dissociated and/or the spatial arrangement of protein is disrupted.
- **The Tertiary structure** denaturation involves the disruption of covalent interactions, Non-covalent interactions and Van Der Waals interactions.
- In **secondary structure** denaturation, proteins lose all regular repeating patterns
- Primary Structure, such as the sequence of amino acids held together by covalent peptide bonds, is not disrupted by denaturation

**Loss of function due to Denaturation:** Most biological substrates lose their biological function when denatured. For example, Enzymes lose their activity.

## REVERSIBILITY AND IRREVERSIBILITY

In very few cases, denaturation is reversible (the proteins can regain their native state when the denaturing influence is removed). This process can be called renaturation.

### Various Denaturants

Acids: Acidic protein denaturants include: Acetic Acid,

Bases: Bases work similarly to acids in denaturation e.g. Sodium Bi-carbonate.

Solvents: Most organic solvents are denaturing, including: Ethanol.

Physical: Thermal denaturation, Beads mill, Radiation.

## COAGULATION

Unfolding of protein molecule exposes the reactive groups along the polypeptide chains when it is denatured. Rebinding between the reactive groups on the same or on adjacent denatured protein molecules may follow. When this rebonding takes place and enough molecules unite so that the protein is no longer dispersed as a sol, the protein is said to be Coagulated.

Coagulation of the protein of the muscle fibers converts the colloidal sol into a gel and causes the fibers to shrink. The higher the temperature of the meat and the longer the cooking time the coagulation will be more and the meat will be less juicy.

The coagulation of egg starts just after denaturation, when heated. The egg white, the transparent viscous sol, when heated , coagulates to form an opaque, white gel.

The pH of fresh milk is 6.6. Lowering of the pH of milk as acid accumulates disrupts the stability may result in coagulation of the milk.

The main ingredients in custard are eggs, sugar, milk. Higher temperature is required to coagulate the egg because the protein in egg is diluted with milk. Two egg yolks instead of one will require more temperature for coagulation.

## FUNCTIONAL PROPERTIES OF PROTEINS

The main functional properties of proteins are Hydration (i.e. Solubility and viscosity):

### Protein

Protein interaction (i.e. Gelation and Precipitation) and Surface Properties (i.e. Foaming and Emulsification).

### Gelation

The globular proteins' gelling properties are of great importance in foods. Protein gelation is one of the most acceptable functional properties for the modification of texture of food items. It is due to the gelation of eggs that items like cakes, omelets and confectionery acquire acceptable texture. Globular proteins e.g. egg white and soybean protein, form gels on heating . For a gel to form it is important that the functional groups (e.g. hydrophobic groups) within the protein are exposed. This makes it easier for the groups to interact and form a three dimensional network.

Gel formation is complicated, and affected by:

- The concentration of protein,
- Amount of water,
- Ionic strength,
- Time

- Temperature
- pH and
- Interaction with other components in the food system.

The process for **gelation** in short, is:

Native protein ⇨ Protein Denaturation ⇨ Gel formation

The heat will make the native protein to denaturate, and during the denaturation, disulfide bonds will be formed and hydrophobic amino acid residues are exposed. After denaturation and further heating, the proteins will aggregate and interact with other proteins and form either a gel or a coagulum. Which type that is formed depends on conditions like molecular weight, heating time and protein concentration?

## SOLUBILITY

The solubility of a protein is the most important functional property since the protein needs to be soluble in order to be applicable in food systems. Other functional properties like emulsification, foaming, and gelation are dependent on the solubility of proteins. Solubility can be described as when equilibrium exists between hydrophilic and hydrophobic interactions. The solubility of a protein is related to the pH, where it is minimal at the isoelectric point, making the environmental pH the most important factor when it comes to the degree of protein solubility. The solubility is also influenced by temperature and ionic strength, (Bolontrade et al., 2013). Freezing, heating, drying and shearing are also factors that have an influence of protein solubility in food systems (Vaclavik and Christian, 2003). Insoluble proteins are not good for food applications and thus it is important that denaturation caused by e.g. heat is controlled so that the protein solubility not will be affected in a negative way (Raikos et al., 2007).

## EMULSIONS

The word "emulsion" has been derived from the Latin word "to milk", the reason being milk is an emulsion of fat and water.

An **emulsion** can be described as a mixture of two or more liquids that are un-mixable. Emulsions are part of a more general class of two-phase systems of matter termed as Colloids. But in culinary world the term Emulsion is used as both phases, dispersed and continuous, are liquids. Therefore, in an emulsion, one liquid or the dispersed phase dispersed in the another phase or the continuous phase.

Emulsion in the food production can take two different forms:

- Fat dispersed into water and
- Water dispersed into fat.

Common fat in water emulsifications include hollandaise, mayonnaise, aioli, milk, cream, and pan sauces.

Other examples include Mayonnaise Sauce, Vinaigrette Sauce etc.

To get a stable emulsion (both in a short and long term perspective) it is of great importance to add an emulsifier. An emulsifier is a surface-active molecule that allows the two phases to homogenize. Surface-active molecules are mostly amphophilic i.e. they have both hydrophobic and hydrophilic parts, which allow the two liquids to blend together.

## Foaming

Foams consist of bubbles of gas phase, a liquid phase and a surfactant such as proteins and whipping or shaking form foams. It is the bubbles of gas trapped in a liquid wherein the liquid is in continuous phase and the gas in dispersed phase. The examples of foaming in the culinary world are—

- Whipped toppings,
- Meringues,
- Ice creams,
- Chiffon desserts and
- Angel cakes (solid foam).

Foams are formed through unfolding and absorption of the protein, at the air-water interface, as well as film formation around the air bubbles.

Different proteins have different abilities to form and stabilize foams, and just as in the case of proteins and their different emulsifying properties. Foaming is one of the physical properties of the proteins. Good foaming property of a protein is determined by its solubility and gas trapping quality.

The factors that affect the foaming properties are

- pH,
- Temperature and
- Iconic strength.

The stability of Foam depends on the proteins ability to form a rigid film around the trapped bubble of gas so that it does not break. The surface tension is a determinant in this case.

## Viscosity

The viscosity of a fluid is a measure of its resistance to gradual deformation by shear stress or tensile stress. For liquids it corresponds to the informal concept of "thickness", e.g. honey has a much higher viscosity than water. Higher viscosity item have higher consistency and lower viscosity product will have lower consistency.

The high proportion of polar residues confers on gelatine molecules great affinity for water. As a sol of gelatine cools it becomes more viscous. The effectiveness of gelatine as a gelling agent comes from its unique amino acid make up.

## COMMERCIAL USES OF PROTEINS IN DIFFERENT FOOD PREPARATIONS

Now-a-days the animal, plant and microbial proteins are extracted and then modified used in many manufactured food products. This is because not only proteins have great nutritional value but also displays many functional properties such as solubility, viscosity, elasticity, dispensability, foam ability, emulsifying effects etc.

**Egg gels**: Ovalbumin, the main protein in egg white, is a globular protein readily denatured by heat. Egg white coagulated by heat changes from a transparent viscous sol to an opaque, white gel as the water in the white is trapped by the protein.

Eggs act as

- an emulsifier in Mayonnaise sauce and cheese Souffle
- As a gelling agent in Custards
- As a coating agent in Croquettes
- As a thickening agent in Pie
- As a structural material in Cakes.
- As a means of incorporating air in Meringues, sponges, Angel cakes etc.

### Gelatine Gels

Gelatine molecules contain high proportions of three groups of amino acids. The use of gelatine in the commercial food preparation cannot be overemphasized.

Following are the ways Gelatine is used in the food preparations:

- Gelatine is used as an agent to increase the viscosity of cream which is otherwise too thin to be whipped.
- Gelatine is used as a stabiliser to prevent the growth of large crystals in the ice cream.
- It is used as a setting agent in moulded gelatine desserts (plain or with fruits), in moulded vegetable salads and aspics, sponges and creams.
- As a gelling agent in various foods as one part gelatine can set 99 parts of water by weight.

### Cakes

**Sponge and Angel cakes** are sometimes referred to as 'foam' cakes. The reason being foam is formed first by beating the egg whites and then adding sugar. The best description should be 'meringue' cake. The coagulated egg protein helps to form the structure of these cakes.

### Meringue

Lesser number of ingredients is required for meringue types of cakes than the angel cakes. Sugar is added to the beaten eggs to stabilize the foam.

### Confectionery items

Confectionery items are divided into two categories—

- Sugar-based e.g. nuggets, fondants, caramels, toffees and jellies.
- Chocolate-based e.g. chocolate covered fruits, nuts, creams and chocolate bars etc.

The ingredients used are milk products, egg whites, starch, fats, nuts etc. The proteins in gelatine and egg white confer the whipping and toughening properties e.g. Marshmallows and Nuggets.

### Custards

The ingredients in Custards are eggs, sugar, milk and flavors. Molecules of protein of egg get denatured by the heat and encompass the fluid milk to form a gel. This property is used to manufacture powdered egg custard in commercial food production.

### TVP or Textured Vegetable Protein

Textured protein items or Protein Analogs are produced from Plant Proteins. The examples of TVP include protein from Soya beans, groundnuts, oilseeds etc. from which oil has been removed. TVPs are excellent alternatives of animal proteins for the vegetarians. Such proteins are also extracted from grass, green vegetables, yeasts, bacteria etc., and tastes equally good as meat. Soya beans and other such items are available through various brands in the markets; they also come in inexpensive packets in the form of balls, nuggets and granules.

Some other important terms:

### Native Proteins

Native proteins are the proteins found in the cells and in its fluids of the living tissues of the plants and animals.

### Biological Value or BV

Biological Value may be defined as the proportion of nitrogen absorbed that is retained by the body for the growth and maintenance. This helps to determine the Protein Quality.

## KEY TERMS

- *Protein*: Proteins are made by amino acids. The amino acids are made up mainly of Carbon, Hydrogen, Oxygen and Nitrogen. Though, Sulfur and other elements are also found in some amino acids.
- *Biological Value or BV*: Biological Value may be defined as the proportion of nitrogen absorbed that is retained by the body for the growth and maintenance. This helps to determine the Protein Quality.
- *Native Proteins*: Native proteins are the proteins found in the cells and in its fluids of the living tissues of the plants and animals.

- *Viscosity:* The viscosity of a fluid is a measure of its resistance to gradual deformation by shear stress or tensile stress. For liquids it corresponds to the informal concept of "thickness", e.g. honey has a much higher viscosity than water. Higher viscosity item have higher consistency and lower viscosity product will have lower consistency.
- TVP *or Textured Vegetable Protein*: Textured protein items or Protein Analogs are produced from Plant Proteins. The examples of TVP include protein from Soya beans, groundnuts, oilseeds etc. from which oil has been removed.
- *Foaming*: Foams consist of bubbles of gas-phase, a liquid-phase and a surfactant such as proteins and whipping or shaking form foams. It is the bubbles of gas trapped in a liquid wherein the liquid is in continuous phase and the gas in dispersed phase.
- *Emulsions*: The word "emulsion" has been derived from the Latin word "to milk", the reason being milk is an emulsion of fat and water. An emulsion can be described as a mixture of two or more liquids that are un-mixable. Emulsions are part of a more general class of two-phase systems of matter termed as Colloids.
- *Coagulation*: Unfolding of protein molecule exposes the reactive groups along the polypeptide chains when it is denatured. Rebinding between the reactive groups on the same or on adjacent denatured protein molecules may follow. When this rebonding takes place and enough molecules unite so that the protein is no longer dispersed as a sol, the protein is said to be Coagulated.
- *Denaturation*: Denaturation is a process in which proteins or amino acids lose the structure (secondary structure, quaternary structure and tertiary structure) which is present in their Native state, by application of some external stress or compound such as a strong acid or base, radiation or heat etc. When a protein is denatured, secondary and tertiary structures are altered but the Peptide Bond of the primary structure between the amino acids are left intact.
- *Isoelectric point*: The +ve and –ve charged molecular species represent equal concentration or the number of negative and positive charge balance each other. Hence the protein molecule is said to be in "Isoelectric Point".
- *Electrophoresis:* Electrophoresis is a technique by which the distribution of charged species can be shown by noting the movement of solute molecules in an Animal/Complete Proteins: A Complete protein is the one that contains all of the essential amino acids required for life and growth from this sole source in right amounts and proportions. The Biological Value of these proteins are very high. These proteins are found in animal foods such as poultry, fish, meat, milk and eggs. But gelatine contains limited amounts of Isoleucine, Threonine and Methionine and zero Tryptophan.
- *Plant Proteins/Incomplete proteins:* Plant proteins are generally not as high in Biological value as the Animal proteins. This is because they have amino acid limitations. Electric field.

## PROJECT BASED LEARNING (PBL)

The students may be given the following tasks:

1) A chart may be prepared showing the percentage of protein contents of the specific food items mainly used in the catering industry e.g. milk, eggs, chicken, mutton, pulses, gelatine, *paneer*, soybeans etc.
2) A chart may be prepared showing how proteins in food are used in the kitchen as well as in the food and beverage processing industry.

## IMPORTANT QUESTIONS:

Q.No.1. Discuss the various properties of protein.

Q.No.2. Explain the types of proteins based on their origins.

Q.No.3. Explain the effects of heat on protein.

Q.No.4. What are the functional properties of proteins?

Q.No.5. Explain the commercial use of protein in food preparation.

Chapter 5

# Food Processing

After reading this chapter, the learner will be able to:

- *Define Food Processing*
- *State the objectives and benefits of food processing*
- *Learn various types of treatments of food processing*
- *Understand the effects of factors like heat, acid, alkali on food constituents.*

## INTRODUCTION

Food processing may be defined as the conversion of raw food ingredients into food by using physical or chemical means. Therefore food processing is a technique in which ready-to-eat or convenience food products are produced for a target market from various raw ingredients. Food processing may include various common operations such as agitating, blending, beating, mincing, emulsifying, pasteurization, homogenizing, kneading, stirring, whipping, various cooking methods etc. other than cleaning, coating, concentrating, disintegrating, drying, evaporation fermentation et al.

## OBJECTIVES AND BENEFITS OF FOOD PROCESSING

Food processing has paved way for many industries, giving lots of job opportunities to the population. It has eliminated seasonal food choice and provided many tasty, ready-to-eat food items available throughout the year. Some of the benefits and objectives of food processing are given below:

1) Toxin elimination: Food processing helps to kill various pathogens such as Salmonella, present in the raw ingredients. Thus it helps to make the food safe to eat and reduces the food borne diseases.
2) Preservation: Food processing makes the food less prone to spoilage and increases the shelf-life.
3) Easy marketing: Marketing of processed food is comparatively easy because of its increased shelf-life. As the food is not going to get spoiled soon so the marketing people get enough time to sell the product and will enjoy less pressure.

4) Easy Distribution: Easy Distribution and transportation is another benefit.
5) Increases food consistency: It helps maintain quality and quantity consistency.
6) Elimination of seasonality of food --It helps to get many seasonal food items readily available throughout the year. Thus, it helps in eliminating seasonality of foods.
7) Enables transportation and Distribution of delicate perishable foods across long distances: Transportation and distribution of exotic perishable foods has enabled the modern buyers an easy access which was not possible earlier.
8) Variety in diet for the present day demanding customers: The extremely varied modern diet is only truly possible on a wide scale because of food processing.
9) Elimination of food shortages and improve the overall nutrition of populations: When they were first introduced, some processed foods helped to alleviate food shortages and improved the overall nutrition of populations as it made many new foods available to the masses
10) The processing of food improves the taste of food as per market demand.
11) Mass production of food is much cheaper: bulk production of processed food helps in bringing down the selling price.
12) Time saving: The processed food helps people to save their valuable time which they can invest for other activities.
13) Convenience: Ready-to-eat natures of processed foods are very convenient in the modern day busy life style.
14) Improves quality of life: The processed food manufacturing companies has come up with foods that take care of Diabetes, allergies, high/low blood pressure problems etc.

Food processing and preparation broadly encompasses three main areas:

(1) The food preservation by
    (a) Modern techniques such as: refrigeration, canning and irradiation etc. and
    (b) Traditional techniques such as drying, salting, smoking and fermentation;
(2) Food additives.
(3) Food Packaging.

## FOOD PRESERVATION

Food preservation is a process by which effectively eliminate or minimize all the factors responsible for food deterioration. The factors which are responsible for the deterioration of food may include:-- Growth of microorganisms such as bacteria, yeasts and molds: activities of food enzymes and various chemical reactions in the food, infestation pests; wrong storage temperature; presence of moisture; oxidation; effect of light; wrong handling etc.

**Food Preservation Methods**

(Foods are preserved in combination of two or more of the following methods)

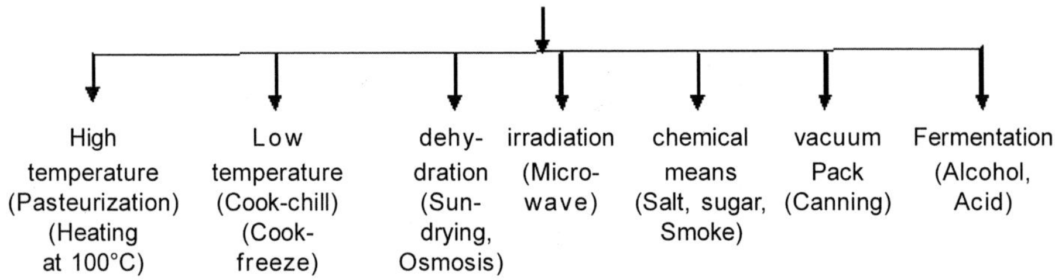


**Diagram. Classification of methods of food preservation**

## BASIC PRINCIPLES OF FOOD PRESERVATION

The basic principle for preservation of food for short period of time are---

a) The plants and animal food items should be cut or killed only just before the cooking.

   For example the fish, poultry, fruits, vegetables etc. should be kept alive as long as possible.

b) If the possibility for keeping the plants and animals alive is limited then it should be cleaned, hygienically covered and stored at proper temperature as quickly as possible.

The basic principles of food preservation for longer period of time are---

a) Follow the above two principles and along with these further precautionary measures should be taken.

b) Inactivating or controlling microorganisms through heat, cold, radiation, chemicals, salt, sugar etc.

c) Controlling or inactivating enzymes within the food.

d) Eliminating or controlling chemical reactions responsible for the spoilage of food.

**Drying** is one of the oldest methods to eliminate or control the deterioration of food. Drying of food will also remove the water from the cells of bacteria. This will stop their multiplication. Bacteria and Yeast usually need more moisture than molds for growth and multiplication. In the olden days the method of the Sun drying were practiced to preserve foods. Fish, Vegetables and fruits are naturally dried by the sun and wind. Still houses with the provision of fire place to dry fruits, vegetables, fish and herbs were constructed in areas where enough Sun light is not available. The uncontrolled drying leaves food items with only 2% to 3% water. A mild drying will keep the nutrients, texture, color and flavor of the food intact. Dried milk powder, instant coffee, freeze-dried fruits for cereals etc. are example of products prepared by this method.

**Salting and sugar** solution acts as preservatives on the principle of Osmosis. **Osmosis** is a process in nature in which the water moves through the perm-selective membrane from the lower concentration area to a higher concentration area. The bacteria, molds and yeasts are covered with membranes through which water can pass. So when these microorganisms are in the concentrated salt solution or in the concentrated sugar solution, the water in their cell moves out through the semi-permeable membrane to the concentrated syrup or brine. This causes dehydration of the cells and stops the multiplication of the microorganisms. Thus fruits can be preserved by placing them in sugar syrup. Meat products can be preserved by placing them in a salt solution.

**Smoking** is considered as one of the oldest methods of preservations. Smoking generated from the burning of wood will have the effect of heat and smoke. In such case, the heat from fire will destroy the microorganisms. It will also help in drying out the food which will be further effective in preserving the food items. The smoke contains Formaldehyde and other preserving chemicals which help in the preservation of food. But smoke without the heat from the fire may contribute to the developing of flavor but will not be effective as preservative. Meats and fish are generally smoked to preserve.

**Pasteurization** is a process in which the pathogens are killed by heating the liquid to approximately 70°C for half a minute and then cooling it about 10°C. This process kills all the pathogens in the liquids e.g. milk so that milk can be stored at a refrigerator for a week. This process was invented by Mr. Louis Pasteur. This process can satisfy two purposes for example-

- To kill all the pathogens and make it safe for human consumptions e.g. milk.
- To improve the shelf life and preservation of food items mainly liquids. Wines, beers, fruit juices and some other foods are pasteurized for improving the shelf life.

Pasteurization process is generally combined with other process to preserve foods. One of the newer application helps to preserve the oysters.

**Irradiation**: There are various types of electro-magnetic radiation, used for destroying microorganisms which helps in food preservations. The Microwaves, ultraviolet rays, ionizing radiations are examples of processes used for food preservations. This radiation process inactivates the natural enzymes of the foods and sterilizes it. But a stronger radiation may alter the nutritional value of the food and can also affect the texture, color and flavor. Therefore, a milder irradiation will kill all the pathogens and inactivate the enzymes while retaining quality of food.

"Cold Sterilization" or Ionizing Radiation is the modern innovation which kills all the disease-causing microorganisms without raising the temperature.

Pork, poultry, vegetables, fruits are preserved through a combined treatment of Irradiation and Pasteurization.

### Differences between Microwave and Irradiation

1) Food irradiation is used mainly for the preservation of food materials. Microwaves are used in the catering industry, for the purpose of thawing and quick heating.
2) Microwaves are a type of electromagnetic radiations, the wave length ranges 1 mm to 1 mt. it has smaller wavelengths. So, the penetrations in food items

are much deeper. But, in Irradiation, due to larger wavelength, the penetration is shallower in the food items.

3) In Microwave, heating of the food items takes place all over the food starting from the inside. But in Irradiation the food item id heated on the surface area.

## CANNING

Canning was invented by Nicolas Appert, who observed that if the is heated sufficiently in a sealed container, then, the food does not get spoiled if the container is not opened. This became one of the most important and widely used methods of food preservation.

In canning the food is sealed in a can and the can is subjected to a temperature that will destroy all the microorganisms. Thus, the food remains safe as no microorganism gets access inside the sealed and sterilized can.

The foods which contain acid such as fruits are more conveniently canned. In acid foods the Clostridium Botulinum forms spore and may not be destroyed, but due to the presence of acid their growth is arrested. But the meat, fish and vegetables require steam sterilization.

The microorganisms which survive the heat treatment in canning may-

- Produce hydrogen gas inside the can and change the shape or burst the can.
- May turn the content sour
- Sugary foods may be spoiled by yeasts

The canned foods generally retain the nutritive value as they are canned as early as possible after being plucked or slaughtered. However there may be loss of heat-sensitive nutrients such as Thiamin and Vitamin C.

## FREEZING

There is a difference between refrigeration and freezing. The commercial and domestic refrigerators generally maintain temperature ranging from 4.5°C to --7°C. But the Frozen storage will maintain -18°C.

If the food is to be stored for a shorter period of time, then we can store it at 5°C or below.

If the foods are stored at -10°C, then the disease-causing microorganisms become inactive.

If the foods are stored at -18°C, then the enzymes activity is stopped and food quality is retained.

That is why, the domestic freezers, now-a-days, store foods at -18°C.

And the commercial freezers store foods at -29°C.

Therefore, if the foods are to stored for a considerably longer period of time then it should be stored at -18°C or below. At this temperature the enzymes within the foods also get deactivated and thus the texture, color, flavor and taste remain intact. This happens because when the foods are stored the water in the food turn into ice crystals. If the food is subjected to slow freezing the large ice crystals are formed and damage the structure of the food and the food quality deteriorates. But the rapid freezing produces only small ice crystals which do not damage the structure and retains the food quality.

Frozen foods once thawed must be used as soon as possible.

Therefore, f frozen foods are easiest, safest and most efficient method of preservation. The quick frozen foods are as good as the fresh foods.

**Table: Average useful storage life of plant and animal tissues at various temperatures. Average Useful Storage Life (In Days)**

| Foods | 0°C or 32° F | 22°C or 72° F | 38°C or 100° F |
|---|---|---|---|
| Meat | 6-10 | 1 | Less than one |
| Fish | 2-7 | 1 | Less than one |
| Poultry | 5-18 | 1 | Less than one |
| Dry meats and fish | 1000 and more | 350 and more | >100 |
| Fruits | 2-180 | 1-20 | 1-7 |
| Dry fruits >100 | 1000 and more | 350 | d more |
| Leafy vegetables | 3-20 | 1-7 | 1-3 |
| Root crops | 90-300 | 7-50 | 2-20 |
| Dry seeds | 1000 and more | 350 and more | >100 |

**Source**: N. W. Dèsrosier.

## FOOD ADDITIVES

Food Additives may be defined as chemical substances intentionally added to food to increase food quality.

The objectives and uses of Food Additives are:

- it helps in modifying the flavour
- It helps in modifying the texture
- To sweeten the foods
- To colour the foods
- To preserve the foods
- To help in processing the foods
- To nutritionally supplement the foods
- To enhance the storage life of foods
- To control the moisture of the foods
- To control the acidity of the food
- As anti-caking agent
- As anti-foaming agent

- As firming agent
- As Humectants
- As releasing agent
- As liquid freezants.

## CLASSES OF FOOD ADDITIVES

With the rapid growth of the processed food industry in India, the uses of Food Additives are also becoming more and more innovative and useful. At present, there are more than 3000 food additives which fall into 12 broad groups. Some of these are discussed below:

### Preservatives

Preservatives may be defined as substances which are added to foods to prevent spoilage by stopping the growth of microorganisms such as yeasts, bacteria and molds.

**Class I Preservatives**: Class I Preservatives include all those substances, the addition of which are not governed by law. The examples of such preservatives are-sugar, honey, salt, spices, alcohol, vinegar, Acetic acid, glucose, fructose, wood smoke etc.

**Class II Preservatives**: Class II Preservatives include those chemicals which are added up to a certain permitted limit to food to inhibit microbial growth and the use of such chemicals are restricted by law. The examples include the salts of -

- Acetic acid
- Benzoic acid
- Sulphurous acids
- Nisin
- Sodium Nitrates and Nitrites
- Potassium nitrates and Nitrites
- Sorbic
- Propionic etc.

Some of the common preservatives and their uses in foods are given below:

| Preservatives | Used in food products |
|---|---|
| Sodium Benzoate | Aerated Drinks, Acidic foods e.g. Tomato sauce |
| Sodium Propionate | Breads and cakes |
| Calcium Propionate | Breads and cakes |
| Sorbic Acid | Wrappers are cleaned to prevent spoilage of Cheese |
| Sulphur Di-oxide | Fruits and Vegetables (to control browning by enzymes). |
| Potassium Metabisulphate | Lemon squash |
| Borax | To wash vegetables and whole fruits |
| Tetracycline | Added to ice blocks to chill fish. |

### Antioxidants

**Antioxidants maybe defined as substances which are used to stop oxidation of fats**. The antioxidants delay the process of oxidative rancidity in fats. These substances, therefore, save the fats being unpalatable. Tocopherol, a natural antioxidant is found in oils manufactured from the seeds of plants. It is due to the presence of this Tocopherol, that the vegetable oils do not get rancid. Antioxidants are used to prolong the keeping quality of foods containing fats.

Some common antioxidants are:

- Butylated Hydroxyanisole (BHA)
- Butylated Hydroxytoluene (BHT)
- Tertiary Butylated Hydroquinone (TBQH)
- Propyl Gallate
- Ascorbic Acids
- Tocopherols (Vitamin E)

### Sulphur dioxide

These are used to preserve breakfast cereals, potato chips, crackers and other fat containing foods. BHA is very stable even in high temperature. This the reason why it is used in baked and fried food items e.g. crackers, cookies, potato chips etc. Most of the whole grain cereals contain polyunsaturated fat which will otherwise get spoiled if no antioxidant is used. Therefore, it is clear from the above discussion that the antioxidants play a very important role in food production.

### Addition of Nutrients

Some nutrients are destroyed during processing of foods. Such nutrients are added compensate the loss. Vitamin B, Thiamine, Nicotinic Acids, minerals, iron, calcium, and other nutrients are added. Salt, breakfast cereals, wheat flour, fruit juices, baby food are fortified with various nutrients.

### Coloring Agents

Colors are added to foods to increase the eye appeal. The natural and artificial colors are added to make the food more attractive.

The natural coloring agents include Annatto, Caramel, Saffron, Carotene etc.

Natural colors maybe defined as colors found in edible raw material.

Artificial or synthetic coloring agents need to pass the toxicological tests to be used in foods.

Though the artificial colors have better stability, uniformity, variety and brighter.

Red color is extracted from beetroots, grapes, and cranberries.

## Flavoring Agents

Flavor comprises of taste and aroma. For many years the natural flavoring agents were used in the food such as spices, herbs, roots and stems of plants and berries. The spices such as pepper, cloves and ginger were very common additives in the food preparation.

The need for synthetic flavors was felt with the increase in demand of flavoring agents. The synthetic flavors are very inexpensive, convenient and more concentrated. Now-a-days the synthetic flavors are mostly used except for vanilla, orange, peppermint and lemon.

| Flavor Additives | Flavor |
|---|---|
| Benzaldehyde | Almond/Cherry |
| Ethyl Butyrate | Pineapple |
| Methyl Anthranilate | Grape |
| Methyl Salicylate | Wintergreen |

There are more than 1200 different flavoring materials available.

The Flavor Potentiator or Flavor Enhancer are substances which do not have flavor of their own but helps in increasing the flavor of the other compounds present in the food e.g. MSG or Monosodium Glutamate, commonly known as Aji-no-moto.

## Sweeteners

Sugar is considered to be the ideal sweetener. But it has some basic drawbacks such as it is responsible for Obesity and tooth decay. Artificial sweeteners are substances which are sweet but contains few or no calories and non-nutritive. The artificial sweeteners include Aspartame, Saccharin, Isomalt, Xylitol etc.

## Humectants

Humectants are food additives which reduce the effect of humidity on a food by absorbing moisture for example Baking Powder.

## Anti-caking Agents

Anti-caking agents are food additives which do not allow the particles of food to adhere to one another. This helps in increasing the flow properties of food during processing.

## Firming Agents

Firming agents are also food additives used to ensure that the tissues of fruits and vegetables remain crisp and firm.

## Inert Gas

Inert gases are added to packets of instant foods, so that, oxidative changes do not occur.

### Effects of Factors Like Heat, Acid, Alkali On Food Constituents

Preserving the nutrients in different phases such as processing, storage and preservation is an important responsibility of a food scientist. We need to have the knowledge about the effect of heat, acid, alkali on the stability of nutrients in various conditions,

The following table shows that Vitamin A is unstable (U) to acid and heat while Vitamin C is stable (S) in alkalinity and heat. In some cases the loss of nutrients exceeds 75%.

In the modern food processing technology the losses of nutrients are usually not more than 25%. If the loss of nutrients is very high, the law allows enriching the food by adding vital nutrients. Heat, acid, alkali may alter the food value but maintaining proper time and temperature is the key to destroying microorganisms and minimum nutrient loss.

| Nutrients | Neutral pH 7 | Acid <pH7 | Alkaline >pH7 | Heat | Cooking loss |
|---|---|---|---|---|---|
| Vitamin A | Stable | Unstable | Stable | Unstable | 0-40 |
| Vitamin D | Stable | Stable | Unstable | Unstable | 0-40 |
| Folic acid | Unstable | Unstable | Stable | Unstable | 0-100 |
| Vitamin K | Stable | Unstable | Unstable | Stable | 0-5 |
| Vitamin $B_6$ | Stable | Stable | Stable | Unstable | 0-40 |
| Riboflavin ($B_2$) | Stable | Stable | Unstable | Unstable | 0-75 |
| Thiamine ($B_1$) | Unstable | Stable | Unstable | Unstable | 0-80 |
| Lysine | Stable | Stable | Stable | Unstable | 0-40 |
| Mineral Salt | Stable0 | Stable | Stable | Stable | 0-3 |

**Source**: Harris. R.S. and Kamas, E. 1975, Nutritional Evaluation of Food Processing, 2nd ed. AVI Publishing Westport, CT.

## FOOD PACKAGING

Packaging is an integral part of food processing. Proper packaging helps in transportation of food products to far reaching areas.

### Functions of packaging

- It helps in preservation of food products
- Helps in transportation and distribution
- Saves the food from microbial contamination
- It saves from physical damage of the food
- It helps in educating and communicating the consumers
- It helps the buyer to make selection by reading the nutritional value, ingredients, date of manufacture, date of expiry etc.

Following points need to be kept to make the packaging effective:

- The container must not react with the food product
- It should provide complete protection from contamination
- Protect from oxidation
- Easy to open
- Should have dispensing facility where ever required
- Convenient and appropriate size and shape
- Cost should be reasonable
- Should be temper-proof

## MAP or Modified Atmosphere Packaging

Modified Atmosphere Packaging is a technique used to increase the keeping quality of the fresh and processed foods. According to this technique the atmospheric air in the packet is changed to a composition of pure oxygen, carbon dioxide and nitrogen. Thus the fresh condition of the food product remains same for longer period of time. This adjusted combination of gas helps the food to breath. The highly perishable food items like fish, meat, fruits and vegetables can be kept fresh for a longer time.

## CAP or Controlled Atmosphere Packaging

In this Controlled Atmosphere storage the farm fresh products are stored in an air tight room. The combination $O_2$,$CO_2$, $N_2$, temperature and humidity of the storage room is controlled. In this method the dry items as well as the fruits and vegetable or all the agricultural products can be stored.

The differences between the MAP and CAP are:

1) In case of MAP the food is packaged in a container or packet. Whereas in case of CAP he items are kept in a store room.
2) In case of MAP, once the container is sealed, the composition of gas cannot be changed. But in case of CAP the gas composition may be regulated as per requirements.

**Differences between MAP and CAP**

| MAP | CAP |
|---|---|
| 1. Modified Atmosphere Packaging is a technique in which the atmospheric air in the packet is changed to a composition of pure $O_2$, $CO_2$ and $N_2$. | 1. In Controlled Atmosphere Packaging the combination of $O_2$, $CO_2$ and $N_2$ along with temperature are controlled. |
| 2. In MAP, there is no control over the process. | 2. In CAP, there is control over the storage atmosphere. |
| 3. Gas composition changes due to product respiration. | 3. In CAP, gas composition changes due to metabolic activities of fruits and vegetables. |
| 4. Gas composition cannot be regulated once it is fixed. | 4. In CAP, fresh air and nitrogen may be added to get desired composition of gases. |

## KEY TERMS

- *Food processing*: Food processing may be defined as the conversion of raw food ingredients into food by using physical or chemical means. Therefore food processing is a technique in which ready-to-eat or convenience food products are produced for a target market from various raw ingredients.
- *Food Preservation*: Food preservation is a process by which effectively eliminates or minimizes all the factors responsible for food deterioration.
- *Drying*: Drying is one of the oldest methods to eliminate or control the deterioration of food. Drying of food will also remove the water from the cells of bacteria. This will stop their multiplication.
- *Smoking*: Smoking is considered as one of the oldest methods of preservations. Smoking generated from the burning of wood will have the effect of heat and smoke. In such case, the heat from fire will destroy the microorganisms. It will also help in drying out the food which will be further effective in preserving the food items.
- *Pasteurization* -- Pasteurization is a process in which the pathogens are killed by heating the liquid to approximately 70°C for half a minute and then cooling it about 10°C. This process kills all the pathogens in the liquids e.g. milk so that milk can be stored at a refrigerator for a week. This process was invented by Mr. Louis Pasteur
- *Irradiation*: There are various types of electro-magnetic radiation, used for destroying microorganisms which helps in food preservations. The Microwaves, ultraviolet rays, ionizing radiations are examples of processes used for food preservations. This radiation process inactivates the natural enzymes of the foods and sterilizes it.

## ROJECT BASED LEARNING (PBL)

1) Students may be directed to collect various types of food additives available in the market. They will prepare a project file of all these additives and submit to the teacher.
2) Students may visit a food processing unit and prepare a project.
3) Students may visit a packaging unit and prepare a project on it.

## IMPORTANT QUESTIONS

Q. No.1. Define food processing. State the objectives and benefits of food processing.

Q.No.2. Explain the effects of factors like heat, acid and alkali on food constituents.

Q. No.3. Explain the following:

a) Pasteurization

b) Irradiation

c) Freezing

Q. No.4. Discuss about food additives.

Chapter 6

# Evaluation of Food

After reading this chapter the student will be able to:

- *Understand the meaning of evaluation of food*
- *Know the objectives of sensory evaluation of food*
- *Explain the sensory assessment of food quality and its methods*
- *Learn about proximate analysis of food constituents.*
- *Understand the Rheological aspects of food.*

## INTRODUCTION

**Sensory Evaluation of food** (or **Sensory Analysis of food**) is a scientific discipline that applies principles of experimental design and statistical analysis to the use of human responses such as sight, smell, taste, touch and hearing in order to evaluate food products.

Different sensory languages and tests are taught to the students to give an opportunity to evaluate and give feedback on their dishes and test products.

## OBJECTIVES OF SENSORY EVALUATION OF FOOD:

- To develop proper and appropriate sensory languages to understand similarities/differences in dishes or test products or menu items;
- To compare existing dishes of the menu and prepare evaluation sheet.
- To analyse food samples for improvements to match consumer's/guest's liking;
- To analyse response sheet or evaluation sheet of the consumers to a dish or a menu
- To gauge specific characteristics of an ingredient in a dish
- To ensure that prepared dish matches with the original specification in regard to the colour, flavour, taste, texture etc.
- To prepare objective and subjective feedback data to enable informed decisions to be made.

- Further research to develop more inter relationship between Objective measurement and subjective measurements

## SENSORY ASSESSMENT OF FOOD QUALITY

**Sensory evaluation** is a scientific discipline that analyses and measures human responses to the composition of **food** and drink, e.g. appearance, touch, odour, texture, temperature and taste.

Food quality has been defined as the degree of excellence of food which includes many factors such as taste, appearance, and nutritional quality, as well as in bacteriological or keeping quality. Food quality must be maintained in order to ensure that food is admired by larger target clients, maintaining food quality also helps to ensures food safety.

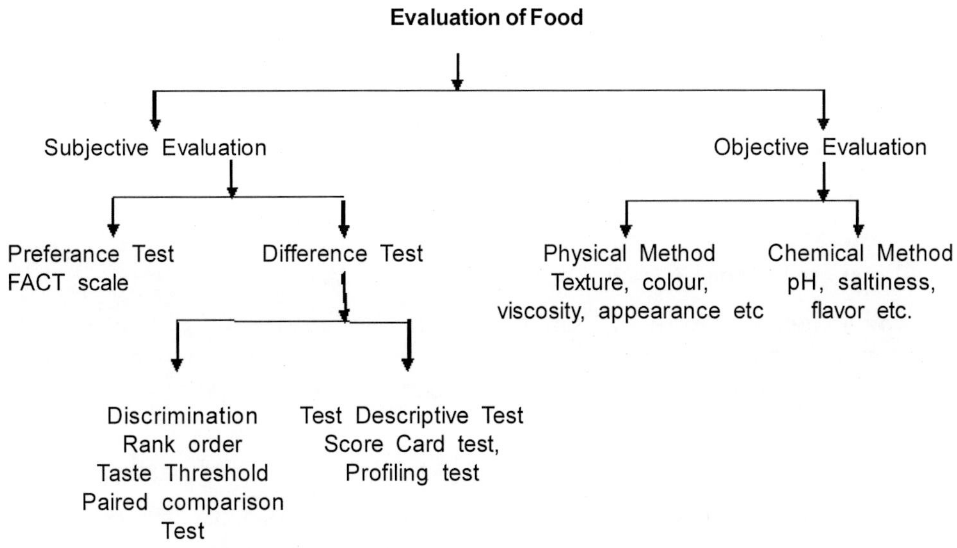


**Diagram: Classification of Evaluation of Food methods.**

The human assessor testes and records the responses and by applying these techniques the food items are judged. Most of the multi-national companies employ human assessors to taste their products before marketing them. Sensory analysis or evaluation of food can mainly be broken down into three sub-sections:

- **Objective testing**: Objective Testing or Effective Testing deals with the objective facts about the food item. Objective measurements are more rapid, reliable and repeatable. The Objective testing includes the physical and chemical tests of the dish.

The Physical Test includes the tests of the

- **Viscosity:** The test for viscosity of liquid items is measured by Viscometer. Farinograph and Amylograph are used for dough and starch pastes respectively.

- **Specific gravity Test:** This test determines the amount of air incorporated in foams such as whipped cream or egg white foam etc. it is a measure of relative density of a dish in relation to the relative density of water.
- **Volume test:** The volume testing is carried out by an equipment called Volumeter.

The chemical Tests include the tests of the:

- The Nutrient Analysis of a dish e.g. kilocalories, proteins, fat, sugar, fibre, vitamins, minerals etc.
- pH tests: This test helps to determine the acidity or alkalinity of a dish which is done by using pH meter or pH paper.
- Saltiness: This is done to determine the salt content by Flame Photometry.
- Sugar test: This is done to determine the level of sugar concentration in the dish,
- Flavour tests: This is done by Chromatography.

  A trained panel of human assessor are appointed to deal with objective facts e.g.

  Do two or more products differ from each other?

  What are the characteristics of two or more products?

  In the **Sensory Profile method**, the human assessor will describe each food item as per the descriptors given in the sensory profile such as bitterness, acidity, etc. and marks them according to the intensity e.g. very week to very strong.

  In the method of **Free Choice Profiling** each assessor builds his own profile.

  In **Holistic method** the overall appearance of the product is taken into consideration.

- **Subjective testing**: Subjective Testing or Affective Testing is also known as Consumer Testing and deals with the subjective facts e.g. preferences or how much the food is expected to be accepted. In this method we gather the Subjective data from a huge panel of usually untrained human testers. Some companies prefer to recruit trained and small group of assessors. The simple questions are put forward such as:

  Which do you prefer, A or B?

  Please rate the "fruity aroma": (dislike, neither, like).

**Preference test** may be defined as a test that gives information on particular aspects determines the preference of the dish. Hedonic scale is used for evaluation.

**Difference testing** helps to determine the differences in two or more dishes.

Name of the dish: Cream of Chicken Soup

| | |
|---|---|
| Appearance | Piping hot, pieces of boiled chicken, drops of cream |
| Colour | Off white |
| Texture | Pieces of boiled chicken, smooth |
| Consistency/taste | Cream consistency, well seasoned, chicken flavour |

**Table: Sample standard specification of Cream of Chicken Soup.**
**Scores**

| Characteristics | Max. Score | Evaluated score & Comments |
|---|---|---|
| Appearance | | |
| Colour | | |
| Texture | | |
| Consistency/Taste | | |

**Table: Sample Score Card for Descriptive Tasting**
**Name of the dish: Cream of Chicken Soup**

Name: Date:

Descriptive Testing (Choose the most suitable term)

| | | | | | |
|---|---|---|---|---|---|
| Appearance | Fat drops | Properly garnished | No/careless garnish | Too much garnish | Spoilt garnish |
| Colour | Dark | Off white | Very white | Very dark | Pale |
| Texture | Lumpy | Smooth | | | |
| Consistency | Thin | Cream consistency | Thick | Dropping | Coating the back of the spoon |
| Taste | Salty | Well seasoned | Too much pepper | Less seasoning | Less salt |
| Flavour | Taste of thickening agent | Distinct chicken flavour | Mild chicken flavour | Strong chicken flavour | Off flavour |

Difference Testing are subdivided into **Discrimination test and Descriptive tests.**

**As the name suggests in the Descriptive tests** the human assessor describes the dish in exact sensory terms taken from the score card.

**Perception:** Perception deals with the biochemical and psychological aspects of sensation. According to Schiffman, the steps involved in the process of perception are:

- The stimulus hits the sense organ and is converted to a nerve signal that travels to the brain.
- The brain then interprets, organizes and integrates the incoming sensations into perception.

- Finally, a response is formulated based on the subject's perceptions.

It should be noted here that often the responses of human assessors differ from each other for the same food item because:

- The sensitivity of sense organs differs from person to person.
- The mental assessment of sensation differs from person to person due to lack of training.

## PROXIMATE ANALYSIS OF FOOD CONSTITUENTS

Proximate principles include chemical analysis of various food constituents such as fats, carbohydrates and proteins. The proximate composition of food means the total calories available through food. The energy is derived from food through the oxidation of fat, protein and carbohydrates.

We know that protein gives us 04 K cal/g; Carbohydrate gives us 04 K cal/g. And fat gives 09 kcal/g. Thus we can find out the total energy derived from the food.

- The value for fat in a food item: This can be determined by chemically extracting the lipid. Ether is used to chemically extract the lipid as lipid dissolves in it.
- The value for protein in a food item: We know that protein contain 16% Nitrogen. Therefore protein content is determined by measuring the Nitrogen content for all food items.
- The value for carbohydrate in a food item: This is determined by subtracting the sum total of moisture, fat, protein, fibre and ash from 100.

Therefore-

Carbohydrate = 100 – (moisture + fat + protein + fibre + ash)

## RHEOLOGICAL ASPECT OF FOOD

The term *Rheology* was first used by Professor Eugene C. Bingham, in 1920. The term was derived from Greek language where Rheo means Flow and Logia means "Study of". Therefore, Food Rheology may be defined as the study of the Rheological properties of food or in other words it is the study of the consistency and flow of food under tightly specified conditions.

The consistency, degree of fluidity, and other mechanical properties are important in understanding

- How long food can be stored,
- How stable it will remain,
- In determining food texture
- In quality control of food during manufacture and processing.

The acceptability of food products to the consumer is often determined by food texture, such as how spreadable and creamy a food product is.

Food can be classified according to its rheological state

a) Solid

b) Gel

c) Liquid

d) Emulsion

These Rheological states are associated with typical rheological behaviors, and its rheological properties can be measured. These properties will affect the design of processing plants, and keeping quality of food items, sensory properties etc. However, food rheology is something we experience every day with our perception of food texture. Tomato Ketchup is commonly used an example of Bingham fluid and its flow behavior can be compared to that of a polymer melt

## KEY TERMS

- *Sensory Evaluation of food (or Sensory Analysis of food*) is a scientific discipline that applies principles of experimental design and statistical analysis to the use of human responses such as sight, smell, taste, touch and hearing in order to evaluate food products.
- Sensory evaluation is a scientific discipline that analyses and measures human responses to the composition of food and drink, e.g. appearance, touch, odour, texture, temperature and taste.
- *Perception*: Perception deals with the biochemical and psychological aspects of sensation. According to Schiffman,
- *Proximate Analysis of Food Constituents*: Proximate principles include chemical analysis of various food constituents such as fats, carbohydrates and proteins. The proximate composition of food means the total calories available through food. The energy is derived from food through the oxidation of fat, protein and carbohydrates.
- Rheological Aspect of Food: The term Rheology was first used by Professor Eugene C. Bingham, in 1920. The term was derived from Greek language where Rheo means Flow and Logia means "Study of". Therefore, Food Rheology may be defined as the study of the Rheological properties of food or in other words it is the study of the consistency and flow of food under tightly specified conditions.

## PROJECT BASED LEARNING (PBL)

Various groups of students may be constituted to take up various types of tests on various dishes. The test reports may be compiled and presented to the subject teacher for verification.

## IMPORTANT QUESTIONS

Q.No.1. Explain the objectives of evaluation of food. What do you understand by sensory assessment of food quality? Explain the methods.

Q.No.2. Explain the following:

a) Proximate Analysis of food constituents

b) Rheological aspects of food.

Chapter 7

# Emulsion

After reading this chapter, the student will be able to:

- *Define emulsion*
- *Understand the theory of emulsification*
- *Learn types of emulsions*
- *Know about emulsifying agents*
- *Know the role of emulsifying agents in food emulsions*

## INTRODUCTION

The word "emulsion" has been derived from the Latin word "to milk", the reason being milk is an emulsion of fat and water.

An emulsion can be defined as a mixture of two or more liquids that are un-mixable. Emulsions are of two-phase systems of matter termed as Colloids. But in food production the term Emulsion is used as both phases, dispersed and continuous, are liquids. Therefore, in an emulsion, one liquid or the dispersed phase is dispersed in another liquid or the continuous phase.

**Emulsion** in the food production can take two different forms:

- Fat dispersed into water and
- Water dispersed into fat.

Common fat in water emulsifications include hollandaise, mayonnaise, aioli, milk, cream, and pan sauces.

Other examples include Mayonnaise Sauce, Vinaigrette Sauce etc.

**Another term used to describe emulsion is:**

A) **Oil and water** (O/W) can form, first, an oil-in-water emulsion, wherein the oil is the dispersed phase, and water is the dispersion medium for example Lipoproteins.

B) They can form **water-in-oil** (W/O) emulsion, wherein water is the dispersed phase and oil is the external phase.

Whether an emulsion of oil and water turns into a "water-in-oil" (W/O) emulsion or an "oil-in-water" (O/W) emulsion depends on the

- volume fraction of both phases and
- the type of emulsifier present.

In general, the **Bancroft Rule** (stated below) applies. Emulsifiers and emulsifying particles tend to promote dispersion of the phase in which they do not dissolve very well. For example, proteins dissolve better in water than in oil, and so tend to form oil-in-water emulsions (that is, they promote the dispersion of oil droplets throughout a continuous phase of water).

Two special classes of emulsions –

a) Micro-emulsion (Droplet size above 100nm. These are Thermodynamically stable).

b) Nano-emulsions (Droplet sizes below 100 nm. These are Kinetically stable).

Other possible emulsions include:

Water-in-oil-in-water emulsion and an

Oil-in-water-in-oil emulsion.

## TYNDALL EFFECT

Emulsions contain both a dispersed and a continuous phase, with the boundary between the phases called the "interface". Emulsions tend to have a cloudy appearance because the many phase interfaces scatter light as it passes through the emulsion. Emulsions appear white when all light is scattered equally. If the emulsion is dilute enough,

Higher-frequency and low-wavelength light will be scattered more, and the emulsion will appear blur – this is called the "Tyndall effect".

**Bancroft Rule**: Bancroft Rule states that "The phase in which an emulsifier is more soluble constitutes the continuous phase."

### Emulsifiers

An Emulsifier is a substance that stabilizes an emulsion.

- An emulsifier is a molecule with one oil-friendly and one water-friendly end.
- Water friendly end in food emulsifier is called Hydrophilic tail and oil-friendly end is called Hydrophobic (or water hating) head. In this way droplets of oil are surrounded by the emulsifier molecule, with the oil core hidden by the water-friendly tails of the emulsifier.
- The best example of a natural emulsion is milk, which is a complex mixture of fat suspended in an aqueous solution.

- Natural emulsifiers are proteins and phospholipids.
- Eggs are widely used as an emulsifier.
- Emulsifiers may also act as Anti-caking agent such as Magnesium Stearate, Sodium, potassium and calcium salts of fatty acids.
- Sorbian mono-stearate is an emulsifier as well as stabilizer.

Examples of food emulsifiers are:

- Egg yolk – in which the main emulsifying agent is Lecithin. The word Lecithin has been derived from the Greek word Lecithos, meaning 'egg yolk'.
- Mustard: The seed hull is the emulsifier.
- Soy: the Lecithin present in Soy is a thickening agent and an emulsifier.
- $NaH_2PO_4$ or Sodium Phosphate: Is used as emulsifier, thickening agent and Leavening agent. An example is processed cheese.
- Sodium Stearoyl Lactylate
- Diacetyl Tartaric acid ester or DATEMis used in bakery.

DATEM: -- Diacetyl Tartaric acid ester of Mono-and-diglycerides is an emulsifier used for producing ice-cream, biscuits etc.

**Emulsifying agents** are substances that are soluble in both fat and water and enable fat to be uniformly dispersed in water as an emulsion. Foods that consist of such emulsions include butter, margarine, salad dressings, mayonnaise and ice cream. Emulsifying agents are used in baking for incorporation of fat into the dough.

Stabilizers are used to stabilize the emulsions.

**Differences between Natural Emulsifier and Synthetic Emulsifier**

| Natural Emulsifier | Synthetic Emulsifier |
|---|---|
| 1. The structure and behaviour of the natural emulsifier changes every time these are made. | 1. The structure and behaviour of the synthetic emulsifier does not change. It is consistent. |
| 2. It may influence the flavour and colour of the emulsion. | 2. It imparts no such effect. |
| 3. NE is costly | 3. SE are much cheaper |
| 4. Availability is a problem | 4. Easily available. |
| 5. It does not alter the density of the emulsion. | 5. It increases the density and adds to the texture of the emulsion. |

## Role of emulsifying agents in Food Emulsion

- Food emulsifiers or Emulsifying agents make the food very appealing.
- Emulsifier ensures that the water and the oil content in food do not get separated.
- Emulsifier gives the freshness and quality to the food.
- Natural food emulsifiers also prevent the growth of moulds in food.

Emulsifiers are used in:

- Creams,
- Sauces,
- Bakery products and
- Dairy products.

They may be derived from the natural products or chemicals. Common emulsifiers are lecithins, mono- and di-glycerides of fatty acids. Esters of monoglycerides of fatty acids.

Natural food emulsifiers are used in variety of foods. Some basic foods having food emulsifiers are:

- Biscuits
- Cakes
- Soft Drinks
- Toffees
- Frozen Desserts
- Bread
- Margarine
- Coffee Whitener
- Caramels

## THEORY OF EMULSIFICATION

There are many theories put forward to explain the ways by which an emulsifier stabilizes an emulsion. But none of these has an universal application to all emulsions.

As Fischer observed "probably a number of factor play a role , and the relative importance of each varies not only in different emulsions but in one and the same emulsion under different circumstances". Various theories of emulsification includes— the Phase-volume theory, Hydration Theory of emulsions, Oriented wedge Theory, Absorbed film and Interfacial tension theory,

Some of the theories involved in the process of emulsification are:

- **Surface Tension Theory** – According to this theory, emulsification takes place by lowering the interfacial tension between two phases. In this case, the emulsifier or the stabilizer lowers the interfacial tension between the two immiscible fluids, thus, reducing the repelling between these two fluids and reducing the attraction of these two fluids.
- **Repulsion Theory** – The emulsifying agent creates a film over one phase that forms globules, which repel each other. This repulsive force causes them to remain suspended in the dispersion medium. According to the DLVO theory (Deryagin, Landau, Vewey, and Overbeek theory), the dispersed particles are

subject to two independent forces i.e. Van der Waals force of attraction and the electrostatic force of repulsion arising from the presence of electrical double layers at the particle surfaces. This electrical double-layer repulsion will stabilize the emulsion when the electrolyte concentration phase is less than a certain value.

- **Viscosity modification**: – It has been observed that some emulsifiers such as glycerin and other polymers increase the viscosity of the medium. This helps in creating and maintaining the suspension of globules of dispersed phase.

It is very important to make a stabilized emulsion for the food production, cosmetic manufacturing, pharmaceutical preparations etc. at the same time; the breaking of emulsion is also required for the recovery of oil in crude oil operations. This is why the emulsion has been a subject of constant investigation.

## USES OF EMULSIONS IN FOOD

Oil-in-water emulsions are common in food products:

- Cream (foam) in Espresso coffee, oil in water (brewed coffee).
- Mayonnaise Sauce and Hollandaise Sauce are oil-in-water emulsions that are stabilized with egg yolk or with other types of food additives.
- Homogenized milk: – Emulsion of milk fat in water and milk proteins
- Vinaigrette Dressings: An emulsion of vegetable oil in vinegar
- Water-in-oil emulsions are less common in food but still exist:
- Butter: An emulsion of water in fat.

## SOME FOOD EMULSIONS

- Salad Dressings: Cooked salad dressings may be termed as acidified liquids, thickened with egg or starch.
- Fats: Melted butters may also be used in preparing Mayonnaise, but the product will be a salad dressing.
- French dressings: French dressings are unstable emulsions.
- Gravies and sauces: Oil, though smaller in quantity is emulsified in water.
- Cream Puffs: Batter/fat emulsion.
- Cakes: oil-in-water emulsions.
- Ice creams and milk: Egg yolk in a mix provides two emulsifiers.

## KEY TERMS

- *Emulsion:* -The word "emulsion" has been derived from the Latin word "to milk", the reason being milk is an emulsion of fat and water.
- An emulsion can be defined as a mixture of two or more liquids that are un-mixable. Emulsions are of two-phase systems of matter termed as Colloids. But

in food production the term Emulsion is used as both phases, dispersed and continuous, are liquids. Therefore, in an emulsion, one liquid or the dispersed phase is dispersed in another liquid or the continuous phase.

- *Tyndall Effect*: Emulsions contain both a dispersed and a continuous phase, with the boundary between the phases called the "interface". Emulsions tend to have a cloudy appearance because the many phase interfaces scatter light as it passes through the emulsion. Emulsions appear white when all light is scattered equally. If the emulsion is dilute enough. Higher-frequency and low-wavelength light will be scattered more, and the emulsion will appear blur – this is called the "Tyndall effect".
- *Bancroft Rule:* Bancroft Rule states that "The phase in which an emulsifier is more soluble constitutes the continuous phase."
- *Emulsifying agents*: Emulsifying agents are substances that are soluble in both fat and water and enable fat to be uniformly dispersed in water as an emulsion. Foods that consist of such emulsions include butter, margarine, salad dressings, mayonnaise and ice cream. Emulsifying agents are used in baking for incorporation of fat into the dough.

## PROJECT BASED LEARNING (PBL)

Students may be directed to prepare a project report on the role of emulsifying agents in food emulsions

Students may be asked to find out the various emulsifying agents available in the super market. They will make a detailed project report based on their findings.

Students may be asked to make a detailed project report on the basis of Tyndal Effect and Bancroft Rule.

## IMPORTANT QUESTIONS:

Q.No.1. Define Emulsion. What are the different types of emulsions?

Q.No.2.What is Tyndall Effect? What is an emulsifier? Give examples.

Q.No.3.What are the theories of emulsification? What are the uses of emulsions in food?

Chapter 8

# Colloids

After reading this chapter, a student will be able to:

- *Define Colloids*
- *Understand the differences in true solutions, coarse solutions and colloids.*
- *Learn about the application of colloid systems in food preparation.*
- *Know the functions of colloidal system in foods.*

## INTRODUCTION

**A colloid** may be defined as a mixture in which insoluble particles of a substance is dispersed throughout another substance.

This term Colloid was coined in the early $19^{th}$ century by the Father of Physical Chemistry, Thomas Graham (1805—1869). The word was derived from Greek word Kolla meaning Glue.

Therefore the colloidal system consists of two parts; -

1) The Dispersed phase or Solute or the fine particles
2) The Dispersion medium or Solvent or the Continuous phase or the second substance.

This field of study was introduced in 1861 by scientist Thomas Graham.

The difference in the size of the particles must be kept in mind:

- True Solution: The size of particles are up to one mill micron
- Colloidal Dispersion: The sizes of the particles are one mill micron to one micron
- Coarse suspension: The sizes of the particles are larger than one micron.

Therefore, the size of the ions or molecules in colloidal system lies in between the true solution and the coarse suspension.

## APPLICATION OF COLLOID SYSTEMS IN FOOD PREPARATION

The majority of foods that we eat everyday are colloidal in nature, especially the ready-to-consume items.

The food colloids serve the following functions:

- Adds nutritional value
- Enhances appearance,
- Improves the texture,
- Provides mouth-feel
- Provides spreading ability
- Transforms from gel to liquid by the warmth of the tongue.

The colloidal systems found in foods may be represented in the table form:

**Table: examples of colloids in foods**

| Collodal system | Solute/Solvent | Examples |
|---|---|---|
| Gel | Liquid/Solid | Jam, Jelly, Curd, Caramel custard etc. |
| Sol | Solid/Liquid | Soups, Gravies, Skimmed Milk, Pouring Custard etc. |
| Emulsion | Liquid/Liquid | Mayonnaise sauce, Various Salad Dressings, Butter, whole milk etc. |
| Foam | Gas/Liquid | Whipped Cream, Whipped white of eggs, |
| Aerosol | Solid/Gas | Smoke for flavoring |
| Solid Foam | Gas/Solid | Cake, Meringue, Fluffy omelette etc. |

## SOL

A Sol may be defined as a colloidal suspension of very small particles in a continuous liquid medium. The reasons for colloidal particles to remain dispersed as a sol are:

- The water/fluid molecules remain bound to the surface of the colloidal particles
- The particles of having same charge repulse each other and thus stay apart.

The destabilization of protein Sol in milk is desirable in the preparation of cheese. But the same is avoided while preparing Cream of Tomato Soup and Scalloped Potatoes.

Soups, Gravies, Skimmed Milk, Pouring Custard etc. are the examples of sols in the food production.

**Gelatin is a sol when hot, and is a Gel when cooled.**

Rigidity is a characteristic of a gel just as fluidity is a characteristic of a Sol.

## GEL

A Gel may be defined as solid jelly-like material that can have properties ranging from soft and weak to hard and tough. Therefore, Gels are a substantially dilute cross-linked system, which does not flow when in steady state.

The molecules of protein in eggs gets denatured by the action of heat and enmeshes the fluid milk forming a gel. Thus custard is formed. Custard is a fragile gel.

A soft custard or pouring custard does not become as firm as a baked custard because stirring disturbs the gel formation.

Gelatin molecules disperse easily in warm water. The dried gelatin is used in domestic purposes. These may be packed in granular form. However, one thing must be kept in mind that raw pineapple contains an enzyme called Bromelin, which hydrolyses gelatin, therefore must be avoided.

Starch-thickened puddings and soft pie-fillings are gels.

Fruit pectic gels or jellies are made by boiling fruit juices and right quantities of sugar.

Jam, Jelly, Curd, Caramel custard etc. are examples of gels.

An ice-cream may be called a complex mixture of an emulsion, a semisolid foam and a gel.

## KEY TERMS

- *Colloid:* A colloid may be defined as a mixture in which insoluble particles of a substance is dispersed throughout another substance.
- *Sol:* A Sol may be defined as a colloidal suspension of very small particles in a continuous liquid medium.
- *Gel*: A Gel may be defined as solid jelly-like material that can have properties ranging from soft and weak to hard and tough. Therefore, Gels are a substantially dilute cross-linked system, which does not flow when in steady state.
- *True Solution*: The size of particles are up to one mill micron
- *Colloidal Dispersion*: The sizes of the particles are one mill micron to one micron
- *Coarse suspension*: The sizes of the particles are larger than one micron

## PROJECT BASED LEARNING (PBL)

Students may be directed to prepare a project report on "Some Common Food Emulsions".

## IMPORTANT QUESTIONS

Q.No.1. Define colloids. Explain the application of colloidal systems in food preparations.

Q.No.2. Explain the functions of colloidal system in foods.

Chapter 9

# Flavours

After reading this chapter, the student will be able to:

- *Define Flavour*
- *Describe various food flavours*

## INTRODUCTION

**Flavour**, is the sensory impression of food or other items, and is determined primarily by the chemical senses of taste **and** smell. The Trigeminal senses help us in flavour perception by detecting chemical senses in the mouth along with temperature and texture. The flavour of the food can be changed with natural or synthetic flavouring agents. A food's flavour, can be altered by changing its smell while keeping its taste similar for example aerated water, candies, which, while made of bases with a similar taste, have different flavours due to the use of different scents or fragrances.

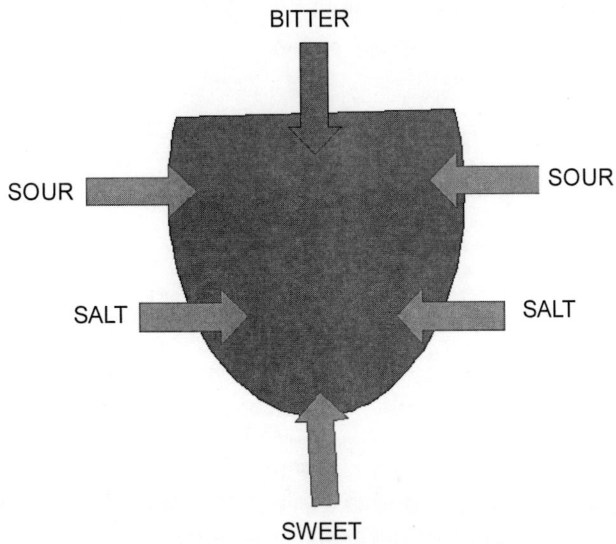


**Diag.: Different areas of tongue responsible for detecting different tastes**

**Natural** flavours must be extracted from **natural** materials. They may not be synthesized chemically. **Nature identical** flavours are the same chemical compounds as **natural** flavours but they can be synthesized chemically from the cheapest and easiest source.

Of the three chemical senses, smell is the main determinant of a **food** item's **flavour**. While the taste of **food** is limited to sweet, sour, bitter, salty, umami, and other basic tastes, the smells of a **food** are potentially limitless

## TASTE

Thousands of taste buds are present on the tongue to detect the four basic tastes i.e. sweet, sour, bitter and salt. The sensitive cells of taste buds come in contact with the stimulating substances. The message is then relayed to the brain. This how we detect the tastes of different food items. The areas of the tongue that distinguishes different tastes are shown in the diagram.

## SMELL

There are millions of olfactory receptor cells in the nasal cavity to detect the smell or odour. Liquids such as alcohol are volatile in nature and therefore excite the sense of smell. When food is put in the mouth, the volatile flavour compounds excite the nasal cavity and stimulate the olfactory hairs. This sensation gets combined with the taste of the food in the mouth to produce a combined impression of the flavour of the food.

Food flavours are divided into the following types:

a) Natural Flavours e.g. herbs and spices, fruits and vegetables

b) Processed Flavours e.g. toasted (breads), roasted (meats), fermented (wines)

c) Added Flavours is further classified as:

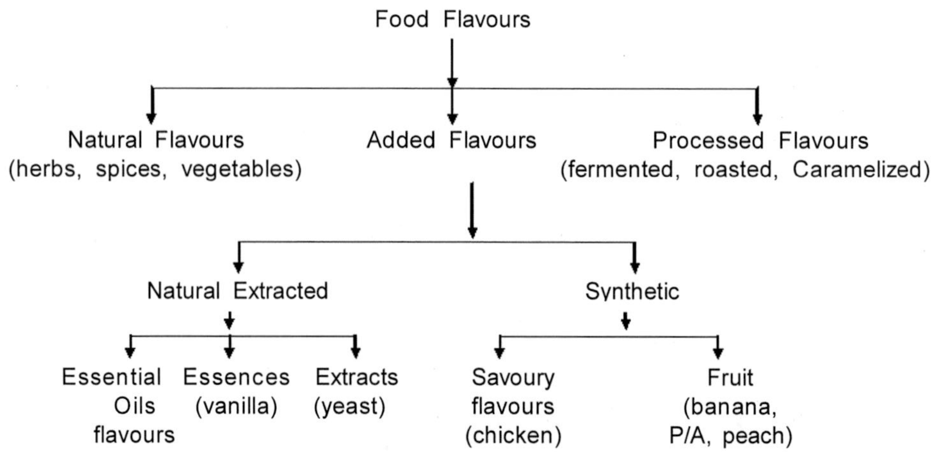


**Dia. Classification of Flavours.**

i) Natural Extracted Flavour e.g. Essential oils (menthol), Essences (vanilla, strawberry), Extracts (yeasts).

ii) Synthetic Flavours e.g. Fruit flavours (pineapple, banana), Savoury flavours (chicken, smoked).

**Natural** flavours must be extracted from **natural** materials. They may not be synthesized chemically. The dominant widely used flavoursome plants products are Parsley, thyme, mint, *Tulsi* etc. amongst the herbs; lemon, pineapple, orange etc. amongst the fruits; cinnamon, cardamom, cloves etc., amongst the spices; onion, cabbage, garlic etc. amongst the vegetables.

**Added Flavours** can be both synthetic or Natural flavours.

**Processed Flavours** develop at the time of processing of the food. Processed flavours may develop due to enzyme action or during fermentation or due to action heat. Unacceptable flavour may also develop due to oxidation.

## DESCRIPTION OF FOOD FLAVOURS

Food flavours are as complex as food colours.

There are more than 800 constituents in coffee alone which plays a role in its aroma and flavours. These constituents are basically organic chemicals and are influenced by the action of heat, air etc.

When the foods are processed the flavours of the food becomes less desirable. Thus the flavour and aroma of coffee, cooked meats, fish, tea etc. changes continuously during acquisition, processing and storing.

However, when wine is matured or cheese is ripened the flavour is improved.

Instrumental approach to analyse the flavour are done by gas chromatography and mass spectrometry,

The freshly brewed coffee will have full flavour.

Crocker and Henderson proposed four components of flavour:

- Fragrant or Fruity or Flowery
- Acid or Sharp
- Burnt or Tarry or Scorched
- Coprylic or goat-like

The sensation known as Sour is due to Hydrogen ions present in acids of fruits and vegetables.

Salt taste is due to ions of salt or Sodium Chloride.

Alcohol, certain amino acids taste sweets. Sweetness is due to the Hydroxyl (-OH) radicals in the sugar molecules.

Alkaloids such as Caffeine are bitter in taste.

In addition to the taste and smell there are other sensitive organs in the mouth. These respond to the various flavours of various foods e.g.:

Astringency of wines, The pungency of mustard,

"Coolness" of the peppermint, Crispness of cornflakes

Pungency of pepper and spices, Smoothness of ice-cream,

Stickiness of toffee, Bitterness of caffeine in coffee,

Sourness of lemon and vinegar, Sweetness of cane sugar,

Tainted flavour decomposed meat Fruity flavours of ripe fruits

Basil has pungent flavour, Coriander with piquant taste

Curry leaves with curry flavour Lemon grass with lemony flavour,

Tamarind has fruity flavour and sour taste

Onions, garlic and cabbage owe their flavour to sulphur-containing compound.

Fruits and vegetables owe their flavours to esters, aldehydes, ethers, ketones etc. found as essential oils in all natural foods.

## PROJECT BASED LEARNING OR PBL:

Charts may be made on the diagrams given in this chapter.

The students may be directed to find out different types of flavours available in the market for commercial purposes and a project may be made on the basis of the findings.

## IMPORTANT QUESTIONS

Q.No.1. Define flavours. Classify flavours.

Q.No.2. Describe different food flavours.

Chapter 10

# Browning

After reading this chapter, the student will be able to:

- *Define Browning*
- Know different types of browning
- understand role of browning in food preparation
- *learn how to prevent undesirable browning.*

## INTRODUCTION

**Browning** may be defined as the process of food turning brown because of the chemical reactions that take place within the food. The chemical reactions that take place in the food during the process of browning is explained through the food chemistry. Browning in food particularly falls into the following categories:

- Enzymatic Browning and
- Non-enzymatic Browning

Following points should be remembered about Browning:

- Browning of food takes place due to chemical reactions in the food.
- These reactions are explained in food chemistry.
- Browning reactions are of two types—enzymatic browning and Non-enzymatic Browning.
- Browning of food may have desirable or undesirable effects.
- Browning in the food industry is important because it relates to cost factor, nutrition and customer's acceptability.
- There are various methods to prevent/control browning of food to increase the shelf life of food products.

## TYPES OF BROWNING

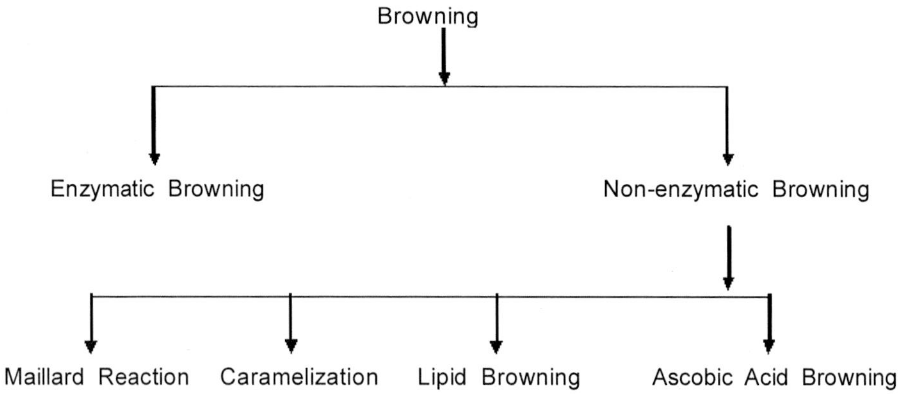


**Diagram: Classification of Browning Reactions in Food.**

## ENZYMATIC BROWNING

As the name suggests, this type of browning is caused by enzymatic oxidations of **polyphenols** and other susceptible compounds. Such browning reactions take place in many fruits, vegetables and in seafood. Enzymatic browning affects the taste, colour, and value of these foods. A number of fruits such as bananas, apples, pears, peaches etc. change from creamy white to undesirable brown colour when bruised or cut. Enzymatic browning also known as 'oxidation of foods' needs contact of Oxygen. The oxygen may be from air or from the intercellular spaces of the tissue. It begins with the oxidation **of Phenolic compounds by Phenol Oxidase into Quinone**, in a series of reactions, eventually resulting in the formation of brown pigments on the surface of the food.

The above mentioned process may be represented in the following reaction:

**$O_2$ (from air or intercellular spaces within the tissues)**

Phenolic Compound ⟶ Quinone

Phenol Oxidaise (Enzyme)

**Diagram: Enzymatic Browning Reaction**

## BENEFICIAL EFFECTS OF ENZYMATIC BROWNING:

- It improves and develops the flavour and colour in Tea, coffee etc.
- It improves and develops colour and flavours in many dry fruits e.g. Raisins.

### Negative Effects of Enzymatic Browning

- Light-coloured fresh fruits and vegetables (such as apples, bananas, potatoes etc.) when cut changes colour, tastes etc. to an unacceptable one.
- Polyphenols oxidizes is the major biochemical reaction in the formation of melanosis in crustaceans e.g. shrimp.

## PREVENTION OF UNDESIRABLE ENZYMATIC BROWNING

1) Addition of Lemon juice and other Acids: undesirable enzymatic browning can be prevented by adding lemon juice or other acids such as Ascorbic acid, Malic acid etc. as these will lower the pH value to 2.5 to 2.7.

2) Blanching or cooking fruits and vegetables: The enzymatic browning may be prevented by blanching or cooking the fruits and vegetables. This possible due to the fact that enzymes are proteins. So by the action of heat the protein will get denatured, inactivating the enzymes, and thereby the browning reaction will not take place.

3) Lowering the temperature: The activity of Phenol Oxidise is can be retarded by lowering the temperature. The activity of enzyme is dependent on the temperature. The optimum temperature for the activity of enzyme is 43°C or 109°F. Foods stored at a temperature below this will slow down the enzymatic browning reactions. But fruits should be treated to prevent browning even if kept in the cold storage.

4) Coating the fruit with sugar or sugar syrup: Coating the fruits with sugar or sugar syrup will prevent the contact with atmospheric oxygen and thus will prevent enzymatic browning. However, the intercellular oxygen will still create problem.

5) Coating with Brine Solution: covering vegetables with brine solution will prevent brining.

6) Covering in water: Covering the vegetables in water will prevent undesirable discolouration.

7) Vacuum Packing: Vacuum packing foods will prevent foods coming in contact with oxygen and thereby will prevent browning.

8) Sulpher D-oxide treatment: Sulphe di-oxide prevents browning, though the exact reason for the same is not yet clear.

### Non-enzymatic Browning

Non-enzymatic Browning, as the name suggests, is a process that results in brown colouration in the food items but without the activity of enzymes The main forms of non-enzymatic browning are the Maillard Reaction, Caramelization, Lipid browning and Ascorbic Acid browning.

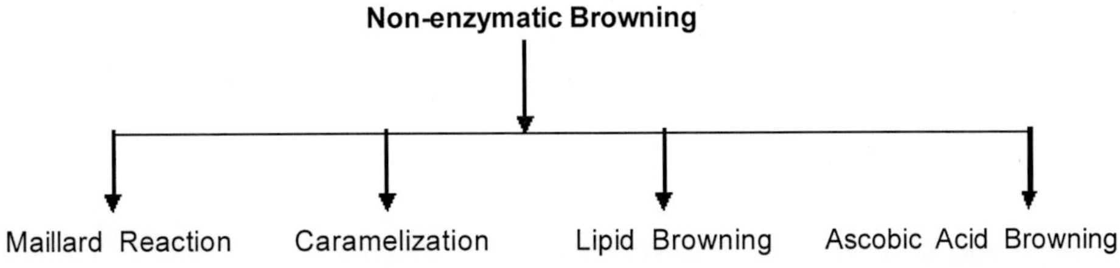

## MAILLARD REACTION

It was Maillard, in 1913, who described in a published paper, about the browning in a mixture of amino acid and reducing sugar at elevated temperature. After 40 years, John E Hodge, a chemist, established chemical reactions of Maillard Reaction.

Following points should be kept in mind:

- The Maillard Reaction may be defined as a chemical reaction between an Amino Acid and a reducing sugar at an elevated temperature ( sugar-protein reaction).
- It is type of Non-enzymatic Browning.
- The reaction may be represented in the following way:

The Reactive Carbonyl Group of the Sugar

+

Nucleophilic Amino Group of the Protein

↓ Many stages of reactions
Takes place (140 to 165 °C (280 to 330 °F)

Brown pigment results.

**FIG.: Maillard Reaction**

- The whole flavouring industry is based on Maillard Reactions.
- Different food items will have different flavour compounds, giving distinct flavour to each item.
- The artificial flavours are also developed by the scientists from these compounds only.
- Various favourable conditions for Maillard Reactions are-
  I) Elevated temperature,
  II) Moisture
  III) Catalysts such as Copper, Iron
  IV) Increased Alkalinity or pH value above 7.8
  V) Type of Amino acid and sugar present and their concentration.
- Appreciable changes are noticed in dry fruits, coffee beans, baked breads, breakfast cereals etc.
- Undesirable changes are also noticed such as loss of nutritive value, loss of Lysine and Methionine in cereals etc.

### Caramelization

Caramelization may be defined as a process that involves **Pyrolysis** of sugar.

- The process involves sugar only.

- Caramelization of sugar occurs at 163—170°C by the action of heat.
- The chemical representation of the process is given below-

$$\text{Sucrose} \xrightarrow[\text{Decomposition, Dehydration \& Polymerization}]{\text{High Temperature}} \text{Caramel+ Acid}$$

**Fig.: Caramelization**

- When sugar is boiled it passes through seven stages to get caramelized. These stages are—small threads (102°C), large threads (103°C), pearl (106°C), soft balls, hard ball, soft crack, hard crack (156°C) and finally Caramel ( at 163 – 170°C).
- The browning will depend on the pH value, types of sugar, presence of catalysts and temperature,
- This process is widely used to flavour and colour soups, gravies sauces, alcoholic beverages, coffee products etc.

## ASCORBIC ACID BROWNING

The ascorbic acid present in many fruit preserves such as Kokum, strawberry preserves get a brown pigmentation due to oxidation.

Prevention: Low storage temperature and addition of Bisulphate's.

## LIPID BROWNING

As is clear from the name itself, this type of browning is found in fats. The amino group of phospholipids and lipoproteins reacts with reducing sugar and aldehydes to form this undesirable browning reaction.

Prevention: Not to store fat for long periods of time.

## ROLE OF BROWNING IN FOOD PREPARATION

Browning of may be desirable in some food preparations, but in some cases the browning need to be prevented. Therefore the role of browning reactions will include examples from both the cases.

- Enzymatic Browning produces an unacceptable condition to the fruits and vegetables. Therefore, it should be prevented. Enzymatic browning of various fruits and vegetables such as bananas, apples, peaches and potatoes produce a brown pigmentation. These fruits and vegetables cannot be used in fruit salads or in Gueridon service due to the discolouration.
- The browning that takes place during the normal cooking methods such as baking, grilling, roasting etc. are highly acceptable to the guests. It produces a colour, texture and flavour that is savoured by the customers. Therefore, roasted chicken or grilled fish or baked beans on toasts are highly popular

dishes.

- There are desirable and undesirable browning reactions take place in Maillard Reactions. The desirable effects of Maillard reactions are noticed in baked breads, roasted coffee beans etc. whereas in baked and roasted foods and also in milk, Lysine and Methionine are lost.
- In case of Ascorbic acid browning the acid is lost from strawberries and citrus juices.
- The attractive golden brown colour of French Fries or cakes or breads are due to browning reactions only.

Therefore it is clear that the undesirable effects of browning in food preparation must be prevented and the desirable effects must be controlled. If a chef is able to do that, he can produce highly attractive food items. The loss that is suffered by the catering industry due undesirable effect of browning can also be prevented by taking proper preventive measures.

## KEY TERMS

- *Browning:* Browning may be defined as the process of food turning brown because of the chemical reactions that take place within the food. The chemical reactions that take place in the food during the process of browning is explained through the food chemistry
- *Enzymatic Browning*: As the name suggests, this type of browning is caused by enzymatic oxidations of polyphenols and other susceptible compounds. Such browning reactions take place in many fruits, vegetables and in seafood.
- *Non-enzymatic Browning*: Non-enzymatic Browning, as the name suggests, is a process that results in brown colouration in the food items but without the activity of enzymes.
- *Maillard Reaction*: It was Maillard, in 1913, described in a published paper, about the browning in a mixture of amino acid and reducing sugar at elevated temperature. After 40 years, John E Hodge, a chemist, established chemical reactions of Maillard Reaction.
- *Caramelization*: Caramelization may be defined as a process that involves Pyrolysis of sugar.
- *Ascorbic acid browning*: The ascorbic acid present in many fruit preserves such as Kokum, strawberry preserves get a brown pigmentation due to oxidation.
- *Lipid Browning*: As is clear from the name itself, this type of browning is found in fats. The amino group of phospholipids and lipoproteins reacts with reducing sugar and aldehydes to form this undesirable browning reaction. Prevention: Not to store fat for long periods of time.

## PROJECT BASED LEARNING OR PBL

Students may be asked to prepare a project report on Mailalard Reaction.

They may be told to prepare a project report on Caramelisations.

A project report may be prepared on the Role of Browning in Indian Food Preparation.

## IMPORTANT QUESTIONS

Q. No.1. Define Browning. Classify browning.

Q. No.2. Explain Enzymatic Browning. How will you prevent it?

Q. No.3. What is Non-enzymatic browning? How will you prevent it?

Q. No.4. Explain the role of browning in food preparations.

Chapter 11

# Glossary

**Anti-caking Agents**: Anti-caking agents are food additives which do not allow the particles of food to adhere to one another. This helps in increasing the flow properties of food during processing.

Antioxidants: Antioxidants maybe defined as substances which are used to stop oxidation of fats.

**Autoxidation: Autoxidation** may be defined as the oxidation that takes place in open air or in the presence of oxygen and forms peroxides and hydro-peroxides.

**Bancroft Rule**: Bancroft Rule states that "The phase in which an emulsifier is more soluble constitutes the continuous phase".

**Basal Metabolism: Basal Metabolism is a term used for the maintenance of vital body functions such as respiration, blood circulation, kidney function, beating of the heart, regulating body temperature etc. Basal metabolism is affected by many factors such as gender, growth, age, body size, body temperature, body composition, stress etc.**

Basic Structure: $C_X(H_2O)_Y$

**Biological Value or BV:** Biological Value may be defined as the proportion of nitrogen absorbed that is retained by the body for the growth and maintenance. This helps to determine the Protein Quality.

$$BMI = \frac{\textit{Body weight in kilograms}}{(\textit{height in meters})2}$$

**BMR or Basal Metabolic Rate: BMR or BEE( basal energy expenditure) may be defined as one " measure of the minimum amount of energy that an awake, resting body requires to maintain the basic life-sustaining, vital functions".**

**Body Mass Index or BMI:** Body Mass Index or BMI is a way of finding out the desirable body weight of an adult.

**Browning** may be defined as the process of food turning brown because of the chemical reactions that take place within the food.

**Carbohydrates** may be defined as a class of chemicals (or Organic Compounds) found in foods which contain Carbon (hence Carbo), Hydrogen and Oxygen (hence Hydrate). The ratio of Hydrogen and Oxygen in Carbohydrates are always in the proportions found in water i.e. 2:1

**Coarse suspension**: The sizes of the particles are larger than one micron.

**Colloid**: A colloid may be defined as a mixture in which insoluble particles of a substance is dispersed throughout another substance.

**Colloidal Dispersion**: The sizes of the particles are one millimicron to one micron

**Denaturation**-when the unique spatial arrangements of the helix or the polypeptide chain is altered, a protein molecule is said to be Denatured.

**Dextrinization**: When dry heat is applied to starch the starch gets converted into dextrins which is brown in colour. This process is known as Dextrinization.

**Difference testing** helps to determine the differences in two or more dishes.

**Emulsifying agents:** are substances that are soluble in both fat and water and enable fat to be uniformly dispersed in water as an emulsion.

**Emulsion:** An emulsion can be defined as a mixture of two or more liquids that are un-mixable. Emulsions are of two-phase systems of matter termed as Colloids. But in food production the term Emulsion is used as both phases, dispersed and continuous, are liquids. Therefore, in an emulsion, one liquid or the dispersed phase is dispersed in another liquid or the continuous phase.

Energy Balance: When the amount of energy consumed by the body through diet equals to the amount of energy expanded by the body, the state is called Energy Balance.

**Energy:** Energy has been defined by Oxford Dictionary as "the strength and vitality required to keep alive." Therefore, energy is the ability or capacity to do work.

**Enzymatic Browning**: As the name suggests, this type of browning is caused by enzymatic oxidations of polyphenols and other susceptible compounds.

**Fire Point**: After the flash it burns and is called **the fire point**.

**Firming Agents**: Firming agents are also food additives used to ensure that the tissues of fruits and vegetables remain crisp and firm.

**Flash Point:** Further heating leads to flash and is called **flash point**.

**Flavour reversion:** –The Fats undergo peculiar changes before it gets rancid. The characteristic flavour associated is lost and the fat and oil has a flat taste and a greasy feel on the tongue. This is known as **flavour reversion and precedes rancidity changes**.

**Flavour:** Flavour, is the sensory impression of food or other items, and is determined primarily by the chemical senses of taste and smell.

**Food Additives:** Food Additives may be defined as chemical substances intentionally added to food to increase food quality.

Food chemistry: - Food chemistry **may be defined as the science that deals with the study of** the chemical **processes and interactions of all biological and non-**

**biological components of foods. Therefore, this branch of science helps us understand**

Food microbiology: **Food Microbiology may be defined as the branch of science that deals with the study of the** various micro-organisms **that grow and multiply in the food and contaminates food. It includes the microorganisms responsible for spoilage of food.**

Food preservation: Food preservation is a process by which effectively eliminate or minimize all the factors responsible for food deterioration.

**Food processing:** Food processing may be defined as the conversion of raw food ingredients into food by using physical or chemical means. Therefore food processing is a technique in which ready-to-eat or convenience food products are produced for a target market from various raw ingredients.

Food Rheology: Food Rheology may be defined as the study of the Rheological properties of food or in other words it is the study of the consistency and flow of food under tightly specified conditions.

**Food Science:** -The Institute of Food Technologists has defined Food Science as "the discipline in which the engineering, biological, and physical sciences are used to study the nature of foods, the causes of deterioration, the principles underlying food processing, and the improvement of foods for the consuming public". The Textbook of *Food Science* defines food science in simpler terms as "the application of basic sciences and engineering to study the physical, chemical, and biochemical nature of foods and the principles of food processing"

**Food scientists: Food Scientists** develop foods that are both safe and nutritious. They are also responsible for the food packaging

**Gel:** A Gel may be defined as solid jelly-like material that can have properties ranging from soft and weak to hard and tough.

**Gelatinization**: When starch is heated with water, it absorbs water, swells, forms a past and then stiffens forming a gel, this is called Gelatinization of starch.

**Humectants:** Humectants are food additives which reduce the effect of humidity on a food by absorbing moisture for example Baking Powder.

**Hydrogenation:** Hydrogenation may be defined as a process by which the oils in the liquid state are converted into solid fats by the addition of Hydrogen.

**Hydrolytic Rancidity:** It is the hydrolysis of Triglyceride molecules to glycerol and fatty acids in the presence of moisture. The process of hydrolysis may get faster due to the presence of microorganisms and/or enzymes.

Important types of Carbohydrates in the foods are: Sugar, Dextrin, Starch, Cellulose, Pectin etc.

**Kilocalorie (Kcalories):** Energy is also measured in Kilocalorie (Kcalories). Kilocalorie may be defined as the heat required to raise the temperature of 01kg. of water by one degree of Celsius.

**Kilojoules:** Is measured as the amount of work done to move a 01kg. Object to a distance of 01 meter under the force of gravity.

**Lipid Browning**: As is clear from the name itself, this type of browning is found in fats

**Lipids:** Fats and oils are organic compounds, they are commonly called Lipids.

**Melting Point**: Fats when heated gradually reach the **melting point** and softens.

**Native Proteins**: Native proteins are the proteins found in the cells and in its fluids of the living tissues of the plants and animals.

**Non-enzymatic Browning:** Non-enzymatic Browning, as the name suggests, is a process that results in brown colouration in the food items but without the activity of enzymes.

or 2H : O.

**Oxidative Rancidity**: Oxidation of Unsaturated Fats (Oils) leads to oxidative rancidity.

**Pasteurization: Pasteurization** is a process in which the pathogens are killed by heating the liquid to approximately $70^0$C for half a minute and then cooling it about $10^0$C

**Perception:** Perception deals with the biochemical and psychological aspects of sensation.

**Preference test**: Preference test may be defined as a test that gives information on particular aspects determines the preference of the dish. Hedonic scale is used for evaluation.

**Preservatives:** Preservatives may be defined as substances which are added to foods to prevent spoilage by stopping the growth of microorganisms such as yeasts, bacteria and molds.

**Rancidity**: – Spoilage of fats results in unpleasant flavour and the fat becomes unfit for consumption. These changes are termed as rancidity of fats.

**Retrogradation:** The Amylose (the linear starch) in the cooked starch paste remain in dispersed form and the paste can flow or viscous as long as it is hot. But when the paste cools off the amylose re-bond together and become rigid. This recrystallization of the gelatinized starch is called Retrogradation.

**SDA or Specific Dynamic Action**: SDA or specific dynamic action refers to that amount of the energy expenditure of the body which needs energy for digestion ingestion absorption transportation utilization storage and exertion. The other terms used to donate this is Calorigenic effect of food or Thermic effect of food or Diet-induced Thermogenesis.

**Sensory Evaluation:** Sensory evaluation is a scientific discipline that analyses and measures human responses to the composition of **food** and drink, e.g. appearance, touch, odour, texture, temperature and taste.

**Sol:** A Sol may be defined as a colloidal suspension of very small particles in a continuous liquid medium.

**Starch**: When the glucose units in a molecule exceed a certain number, the resulting high polymer is called **"starch"**.

**Subjective testing**: Subjective Testing or Affective Testing is also known as Consumer Testing and deals with the subjective facts e.g. preferences or how much the food is expected to be accepted.

**SYNERESIS:** The bulk of the water in cooked starch paste is held in the spaces formed by the network of swollen starch grains and precipitated amylase. When a Gel is cut or even as it ages, some of the liquid will seep from the interstices. This leakage of liquid from a gel is known as Syneresis.

- The chemical reactions that takes place in the food
- The composition of food items
- The structures of the food components.
- The various properties of food items

**The smoke point: The smoke point** of an oil or fat is the temperature at which, under defined conditions, enough volatile compounds emerge when a bluish gas or smoke becomes clearly visible from the oil.

**True Solution**: The size of particles are up to one mill micron

**Tyndall Effect:** Emulsions contain both a dispersed and a continuous phase, with the boundary between the phases called the "interface". Emulsions tend to have a cloudy appearance because the many phase interfaces scatter light as it passes through the emulsion. Emulsions appear white when all light is scattered equally. If the emulsion is dilute enough, Higher-frequency and low-wavelength light will be scattered more, and the emulsion will appear blur – this is called the "Tyndall effect".

**Underweight: Underweight** is a term describing a person whose body weight is considered too low to be healthy. The definition usually refers to people with a BMI of under 18 or a weight 15% to 20% below that normal for their age group.

**Viscosity:** The viscosity of a fluid is a measure of its resistance to gradual deformation by shear stress or tensile stress. For liquids it corresponds to the informal concept of "thickness", e.g. honey has a much higher viscosity than water. Higher viscosity item have higher consistency and lower viscosity product will have lower consistency.

**Winterization:** Winterization is a process in which oils are quickly cooled ensuring no movement so that the crystals of Triglycerides fall apart and chilled, viscous oil is obtained. This pre-cooling treatment to remove fat crystals is known as Winterization. And this oil is said to be **winterized.**

Chapter 12

# Question Bank

**NATIONAL COUNCIL FOR HOTEL MANAGEMENT AND CATERING TECHNOLOGY**

**PRINCIPLES OF FOOD SCIENCE**

**Academic year - 2015—2016**

**Time allowed—03 hours** **Max. Marks—100**

Q.1. Define food science and discuss the relationship of food science with food chemistry, food microbiology and food processing. (10)

Q.2. Define emulsion. discuss two types of emulsion (o/w), w/o). State the role of emulsifying agents. (10)

Q.3. What are fats and oils? differentiate between them.

OR

Discus the functional properties of proteins i.e. viscosity, foamability, gelation and emulsification. (10)

Q.4. Differentiate between amylose and amylopectin. explain the factors affecting starch gel formation. (10)

Q.5. Define enzymatic browing in food. How will you prevent enzymatic browing reactions? (10)

Q.6. Give brief description of the following:

a) Dextrinisation b) Gelatinization (5+5=10)

Q.7. Explain the sensory evaluation of food quality.

OR

Discuss the types of colloidal system. (10)

Q.8. Explain the following terms (*any five*)

A) Pasteurisation B) Winterisation

C) Denaturation of proteins D) Syneresis

E) Food rheology F) Food enzyme (5X2=10)

G) Reaction maillard

Q.9. Explain the classification of food flavours.

Or

What are the objectives of food processing? Describe two food preservation methods. (10)

Q.10. Fill in the blanks (10X1=10)

A) HTST stands For——————

B) Rancidity Occurs In ————

C) Polyphenolase is———which causes enzymatic browning.

D) ——-is natural emulsifying agent.

E) ——-compound is formed in maillard reaction.

F) The protein gluten is present in ————

G) ————is the natural pigment in tomatoes.

H) ————is a crystalloid.

I) ————-is a proteolytic enzyme present in pineapple.

J) Dry heating of starch is known as —————

## NATIONAL COUNCIL FOR HOTEL MANAGEMENT AND CATERING TECHNOLOGY

## PRINCIPLES OF FOOD SCIENCE

## ACADEMIC YEAR - 2014-2015

Time Allowed—03 HoURS Max. Marks—100

Q.1. A) Define food science.

B) Enumerate its importance for catering establishments. (3+7=10)

Q.2. A) Classify Carbohydrates

B) Describe any five functions of carbohydrate in food productions (5+5=10)

OR

Explain the process of gelatinization and with the help of an illustration state. The factors affecting it. (10)

Q.3. A) Describe three types of dispersions.

B) Explain some colloids that can be formed during food preparations.

(5+5=10)

OR

Define the role of emulsifying agents in food and explain the characteristics of emulsions. (10)

Q.4. Illustrate the basic structure of proteins. state the properties of proteins that are useful for food preparations. (5+5=10)

Q.5. What is the importance of antioxidants in food? explain any two types of spoilage conditions seen in fats and list some preventive measures. (3+7=10)

Q.6. How is the proximate analysis of food constitutes conducted in the food industry? (10)

OR

Define sensory assesment of food quality. draw a standard format of a score. Card used for sensory evaluation of food. (3+7=10)

Q.7. Why is the demand for food processing greatly increasing? Explain the types of processing methods by application of heat. (3+7=10)

OR

Explain the science behind the detection of flavour by the five sensory organs of the body. (10)

Q.8. List atleast two differences:

A) Winterisation and homogenization

B) Microwave and irradiation

C) CAP and MAP

D) Leavening and shortening agents

E) Natural and synthetic emulsifiers (5X2=10)

Q.9. Answer in brief (5X2=10)

A) Flavour of tea

B) Fermentation

C) Taste panel

D) Refining of fat

E) Synthesis

Q.10. Fill in the blaks: (5X2=10)

A) ——————————-is the enzyme responsible for undesireable browning in food ( phenol oxidase, amylase, papin)

B) Cream is an example of ———————————————- (aerosol, emulsion, solid foam),

C) Masticometer is a device used to measure the ————————————- of a product (chewiness, flow, colour).

D) A processing technique applying heat which kills only the disease causing micro-organism is ————————————— (sterilisation, pasteurisation, drying).

E) A flavour component in wine which contributes to the mouth feel and colour and breaks down during aging is ———————————— (nicotine, caffeine, and tannin).

# NATIONAL COUNCIL FOR HOTEL MANAGEMENT AND CATERING TECHNOLOGY

## PRINCIPLES OF FOOD SCIENCE

## ACADEMIC YEAR - 2012—2013

**Time Allowed—03 Hours** **Max, Marks—100**

Q.1. A) Explain the importance of food science in the hospitality industry.

B) Describe the inter-relationship of food science with other related fields. (5+5=10)

Q.2. A) Illustrate the effect of heat on proteins with the help of a suitable diagram.

B) Explain any two functions of protein with suitable examples.

OR

A) Classify proteins based on their origin.

B) State the uses of protein in various food preparations. (5+5=10)

Q.3. State the factors affecting the texture of carbohydrates and name any two carbohydrates that can be used to thicken food preparations. (5+5=10)

OR

Explain the process of gelatinization and explain any two classes of carbohydrates. (10)

Q.4. Define the term rancidity. What are the factors affecting autoxidation? How can it be prevented?

OR

With the help of a neat flowchart classify fats and oils and state any two uses of fats in commercial preparations (8+2=10)

Q.5. Food processing is of great importance. elaborate on the various processing treatments that can be applied to food. (10)

Q.6. A) What are the steps to be followed while conducting sensory evaluation of food?

B)state the various types of objective evaluations that are executed on food? (5+5=10)

Q.7. Give one word for the following statements: - (5X2=10)

A) Study of the flow properties of food.

B) A mixture of egg white and sugar beaten stiffly.

C) Light rays getting deflacted when passed through a liquid.

D) Pigment responsible for the green colour of vegetable.

E) Treatment given so that oils remain fluid at refrigerator temperature.

Q.8. Answer in breif (ANY FIVE):

A) Flavour reversion in fats.

B) Flavour in spices with four examples.

C) Format of a sample score card for sensory evaluation.

D) Objectives of food procesing.

E) Structurs of protiens.

F) Theory of emulsification. (5X2=10)

Q.9. Differentiate between the following:

A) hydrolysis and hydrogenation.

B) enzymatic and non enzymatic browning.

C) denaturation and dextrinization.

D) differnce and decriptive tests.

E) jams and marmalade. (5X2=10)

Q.10. Match the following: (10X1=10)

| | |
|---|---|
| A) Capsaicin | (1) Heating fats |
| B) Monosaccharide | (2) Milk |
| C) Flash Point | (3) Foam |
| D) Homogenization | (4) Chilles |
| E) Brine | (5) Micro-organism |
| F) Egg yolk | (6) Wheat flour |
| G) Red Wine | (7) Carbohydrates |
| H) Marshmallow | (8) Lecithin |
| I) Gluten | (9) Tannins |
| J) Yeast | (10) True Solution |

## NATIONAL COUNCIL FOR HOTEL MANAGEMENT AND CATERING TECHNOLOGY

## PRINCIPLES OF FOOD SCIENCE

## ACADEMIC YEAR - 2011—2012

TIME ALLOWED—03 HOURS MAX, MARKS—100

Q.1. DEFINE FOOD SCIENCE. DISCUSS THE SCOPE OF FOOD SCIENCE AND THE ROLE IT PLAYS IN TODAY'S GROWING INDUSTRY. (3+7=10)

Q2. WHAT IS GEL FORMATION? WHAT ARE THE FACTORS AFFECTING GEL FORMATION? (2+8=10)

Q3. WRITE BRIEFLY ON THE TYPES AND PROPERTIES OF COLLOIDS. (10)

Q4. GIVE THE FUNCTIONAL PROPERTIES OF PROTEIN.

OR

WRITE DOWN THE THEORIES OF EMULSION. (10)

Q5. DEFINE ENZYMATIC BROWNING. HOW WILL YOU PREVENT ENZYMATIC BROWNING REACTIONS? (2+8=10)

Q6. DISCUSS ABOUT THE ROLE OF FAT AS: (5+5=10)

(a) LEAVENING AGENT

(b) SHORTENING AGENT

OR

DESCRIBE THE CHANGES OCCURRING IN PROTEIN FOODS DUE TO ACTION OF HEAT AND ACID. (10)

Q7. WHAT ARE THE OBJECTIVES OF FOOD PROCESSING? DESCRIBE PASTEURIZATION METHODS? (7+3=10)

OR

NAME SOME PIGMENTS FOUND IN FRUITS AND VEGETABLES. WHAT CHANGES OCCUR IN THEM DUE TO ACTION OF HEAT, ACIDS AND ALKALIS? (5+5=10)

Q8. GIVE BRIEF DESCRIPTION OF THE FOLLOWING: (5+5=10)

(a) GELATINIZATION

(b) CARAMELIZATION AND MAILLARD REACTION

Q9. EXPLAIN THE CLASSIFICATION OF FOOD FLAVOURS.

OR

EXPLAIN THE SENSORY CHARACTERISTICS OF FOOD (10)

Q10. FILL IN THE BLANKS: (10x1=10)

(a) ______________ IS THE FATHER OF COLLOIDAL SYSTEM.

(b) AN EXAMPLE FOR EMULSION IS ______________.

(c) HEATING OF DRY STARCH IS KNOWN AS ____________.

(d) __________ IS AN ENZYME WHICH CAUSES ENZYMATIC BROWNING.

(e) HTST STANDS FOR ____________.

(f) LACTOSE IS AN ___________.

(g) ____________ IS AN EXAMPLE FOR ESSENTIAL AMINO ACID.

(h) THE UNPLEASANT ODOUR OF FAT RESULTS ____________.

(i) SOL IS A ____________ GEL.

(j) ____________ IS A NATURAL PRESERVATIVE.

# NATIONAL COUNCIL FOR HOTEL MANAGEMENT AND CATERING TECHNOLOGY

## PRINCIPLES OF FOOD SCIENCE

## ACADEMIC YEAR - 2011—2012

TIME ALLOWED—03 HOURS MAX, MARKS— 100

Q1. WHAT IS FOOD PROCESSING AND IT'S OBJECTIVE? (10)

OR

EXPLAIN ANY FIVE SUBJECTIVE EVALUATION METHODS FOR FOOD.

Q2. CLASSIFY CARBOHYDRATES AND EXPLAIN THE EFFECT OF MOIST HEAT ON STARCH AND FACTORS AFFECTING IT.

OR

CLASSIFY PROTEINS. EXPLAIN THE VARIOUS STAGES OF EGG FOAM FORMATION. (10)

Q3. (A) DEFINE FOOD SCIENCE.

(B) DEFINE FLAVOUR AND CLASSIFY IT. (5+5=10)

OR

ENZYMATIC BROWNING CAN BE PREVENTED. HOW?

Q4. WRITE SHORT NOTES ON THE FOLLOWING:

(A) EMULSIFICATION (B) RANCIDITY

(C) DENATURATION (D) USE OF CAROHYDERATES IN FOOD PREPARATION

(E) MAILLARD REACTION (5X2=10)

Q5. DISCUSS THE TYPES OF RANCIDITY COMMONLY OBSERVED IN FOOD. (10)

Q6. DIFFERENTIATE BETWEEN A SOLUTION, COLLOIDAL DISPERSION AND A SUSPENSION. (10)

Q7. EXPLAIN THE ROLE OF BROWNING AND FLOVOURS IN FOOD PREPARATION. (10)

Q8. DISCUSS THE NEWER TRENDS OF FOOD PACKAGING IN INDIA. (10)

Q9. (A) WHAT IS HYDROGENATION? WHAT ARE ITS ADVANTAGES?

(B) EXPLAIN THE COMMERCIAL SIGNIFICATION OF FATS AND OILS.

(5+5=10)

Q10. FILL IN THE BLANKS: (10x1=10)

(A) THE CONTINOUS PHASE IIN SOL IS ______________ (GAS/SOLIDS/ LIQUIDS)

(B) EMULSIFICATION AGENT NATURALLY PRESENTS IN THE YOLK IS _________. (YORK/EGG WHITE/LECITHIN)

(C) DEXTRIN IS A __________ (MONOSACCHARIDE, DISACCHARIDE, POLYSACCHARIDE).

(D) GELATINIZATION REQUIRE_____________ HEAT (DRY, SEMIDRY, MOIST).

(E) PEPTIDE LINKAGE OCCUR IN_______________ NUTRIENT (FAT, PROTEIN, CARBOHYDRATE).

(F) DISAGREEABLE ODOUR AND FLAVOUR IN FATS AND OILS IS CALLED ____________.( REVERSION, WINTERIZATION, RANCIDITY).

(G) _________ EXZYME IS RESPONSIBLE FOR ENZYMATIC BROWNING (PHENOL OXDIASE, PHENOL NITRATE, PHENOL CARBOXLASE).

(H) DANGER ZONE TEMPERATURE RANGE FOR FOOD PRODUCT ARE __________ °C. (1-4°C, 20-40°C, 5-63°C).

(I) TRIANGLE TEST IS A ___________TEST (DESCRIPTIVE, DISCRIMINATION, CHEMICAL).

(J) ADDED FLAVOURS ARE___________ (NATURAL EXTRACTED, SYNTHETIC, BOTH NATURAL AND SYNTHETIC).

## NATIONAL COUNCIL FOR HOTEL MANAGEMENT AND CATERING TECHNOLOGY

## PRINCIPLES OF FOOD SCIENCE

## TERM END EXAMINATION—2015-2016

TIME ALLOWED—03 HOURS MAX. MARKS— 100

Q1. (A) DEFINE FOOD SCIENCE. WHAT IS ITS SCOPE?

(B) NAME AND DEFINE **ANY FIVE** FIELDS OF SCIENCE RELATED TO FOOD SCIENCE. (5+5=10)

Q2. DRAW A CHART OF THE VAROUS KINDS OF CARBOHYDRATES BASED ON NUMBER OF SUGAR UNITS AND THEIR COMPLEXITY. GIVE ONE EXAMPLE OF EACH

OR

WHAT IS GELATINIZATION? WHAT FACTORS EFFECTS GELATINIZATION OF STARCH? (10)

Q3. WHAT ARE THE DIFFERENT TYPES OF FATS BASED ON DEGREE OF SATURATION? GIVE ONE EXAMPLE OF EACH TYPE?

OR

A) WHAT DO YOU MEAN BY SHORTENING VALUE OF FATS?

B) WHY IS REFINING OF FATS DONE AND HOW?

Q.4. EXPLAIN THREE FUNCTIONAL PROPERTIES OF PROTEINS (GELATION, EMULSIFICATION, FOAMABILITY, VISCOCITY)

OR

EXPLAIN IN DETAILS THE PROCESS OF DENATURATION AND COAGULATION OF PROTEINS WITH THE HELP OF SUITABLE EXAMPLES. (10)

Q.5. NAME AND DESCRIBE THE BROWNING REACTIONS THAT OCCUR IN FOOD. NAME FIVE FOOD ITEMS IN WHICH BROWNING IMPROVE THE FLAVOUR. (10)

OR

WHAT CHARACTERISTICS DO COLLOIDS EXIBIT? NAME AND EXPLAIN ANY THREE. (10)

Q.6. WHAT IS SENSORY ASSESSMENT OF FOOD QUALITY AND WHAT ARE THE PARAMETERS USED TO ASSESS THE SAME? (10)

OR

A) DEFINE FOOD PROCESSING. WHAT ARE THE OBJECTIVES OF FOOD PROCESSING?

B) NAME ANY FIVE EFFECTS OF PROCESSING ON NUTRITIVE VALUE OF FOODS AND ALSO STATE FIVE WAYS TO AVOID LOSS OF NUTRIENTS. (5+5=10)

Q.7. DIFFERENTIATE BETWEEN THE FOLLOWING (ANY TWO):

A) SOL and SUSPENSION

B) AUTO OXIDATION AND HYDROLYTIC RANCIDITY

C) STARCH and DEXTRIN

D) FRACTIONATION and WINTERIZATION

Q.8. MATCH NTHE FOLLOWING; -

| | |
|---|---|
| A) ACROLEIN | 1) MICELLE FORMATION |
| B) RHEOLOGY | 2) SYNERISIS |

# NATIONAL COUNCIL FOR HOTEL MANAGEMENT AND CATERING TECHNOLOGY

## NUTRITION

## ACADEMIC YEAR - 2016—2017

TIME ALLOWED—03 HOURS MAX, MARKS—100

Q.1. DISCUSS THE IMPORTANCE OF FOOD IN MAINTAINING THE GOOD HEALTH.

OR

CLASSIFY NUTRIENTS AND DISCUSS THEM BRIEFLY. (10)

Q.2. DEFINE ENERGY. DISCUSS THE VARIOUS FACTORS AFFECTING THE REQUREMENTS OF ENERGY. (10)

Q.3. WHAT ARE THE FUNCTIONS OF CARBOHYDRATES IN OUR BODY?

OR

ILLUSTRATE THE ROLE OF DIETARY FIBRE IN HUMAN DIET. (10)

Q.4. CLASSIFY VITAMINS AND EXPLAIN THE SIGNIFICANCE OF VITAMIN A AND D.

OR

DEFINE AND CLASSIFY PROTEINS. SUGGEST METHODS TO IMPROVE THEIR QUALITY. (10)

Q.5. ENLIST THE VARIOUS FUNCTIONS OF WATER IN MAINTAINING GOOD HEALTH.

OR

DEFINE INVISIBLE SOURCE OF WATER. HOW WATER BALANCE IS MAINTAINED IN OUR BODY? (10)

Q.6. 'BALANCED DIET IS IMPORTANT TO LIVE A HEALTHY LIFE" HOW FAR DO YOU AGREE WITH THIS STATEMENT? (10)

Q.7. WHAT ARE THE VARIOUS FACTORS INVOLVED IN MENU PLANNING IN RELATION TO NUTRITION? (10)

Q.8. DISCUSS THE FAST FOOD TREND IN THE FOOD SERVICE INDUSTRY, WITH REFERENCE TO NUTRITION AND HEALTH. (10)

Q.9. WHAT MEASURES SHOULD BE TAKEN IN THE MASS FOOD PRODUCTIONTO RETAIN MAXIMUM NUTRITIVE VALUE OF FOOD? (10)

Q.10. STATE TRUE OR FALSE:

A) ANOTHER NAME OF VITAMIN-A IS THIAMINE

B) ENERGY IS DEFINED AS THE CAPACITY FOR DOING WORK.

C) COFFEE IS AN INVISIBLE SOURCE OF WATER.

D) LACTOSE SUGAR IS FOUND IN MILK.

E) 1-GRAM OF PROTEIN GIVES 4-KCAL WHEN OXIDISED IN THE BODY.

F) PYRIDOXINE DEFICIENCY CAUSES PELLAGRA.

G) AMLA IS A GOOD SOURCE OF VITAMIN-C.

H) DEFICIENCY OF IODINE CAUSES GOITRE.

I) FATS ARE CLASSIFIED UNDER MICRONUTRIENTS.

J) VITAMIN-B IS SOLUBLE IN WATER.

# PART TWO
# Nutrition

Chapter 13

# Introduction to Basic Aspects of Nutrition

## DEFINITION OF USEFUL TERMS

**Food**: Food has been defined by the Oxford Dictionary as "any substance that people or animals eat or that plants absorb to stay alive." Therefore we can say that foods are those substances which are taken into the body to maintain life and growth. Foods are nourishing, complex and chemical substances that provide fifty or more nutrients required for life, growth and good health.

**An interesting fact** is that there are no two foods in the nature that provide exactly the same and equal quantity of nutrients,

**Health:** Health has been defined by the Oxford Dictionary as "the state of being free from illness."

According to World Health Organization, health is the "state of complete physical mental and social well-being and not merely the absence of disease and infirmity."

**Nutrition**: Nutrition has been defined by the Oxford Dictionary as "the process of eating or taking nourishment." Therefore nutrition can be defined as a process of supplying or receiving of nourishing food. Proper nutrition can be received or supplied by the consumption of right type, right quantity and right quality of food that body requires. The body must be able to digest and absorb all the nutrients provided by the food for desirable growth and maintenance.

**Nutrients**: Nutrients, as per Oxford Dictionary are the "substances essential for life and growth. Therefore, nutrients are those fifty plus highly complex chemical substances required for life, growth and maintenance of the whole body.

Some Other Related Terms

**Diet**: Diet as per Oxford Dictionary is "the food that a person or animal usually eats" or "a limited range or amount of food, adopted to lose weight or for medical reasons".

**Dietetics**: It is defined as the study of diet and its effects on health.

**Dietician**: A dietician is an expert on diet and nutrition.

**Malnutrition**: It can be defined as poor health caused by not having enough food or not enough of the right food. Malnutrition includes both over and under nutrition resulting in a deficiency or excess of nutrient consumption.

## IMPORTANCE OF FOOD

Physiological, Psychological and Social function of food in maintaining good health. Food is highly important for all living beings. The animal and plant kingdom is dependent on food to carry out the essential functions. Following are the various functions of food in maintaining good health.

1. **Physiological Functions**: The plants and animals are made up of atoms bound together to form molecules, which forms cells, cells form tissues and tissues forms the organ and organ system which performs various functions to remain alive. These functions can only be performed if nutrients are provided through food.

   With the help of the energy derived from food, the body performs following physiological functions:

   a) **Respiration**- Respiratory Functions are performed by the lungs, trachea and air passage ways.

   b) **Reproduction**- Food helps in reproductive activities essential for continuation of species.

   c) **Excretory**- The metabolic wastes are removed from the body by kidney, lungs, bladder and skin.

   d) **Immunity**- Food provides immunity. It helps lymph and lymph structure to fight against the foreign invaders.

   e) **Support, Strength and Growth**- Food provides nutrients which helps in the function of muscular and skeletal organ system comprising of bones, cartilage, ligaments, cardiac, skeletal muscles etc.

   f) **Receiving Stimuli**- The nutrients of the food strengthen the nervous system of the body made up of nerves, sense organs, brain, spinal chord etc.

   g) **Controls Body Temperature**- Nutrients of the food helps the Integumentary organ system comprising of hair, nails, skin, etc to cover and protect the body and maintain normal body temperature.

   h) **Regulates Body Function**- The nutrients helps in maintaining endocrine system made up of thyroid gland, pituitary gland, etc which regulates various body functions.

2. **Psychological Functions**- Other than the Physiological and biochemical function, food plays an important role on our psychology too.

   a) **Love**- Food plays an important role in displaying love. When a mother cooks fovourite food for her child, she's actually expressing her love for the child.

b) **Security**- A child feels fully secured when eating food sitting on mother's lap. When we eat homemade food we feel a sense a security about the quality of food.

c) **Happiness**- We generally go out to dine or prepare expensive food items when we're very happy. The same thing is done when we want to reward one of our family member or friend.

d) **Negative Feelings**- When a person is bored, anxious, frustrated or lonely, he/she generally tends to skip a meal or eat less/more.

3. **Social Function**- Other than Physiological and psychological influences, food also plays an important role in the society.

a) **Joint Family Meals**- When all the members of the family sit and eat together, the atmosphere becomes highly relaxed and enjoyable.

b) **Festivals**- Food plays a significant role during festivals. Each festival is generally and typically attached to some particular food items/menus.

c) **Religious Implications**- Food has religious implications. The societal norms are dictated to restrict some foods during some religious ceremonies. Whereas, preparations and consumptions of certain foods are allowed during some of the religious functions.

d) **Respect/Warmth and friendship**- When we invite our friends, to have meals at out homes, we generally cook food of his/her choice. We basically display our respect and warmth by doing that.

e) **Status Foods**- Certain foods are labeled as the food for the children whereas some as labelled as food for the adults. For example- Tea and coffee are labelled as adult food whereas milk and malted beverages are looked upon as children's food.

## CLASSIFICATION OF NUTRIENTS

There are more than 50 or more highly complex chemical substances called nutrients are present in the food. These nutrients are vital requirements for the body. All these

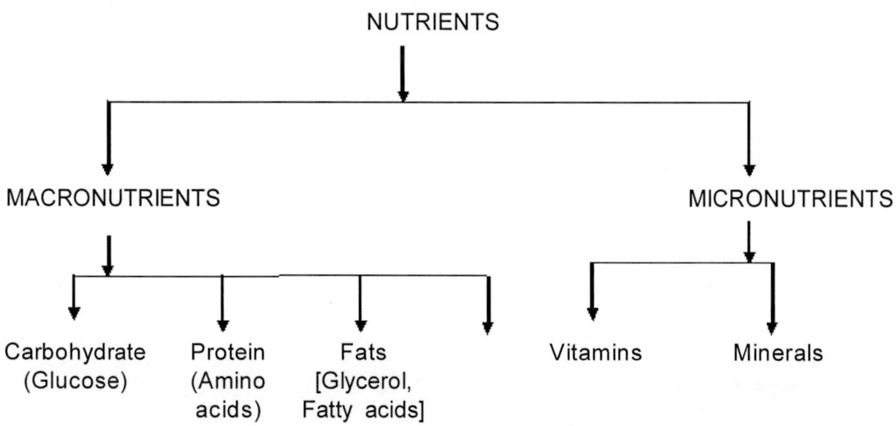


**Dia. Classification of nutrients on the basis of the amounts needed by the body**

chemical substances are part of 6 nutrient classes, namely, water, protein, carbohydrates, vitamins, minerals and lipids. The nutrients may be classified in various ways.

1. **Classification of nutrients on the basis of amounts needed by the body**- The nutrients are divided into micro and macro nutrients on the basis of quantities required by the body on daily basis.

   **MACRO NUTRIENTS** are those nutrients which are needed by the body in large (i.e. macro) amounts. Carbohydrates, fats, proteins and water fall into this category as these nutrients are required in comparatively larger amount.

   **MICRONUTRIENTS** are those nutrients which are required by the by body in small (i.e. micro) amounts. Vitamins and minerals fall into this category. These micro nutrients do not provide any energy but helps in producing the energy from other nutrients.

The requirements of Macronutrients are measured in Kilograms (kg.) or gram (gm.) whereas the requirements of Micronutrients are measured in Milligrams (mg.) or Micrograms (μg).

01 Kilogram (kg.) = 1000grams (gms.) = 2.22 pounds (lbs)

454 grams = 01pounds (lbs) =16 ounces (oz)

01grams = 1000 milligrams (mg.)

01 milligrams = 1000micrograms (μg).

Classification of Nutrients on the Basis of Their Essentiality in the Body:

The nutrients can also be divided into **Essential Nutrients and Non-essential Nutrients.**

**Essential Nutrients** are referred to those nutrients that must be supplied in the daily diet because the body is unable to make them or cannot make them in required quantities e.g. Vitamin A is an essential nutrient for vision, but our body is unable to synthesise it.

**Nonessential Nutrients** are those nutrients which are found in food and can also be produced by the body. For example, Lecithin, required for nerve functions, is a nonessential nutrient because it can be synthesised in the body from other substances.

Classification of Nutrients on the Basis of Their Functions in the Body

Nutrients can be classified on the basis of the various functions they perform in the body.

**Carbohydrate**: The main function of carbohydrates in the body is to provide energy to perform body's work and to produce enough heat to maintain normal body temperature.

**Fats:** After carbohydrate, fat is the second source of energy. It also provides a support or cushion around vital organs e.g. kidneys.

**Proteins**: Proteins are useful for the structure of all cells, for the regulation of body process and also provides energy.

**Vitamins:** Vitamins promote and regulate various chemical reactions and process in the body. Proper vision, bones, blood clotting, connective tissues etc, are dependent on the supply of the vitamins.

**Minerals:** Minerals are part of the structure of every cells, maintains water and acid-base balances, regulates nerve impulses, helps in muscles contractions and are constituents of various regulating compounds.

Water: Water functions as a solvent, a lubricant, a transport medium and a regulator of body temperature. It forms nearly 60% of the human body.

Classification of Nutrients on the Basis of Chemical Properties

All the nutrients can also be classified into Organic Nutrients and Inorganic Nutrients.

The Organic Nutrients are those nutrients which contain carbon element e.g. Carbohydrates, Proteins, Fats, Vitamins.

The Inorganic Nutrients are those nutrients which do not contain carbons e.g. minerals and water.

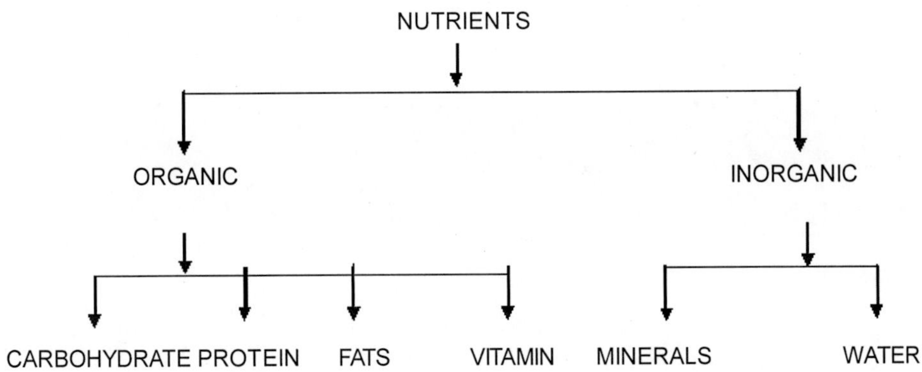

Chapter 14

# Energy

After reading this chapter, the students will be able to:

- *Define energy*
- *Know the units of measuring energy*
- *Explain factors affecting energy requirements*
- *Understand the concept of BMR,SDA, Thermodynamic action of food*
- *Explain dietary sources of energy*
- *Explain concept of Energy Balance*
- *Know about overweight and underweight*
- *Know the health hazards associated with Underweight and overweight.*

## DEFINITION OF ENERGY

Energy has been defined by Oxford Dictionary as "the strength and vitality required to keep alive." Therefore, energy is the ability or capacity to do work.

### POINTS TO BE REMEMBERED

- Energy is required as long as we live
- The requirement of energy by the body cannot be stopped or started at our will
- Energy is required for the three main activities of the body such as
  a) Basic Body Activities
  b) All Physical Activities
  c) For Processing the Diet
- Energy can only be converted from one form to another form but can neither be created nor destroyed
- The following formula depicts how energy is produced in our body

Glucose (from carbohydrate), Glycerol & Fatty Acids (from fats) and Amino Acids(from protein) + $O_2$

Energy (Adenosine Tri-phosphate or ATP) + $CO_2$ + $H_2O$

- The steps to convert food to energy by the body are as follows

Ingestion or eating food Digestion (food breaks down to nutrients) Absorption(transferred nutrients) Transportation Respiration ( provides Oxygen) utilization (uses &functions of nutrients) Storages Excretion ( Removal of wastes).

## UNITS OF ENERGY MEASUREMENTS

The energy is measured for human body in Kilojoules ( Kjouls). Kilojoules is the unit of work.

**Kilojoules is measured as the amount of work done to move a 01kg. object to a distance of 01 meter under the force of gravity**.

Energy is also measured in Kilocalorie (Kcalories). Kilocalorie may be defined as the heat required to raise the temperature of 01kg. of water by one degree of Celsius.

01 Kilocalorie = 04.8 Kilojoules

01Megajoules = 239Kcalories

Kilocalorie is a unit of heat that is used to denote the energy released by foods.

Kilojoules is a measure of work that can be used to denote energy intake as well as energy released.

## ENERGY CONTRIBUTION FROM MACRONUTRIENTS

We know that the macronutrients are the nutrients which are needed by the body in larger amounts. The macronutrients are Carbohydrates, Proteins, Fats and Water.

Carbohydrates provide 04Kcalories or 16.7Kjoules per grams.

Fats provide 09Kcalories or 37.6Kjoules per grams.

Proteins provide 04Kcalories or 16.7Kjoules per grams.

**Water does not provide any energy**.

Factors affecting energy requirements

The total energy requirement of the body is the sum total of the total energy spent for:

- Basal metabolism
- Voluntary physical activities and
- The Caloriegenic effect of food

**A) Basal Metabolism**: Basal Metabolism is a term used for the maintenance of vital body functions such as respiration, blood circulation, kidney function, beating of the heart, regulating body temperature etc. Basal metabolism is affected by many factors such as gender, growth, age, body size, body temperature, body composition, stress etc.

The above-mentioned involuntary activities of the body need nearly 60% to 75% of the total energy requirement of the body.

B) **Voluntary Physical Activities**: This is the second most energy requirement factor of the body. The total energy required for this depend on what kind of activity we perform and for how long. Various voluntary activities such as sitting, walking, running, swimming, dancing, playing chess etc. will need different amount of energy for different individual.

C) **Caloriegenic Effect of Food**: This activity which include ingestion, digestion, absorption, transportation, utilization, storage and exertion. The energy spent for the above activities is very little and ranges between 5% to 10%.

## BMR OR BASAL METABOLIC RATE

BMR or BEE( basal energy expenditure) may be defined as one " measure of the minimum amount of energy that an awake, resting body requires to maintain the basic life-sustaining, vital functions". Those functions include blood circulation, breathing, heartbeat, kidney function, maintaining muscles, maintaining body temperature. The total energy requirement for all these functions is called Basal Metabolic Rate or BMR. About 60% to 75% of the total energy requirement of the body is for the maintenance of these basic body functions.

### Factors Affecting the BMR

Following are the factors that affect the BMR.

- **Age**:- BMR is highest in infants and decreases as an individual grow older.
- **Gender**:- Men have about 10 % higher BMR than women due to more lean body mass.
- **Body shape and size**:- Tall, thin individuals will have higher BMR because of greater surface area for heat loss.
- **Growth:-** Infants, pregnant women, period of adolescence have high BMR due to building of new tissues.
- **Body Composition**:- More the lean body mass greater the BMR. Ex:- an athlete.
- **Body Temperature**:- If the body temperature rises above the normal BMR also increases. BMR rises 13% for each 1 degree C.
- **Stress:-** Stress increases BMR.
- **Hormones**:- BMR increases if Thyroid or growth hormones increases.
- **Starving/Fasting**:- BMR decreases during fasting/starving.

### SDA or Specific Dynamic Action

SDA or specific dynamic action refers to that amount of the energy expenditure of the body which needs energy for digestion, ingestion, absorption, transportation, utilization, storage and excretion. This other terms used to denote this is Calorigenic effect of food or Thermic effect of food or Diet-induced Thermogenesis. The energy requirement for this process is around 5 to 10 per cent of total energy requirement. Therefore SDA can be defined as the increase in energy expenditure that occurs during the digestion, absorption, metabolism and storage of food. It is equal to approximately 5 to 10 per cent of the total daily energy intake.

### Dietary Sources of Energy

Energy has been defined as the ability to do work. Body needs energy constantly throughout the life. The source of energy to the body is actually food. Food is the supply and ATP is the fuel. Carbohydrates provide energy to the body. The carbohydrate in our diet should come from complex carbohydrates such as grains and starchy vegetables and from natural sugar found in milk and fruits. These foods are rich in vitamins, minerals and fibre also other than energy content. Fat is an excellent source of energy. But execs dietary fat should be avoided. Excess energy provided in the diet through fat, carbohydrate and protein gets convert into body fat. The protein need of an athlete are met by the RDA of 0.8 gm/kg/ per day, expressed in energy percentage will account to 12 to 15 % of energy.

Following points must be kept in mind:

- Diet containing higher ratio of water and fibre will automatically have lower energy content. E.g. vegetables and fruits. Fresh fruit contain lower caloric than canned ones in bread, rice, pastas, sugar and candy contains greater amount of digestible carbohydrates. Legumes are a concentrated source of energy containing macro nutrients such as carbohydrates and proteins.
- The maximum concentration of calories is found in foods that contain the greatest proportion of fats whether animal fat or vegetable fat, it will give equal amount of calories. Oil, margarine, butter and cream are high calorie food items. The fat in egg is found mainly in the yolk. Fish, lean meat and chicken provide moderate amount of calorie. Deep fat fried foods are high in calorie. Cakes, cookies, pastries are higher in caloric content due to the ingredients used (sugar, shortening etc).
- After fat, alcohol has the highest caloric content. Regular beer of 12 oz will yield approx. 150kcal. Peanuts, chips etc eaten with alcohol adds up to higher caloric content.

## ENERGY BALANCE

Energy, as we know by now, is the ability to do work or make things happen. The body constantly needs energy to carry out all the basic body functions. We cannot turn on or turn off the energy requirement of the body.

When the amount of energy consumed by the body through diet equals to the amount of energy expanded by the body, the state is called **Energy Balance.**

Enetgy in = energy out

In the above condition, the body weight will remain unchanged.

Therefore, the energy balance may be defined as "the principle that states that the amount of energy consumed in the diet must be equal to the amount expanded for body weight to remain constant."

## OVERWEIGHT

If the energy balance is not maintained then a person may either become overweight or underweight.

If excess energy is consumed through diet, then energy gets stored in the body in the form of fat. **The condition of overweight may be defined as "the body-weight 10% to 20% above the desirable body weight standards."**

**OBESE:** A person may be called obese when the body weight exceeds the standard desirable body weight by more than 20%.

**OBESITY:** The condition of being obese is called obesity.

**Health Hazards Associated to Overweight are-**

High Blood Pressure, High Blood Cholesterol, Diabetes, Cancer on the breast, Heart Disease, cancer in ovary or uterus or prostate, Psychological Problems, Gall Bladder disease, Social problems, Gout, Arthritis etc.

Obese children are teased by the peer group. They remain isolated from the other children of their age.

Obese adults suffer from depression, negative self-image.

Body Mass Index or BMI

Body Mass Index or BMI is a way of finding out the desirable body weight of an adult.

$$BMI = \frac{\textit{Body weight in kilograms}}{(\textit{height in meters})2}$$

## UNDERWEIGHT

If the body weight is 10% or more below the standard desirable weight, then the person is underweight.

Underweight is a term describing a person whose body weight is considered too low to be healthy. The definition usually refers to people with a BMI of under 18 or a weight 15% to 20% below that normal for their age group.

Causes of underweight: an individual may be underweight for various reasons such as

- Hereditary reasons
- Lack of nutritive foods
- Weak metabolism
- Use of drug
- Continuous illness.

- Typical medical complications such as Hyper-thyroids/cancer.
- Eating disorder due to mental stress, over work or excess physical activities.
- TB patients with liver or digestion complication etc.

## TREATMENT FOR UNDERWEIGHT

### Diet

Underweight individuals may be advised to gain weight by increasing calorie intake. This can be done by eating a sufficient volume of sufficiently calorie-dense foods

### Exercise

Another way for underweight people to gain weight is by exercising. Weight lifting exercises are effective in helping to improve muscle tone as well as helping with weight gain

### Appetite stimulants

Certain drugs may increase appetite either as their primary effect or as a side effect.

## KEY TERMS

- *Energy:* Energy has been defined by *Oxford Dictionary* as "the strength and vitality required to keep alive." Therefore, energy is the ability or capacity to do work.
- *Kilojoules*: The energy is measured for human body in Kilojoules ( Kjouls). Kilojoules is the unit of work. Kilojoules is a measure of work that can be used to denote energy intake as well as energy released.
- Kilojoules is measured as the amount of work done to move a 01kg. object to a distance of 01 meter under the force of gravity.
- *Kilocalories:* Energy is also measured in Kilocalorie (Kcalories). Kilocalorie may be defined as the heat required raising the temperature of 01kg. of water by one degree of Celsius.
- 01 Kilocalorie = 04.8 Kilojoules
- 01Megajoules = 239Kcalories
- Kilocalorie is a unit of heat that is used to denote the energy released by foods.
- *MACRONUTRIENTS*: We know that the macronutrients are the nutrients which are needed by the body in larger amounts. The macronutrients are Carbohydrates, Proteins, Fats and Water.
- *Basal Metabolism*: Basal Metabolism is a term used for the maintenance of vital body functions such as respiration, blood circulation, kidney function, beating of the heart, regulating body temperature etc. Basal metabolism is affected by many factors such as gender, growth, age, body size, body temperature, body composition, stress etc.

- *BMR or Basal Metabolic Rate: -_BMR or BEE (basal energy expenditure) may be defined as one* " measure of the minimum amount of energy that an awake, resting body requires to maintain the basic life-sustaining, vital functions".
- *Caloriegenic Effect of Food*: This activity which include ingestion, digestion, absorption, transportation, utilization, storage and exertion. The energy spend for the above activities is very little and ranges between 5% to 10%.
- *SDA or Specific Dynamic Action:* SDA or specific dynamic action refers to that amount of the energy expenditure of the body which needs energy for digestion, ingestion, absorption, transportation, utilization, storage and excretion. This other terms used to denote this is Calorigenic effect of food or Thermic effect of food or Diet-induced Thermogenesis.
- *Energy Balance*: The energy balance may be defined as "the principle that states that the amount of energy consumed in the diet must be equal to the amount expanded for body weight to remain constant."
- *Overweight*: The condition of overweight may be defined as "the body-weight 10% to 20% above the desirable body weight standards."
- *Obese*: A person may be called obese when the body weight exceeds the standard desirable body weight by more than 20%.
- *Obesety:* The condition of being obese is called obesity.
- *Body Mass Index or BMI*: Body Mass Index or BMI is a way of finding out the desirable body weight of an adult.
- $\text{BMI} = \dfrac{\text{Body weight in kg}}{(\text{Height in meters})^2}$
- *Underweight*: If the body weight is 10% or more below the standard desirable weight, then the person is underweight.

## PROJECT BASED LEARNING OR PBL

Find out the BMI of any ten students in your class.

Students may be asked to calculate how much energy they have consumed in their Breakfast/Lunch/dinner.

## IMPORTANT QUESTIONS: -

Q.No.1. Define Energy. What are the units of energy measurements?

Q.No.2. Explain the factors affecting energy requirements. How much energy is provided by different micronutrients?

Q.No.3. Explain the following:

a) BMR b) BMI c) SDA d) Dietary Source of Energy e) Energy Balance

Q.No.4. Explain the following:

a) Overweight b) Underweight.

Chapter 15

# Carbohydrate

After reading this chapter the students will be able to:

- Define Carbohydrate
- Classify Carbohydrate
- Know the dietary sources of Carbohydrates
- Explain functions of carbohydrate in the body
- Define Dietary Fibre
- *Explain significance of Dietary Fibres*

## DEFINITION OF CARBOHYDRATE

Carbohydrates may be defined as chemical compounds containing carbon (hence 'Carbo') as well as hydrogen and oxygen in the same proportion as found in water ( hence 'hydrate').They may also be referred to as hydrates of carbon.

## CLASSIFICATIONS OF CARBOHYDRATES

Carbohydrates are divided into two categories

- **Simple carbohydrates** which includes monosaccharide and disaccharides. 'Mono' means 'one' and 'di' means 'two'.
- **Complex carbohydrates** which include polysaccharides. 'Poly' means 'many'.

### Simple carbohydrates

Simple carbohydrates include monosaccharide and disaccharides. Monosaccharides are the basic unit of carbohydrates having a single (mono) sugar molecule. The most significant monosaccharide present in the foods are glucose, fructose and galactose. All these have different atomic structure , though they contain same numbers of carbon i.e. 06 , hydrogen i.e. 12 and oxygen i.e. 06 . Glucose is known as blood sugar and is produced in plants by photosynthesis process.

Disaccharides are sugar formed by the combination of two (di means two) monosaccharide. Maltose, sucrose are example of disaccharides. Sucrose is the common white table sugar. Refined sugars are termed as empty calories as they contain Kcalories and few other nutrients.

### Complex carbohydrates

Complex carbohydrates or polysaccharides are carbohydrates containing many (i.e. poly) sugar units joined together.

**Fibre** is a mixture of substances, mainly polysaccharides; fibres cannot be digested by the human stomach. Fibres are found in fruits, vegetables and whole grains. Therefore polysaccharides are formed by linking many monosaccharides in long chains. Glycogen is polysaccharide found in animals. Starches and fibres are polysaccharides found in plants.

Glycogen is the storage form of carbohydrates in animals.

Starch is the storage form of energy in plants.

## DIETRY SOURCES OF CARBOHYDRATES

Simple carbohydrates are naturally present in whole food such as milk of fresh fruits. The refined sugar is added to diet, it is obtained by processing to extracts from plants, example sugarcane or sugar beets. Refined sugar is considered as empty calories as they contain mostly calories only.

All grain foods such as breads, quick breads, breakfast cereals, pastas, macaroni, rice etc.

Legumes are high complex carbohydrates, while potatoes, sweet potatoes, corn are full of carbohydrates.

All fruits and vegetable contains simple sugars. The sugary foods such as soft drinks, bakery products, jams, jellies etc contain high sugar.

Cereals: - Oats, corn, wheat, rice, barley, jowar, bajra, ragi.

Fruits and vegetables: Banana, mango, custard apple, potato, green peas, French beans.

Pulses: Bengal gram, kidney beans, lentils, green gram (whole) etc.

Nuts and oilseeds: Cashew nuts, groundnuts, dry coconuts etc.

Other food items: Sago, honey, dates, skimmed milk powder, sugar, jiggery etc.

A balanced diet should supply approximately 60% Kcal of energy from carbohydrates. It is clear from the above discussion that the animal foods do not provide us with carbohydrates. Therefore our diet should contain adequate quantity of plant foods.

## FUNCTIONS OF CARBOHYDRATES

The functions of carbohydrates in body are as follows:-

- Carbohydrates provide glucose which provides energy to cells. This helps the body to maintain normal temperature as well as carry out basic body functions.

- **Protein-sparing effect**: Body derives all its energy requirements from carbohydrates instead of using proteins from diet or body tissues. Therefore carbohydrates spare proteins.
- Galactose makes up a part of nervous tissues.
- Galactose and glucose combine to form lactose in women to produce breast milk.
- Deoxyribose and ribose are components of DNA and RNA which carry genetics information.
- Carbohydrates are required to form part of Cartilage, bones and nervous tissues.
- Carbohydrates help in cellular metabolism of fats.
- Carbohydrates with nitrogen form non essential amino acids.
- Dietary fibres absorb and hold water which helps in bowl movement.
- Lactose in large intestine helps to grow certain bacteria, which synthesis B complex vitamins.

## DIETRY FIBRES

Dietary fibres consist of substances which cannot be digested in stomach and small intestine because humans do not have enzymes which will break the bond. Fibres are of two types: **Insoluble fibre and soluble fibre**. Food sources of insoluble fibre are wheat bran and rye bran, broccoli etc.

Soluble fibres swell or dissolve in water. Food sources of soluble fibre are oat bran, apples, beans, seaweed.

### Crude Fibres

Crude fibre is a fibre that remains after a food has been treated with acids and base.

## SIGNIFICANCE OF DIETRY FIBRE (PREVENTION/TREATMENT OF DISEASES)

Dietary fibres though cannot be digested, plays a significant role in body. Some of these are discussed below:

1. Soluble fibres absorb water, forming a viscous solution which delays the glucose absorption and is beneficial for diabetics and patients of hypoglycaemia.
2. The insoluble fibre increases the bulk in the stomach whereas the soluble fibre holds and increase fluid content. Together it helps in bowel movement. This helps in treating Constipation and Haemorrhoids.
3. The intake of fibre reduces the chance of diverticuli. Diverticuli is the swelling of intestine wall due to difficulty in defection.
4. But a very high fibre diet can cause :

i) Intestinal blockage. To prevent such condition one need to drink a lot of water.

ii) In children, if stomach is full with high fibre diet, the energy needs may not be fulfilled. This may cause nutrients deficiency.

iii) Children with high fibre diet may suffer the deficiency of minerals such as zinc, calcium, iron and magnesium tends to bind with fibre. Supplements may be provided.

5. High fibre intake may produce intestinal gas and cause discomfort. In this case, diet of high nutrients and low in fibre should be given.

## KEY TERMS

- *Carbohydrate*: Carbohydrates may be defined as chemical compounds containing carbon (hence 'Carbo') as well as hydrogen and oxygen in the same proportion as found in water ( hence 'hydrate').They may also be referred to as hydrates of carbon.
- *Simple Carbohydrates*: Simple Carbohydrate which includes monosaccharide and disaccharides. 'Mono' means 'one' and 'di' means 'two'.
- *Complex Carbohydrates*: Complex Carbohydrates which include polysaccharides. 'Poly' means 'many'.
- *Protein:* sparing effect: Body derives all its energy requirements from carbohydrates instead of using proteins from diet or body tissues. Therefore carbohydrates spare proteins.
- *Dietary Fibers:* Dietary fibers consist of substances which cannot be digested in stomach and small intestine because humans do not have enzymes which will break the bond. Fibres are of two types: Insoluble fiber and soluble fiber.

## PROJECT BASED LEARNING OR PBL

Students may be directed various Carbohydrate-rich foods they have consumed in their meals.

They may be asked to find out various dietary source of fiber/carbohydrates in their meals.

They may be asked to prepare a chart on the classifications/functions of carbohydrates.

## IMPORTANT QUESTIONS

Q.01. Define Carbohydrate. Classify carbohydrate and explain.

Q.02. Explain the various functions of carbohydrate.

Q.03. a) Explain the significance of dietary fibre.

b) Explain the dietary source of Carbohydrate.

Chapter 16

# Lipids

After reading this chapter, students will be able to:

- *Define Lipids*
- *Classify Lipids*
- *Explain dietary sources of Lipids*
- *Explain the functions of Lipids*
- *Narrate the significance of fatty acids*
- *Define Cholesterol*
- *Know sources of Cholesterol*
- *Explain the functions of Cholesterol*

## DEFINITION

Lipids may be defined as organic molecules, most of which are insoluble in water. This class of macronutrients is commonly called fats and oils.

### SOME POINTS TO BE REMEMBERED

The term fat means lipids that are solid at room temperature.

- Oils are lipids that are liquid at room temperature.
- Lipids are body's most concentrated source of energy.
- Dietary lipids provide 09 kilocalories per gram energy to the body.
- Lipids are important components of cell's structure mainly of brains and nervous system.
- Lipids provide texture and flavour when added to food.
- Lipids are composed of three chemical elements namely carbon, hydrogen and oxygen. Some lipids also contain phosphorus, nitrogen, protein , oxygen and carbohydrates.

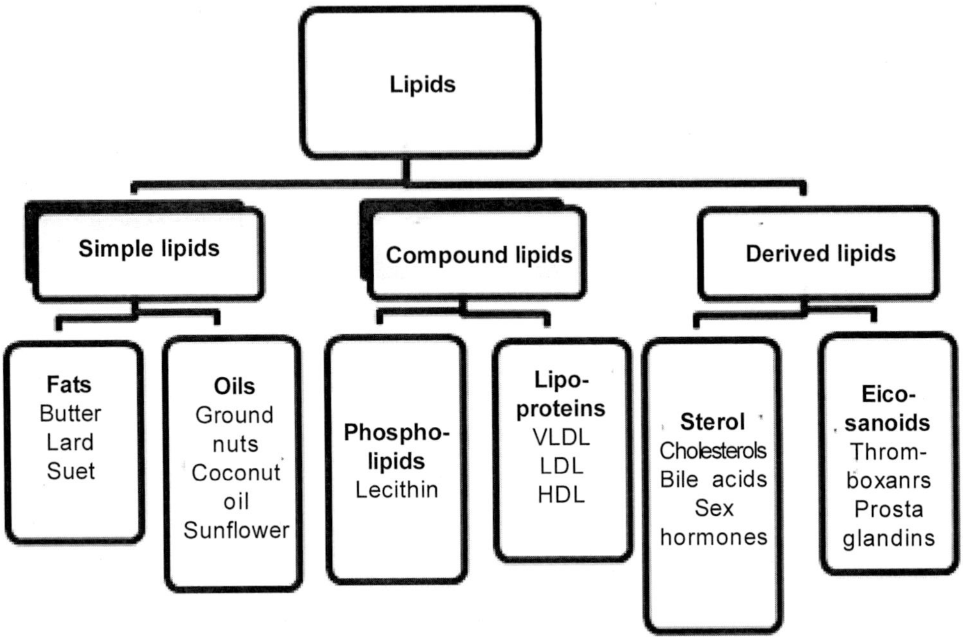


**DIG. Classification of lipids**

## CLASSIFICATION OF LIPIDS

Lipids can be classified into the following main categories:-

- Simple lipids
- Compound lipids
- Derived lipids

### Simple lipids

Simple lipids are commonly known as fats and oils. Fats and oils differ in their composition and properties and a few similarities.

Simple lipids are fatty acids bound to glycerol.

Glycerol+1 fatty acid is termed as monoglyceride.

Glycerol+2 fatty acid is termed diglyceride.

Glycerol+3 fatty acid is termed triglyceride.

### Compound lipids

Compound lipids are the lipids in which at least one of the fatty acids is replaced by another chemical group such as nitrogen, phosphate, carbohydrate or protein. The glycerol is replaced sometimes by another alcohol. Examples include phospholipids, lipoprotein, glycolipids etc.

### *Classes of lipoproteins*

**VLDL**: Very Low Density Lipoproteins. It consists of mainly Triglycerides.

**LDL**: Low Density Lipoproteins. Synthesised by liver. Main carrier of Cholesterol. High-fat diet increases the level.

**HDL**: High Density Lipoprotein. High in protein. Commonly known as good cholesterol. Probably reduces the risk of heart diseases.

## Derived lipids

Derived lipids are fatlike compounds that contain carbon in the shape of ring structures. Derived lipids originate mostly from simple lipids and compound lipids. Examples include sterols {such as cholesterol, sex hormones, bile acids etc}; and the eicosanoids {such as leukotrienes and thromboxanes} vitamins A,D,E and K also come in this category.

### *Dietary sources of lipids*

**Total f**ats: Total fats are clearly visible fats are butter ,margarine, shortenings, oil.

**Invisible fats are** in whole milk, cheese , egg yolk, cake, candy, pie etc.

**Fatty acids**: high in saturated fatty acids are whole milk, cream, ice cream, fatty meats, lamb, pork, ham, butter, coconut oil, palm oil, shortenings etc. Cakes, cookies, chocolates etc.

Mono saturated fatty acids are high in olives ,olive oil, cashew nuts, peanut oil etc.

High in omega 3 fatty acids are fish (salmon, herring, carp etc).

High in essential fatty acids are vegetable oils , fatty fish etc.

### *Cholesterol*

cholesterol is found in animal foods but not in plant foods.

There is no cholesterol in white of eggs and all plant foods.

High in cholesterol are egg yolks, liver, brains, kidney, fish roe, shrimp etc.

## FUNCTIONS OF LIPIDS

Following are the function of lipids:-

- Sources of energy:-Simple lipids or fat is the body's is the preferred source of energy.
- Source of energy:- Smple lipids or fat is the body's preferred source of energy.
- Protein- sparing effect:-Aas fat is the body's preferred source of energy, so its availability reduces the chances of protein being used as a source of energy.
- Stored energy:- The fat deposit in adipose tissue acts as stored energy.

- Thermal insulation:- The layer of fat under the skin acts as thermal insulation to maintain constant body temperature.
- Protects vital organs:-Fat provide the cushion of support around kidneys
- Normal growth in children:- Linoleic acid is essential for normal growth in children. It is also required for healthy skin in children and adult alike.
- Various body functions:-The derived lipids help in contraction of muscles, regulation of blood pressure, immunity etc.
- Body cholesterol is required for brain formation, nervous tissues formation, synthesis of vitamin D and sex hormones etc.

Significance of fatty acids {PUFAS, MUFAS, SFAS, and EFAS} in maintaining health:

The major constituent of most lipids is fatty acids. Fatty acid is made up of chain of carbon atoms with a carboxyl (COOH) group in one end and a methyl ($CH_3$) group on the other end (OMEGA).

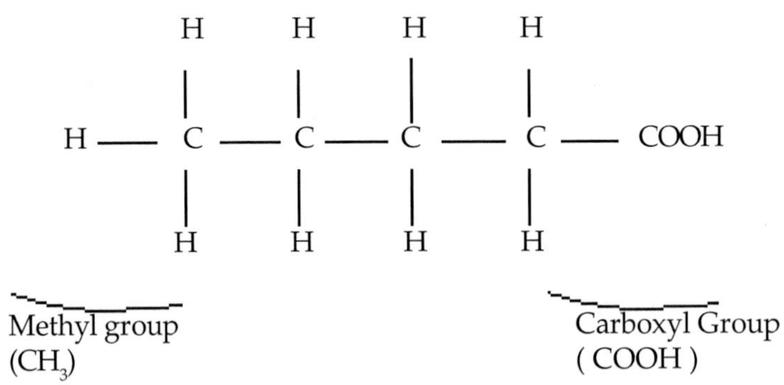


**Dia. Structure of Fatty Acid**

## SATURATED FATTY ACIDS

Saturated fatty acids may be defined as a fat or fatty acid in which the carbon atoms are bonded to as many hydrogen as possible ( hence Saturated ) and contains no carbon-carbon bonds in its chemical structure. We can also say that when each carbon in the middle of the chain has two hydrogen bond to it, the fatty acid may be termed as 'Saturated'.

The common saturated fatty acids are Palmitic Acids, Stearic acids, found in animal products. The vegetable sources of saturated fatty acids are Palm oil, Palm Kernel oil, Coconut oil etc.

## USFA OR UNSATURATED FATTY ACIDS

Unsaturated fatty acids are those fatty acids that contain one or more carbon-carbon double bonds. Such fatty acids can take ip more hydrogen (hence Unsaturated).

**MUFA or Monounsaturated Fatty Acids**: MUFA are those with one double bond.

**PUFA or Polyunsaturated Fatty Acids**: PUFA are those with two or more double bonds.

**EFA or Essential Fatty Acids**: Fatty acids that are essential for the body but cannot be synthesized in required quantity are known as Essential fatty acids.

**Significance:** If essential fatty acids are not adequate in diet then following symptoms are noticed:-

1. Dry Scaly skin
2. Liver abnormality
3. Delayed wound healing
4. Retarded growth in infants
5. Impaired vision
6. Impaired hearing

Omega-6 fatty acids are important for

1. Growth
2. Marinating red blood cell system
3. Fertility
4. Skin health

Polysaturated fatty acids such as Linoleic acid and Arachhidonic acid help in lowering blood cholesterol level and also present Atheroselerosis and coronary heart diseases.

## CHOLESTROL

Cholesterol may be defined as liquid consisting of multiple chemical rings that is only made by animal cells. Cholesterol is the best known sterol.

### Dietry Sources of Cholestrol

Cholesterol is only found in animal food. Plant foods do not contain cholesterol at all. Dietary sources of cholesterol are:-

- Butter - 250mg cholesterol per100g
- Brain - 2000mg cholesterol per 100g
- Liver - 300mg cholesterol per 100g
- Ice cream - 40mg cholesterol per 100g
- Paneer - 19mg cholesterol per 100g
- Whole milk - 14mg cholesterol per 100g
- Egg yolk - 250mg cholesterol per 100g

- Fish - 60mg cholesterol per 100g
- Skimmed milk - 02mg cholesterol per 100g

### Blood Cholesterol

The liver produces cholesterol from carbohydrate, protein, fat. Cholesterol synthesis slows down when insulin level is low. This happens when we take many small diets replacing a heavy meal. So, spreading total food intake into many small meals is an effective way to lower blood cholesterol. Reducing energy intake will also lower blood cholesterol. Cholesterol's harmful effect starts when it forms deposits on the artery walls. This deposits lead to heart attacks and strokes. Intake of the food items high in cholesterol such as meat, egg yolk, poultry, fish etc should be restricted.

### Functions of Cholesterol

1. Cholesterol is required to synthesise vitamin D in skin.
2. Chloric acid is necessary for digestion of fat.
3. Steroid hormones promotes growth and sex characteristics.
4. It is required for glucose synthesis in liver.
5. It forms the coating of nerve cells.

### KEY TERMS

- *Lipids:* Lipids may be defined as organic molecules, most of which are insoluble in water. These classes of macronutrients are commonly called fats and oils.
- *Simple lipids*: Simple lipids are commonly known as fats and oils. Fats and oils differ in their composition and properties and a few similarities.
- *Compound lipids*: Compound lipids are the lipids in which at least one of the fatty acids is replaced by another chemical group such as nitrogen, phosphate, carbohydrate or protein. The glycerol is replaced sometimes by another alcohol. Examples include phospholipids, lipoprotein, glycolipids etc.
- *VLDL:* Very Low Density Lipoproteins. It consists of mainly Triglycerides.
- *LDL:* Low Density Lipoproteins. Synthesised by liver. Main carrier of Cholesterol. High-fat diet increases the level.
- *HDL:* High Density Lipoprotein. High in protein. Commonly known as good cholesterol. Probably reduces the risk of heart diseases.
- *Derived lipids*: Derived lipids are fatlike compounds that contain carbon in the shape of ring structures. Derived lipids originate mostly from simple lipids and compound lipids.
- *Total fats*: Total fats are clearly visible fats are butter ,margarine, shortenings, oil.
- Invisible fats are in whole milk, cheese, egg yolk, cake, candy, pie etc.

- *Fatty acids*: high in saturated fatty acids are whole milk, cream, ice cream, fatty meats, lamb, pork, ham, butter, coconut oil, palm oil, shortenings etc.
- *Cholesterol*: -Cholesterol is found in animal foods but not in plant foods. There is no cholesterol in white of eggs and all plant foods. High in cholesterol are egg yolks, liver, brains, kidney, fish roe, shrimp etc. Cholesterol may be defined as liquid consisting of multiple chemical rings that is only made by animal cells.
- *Saturated Fatty Acids*:- Saturated fatty acids may be defined as a fat or fatty acid in which the carbon atoms are bonded to as many hydrogen as possible ( hence Saturated ) and contains no carbon-carbon bonds in its chemical structure. We can also say that when each carbon in the middle of the chain has two hydrogen bonds to it, the fatty acid may be termed as 'Saturated'.
- *USFA or Unsaturated fatty acids*: Unsaturated fatty acids are those fatty acids that contain one or more carbon-carbon double bonds. Such fatty acids can take ip more hydrogen (hence Unsaturated).
- *MUFA or monounsaturated fatty acids*: MUFA are those with one double bond.
- *PUFA or polyunsaturated fatty acids*: PUFA are those with two or more double bonds.
- *EFA or essential fatty acids*: Fatty acids that are essential for the body but cannot be synthesized in required quantity are known as Essential fatty acids.

## PROJECT BASED LEARNING OR PBL

Students may be asked to

- Find out the cholesterol content of their meals
- A chart may be prepared on classification of lipids

## IMPORTQANT QUESTIONS

Q. 01. Define lipids. What are the characteristics of lipids?

Q.02. Classify Lipids.

Q.03. Explain the dietary sources of lipids.

Q.04. List out the functions of lipids in the body.

Q. 05. Explain the significance of Lipids

Q. 06. Write a short note on Essential Fatty Acid.

Q. 07. Write a short note on Cholesterol.

Chapter 17

# Protein

After reading this chapter, the learner will be able to:

- Define protein
- Classify protein based on amino acid composition
- Know the dietary source of protein
- Learn the functions of protein
- *Understand the methods of improving quality of protein in food( special emphasis on soy protein and whey protein)*

## DEFINITION

Proteins are the large, diverse and complex group of molecules. Proteins are organic compounds. The term protein means 'to take the first place' or 'of first importance'.

Some points to be remembered:

- Protein contains Carbon, Hydrogen, Oxygen and Nitrogen. Approximately 1/6$^{th}$ of protein is nitrogen and that distinguishes it from carbohydrate and fats.
- Amino acid (there are 20 amino acids) is the building blocks of proteins. Each amino acid contains a carbon atom attached to a hydrogen atom, an amino group, an acid group and a side chain. There are three types of amino acids: Essential Amino Acid, Nonessential Amino Acid and Semi-essential Amino Acid. The amino acids which cannot be made by the body in required amount and must be consumed through diet are called essential amino acid (there are 09 essential amino acids out of total 20). The 11 amino acids which body can synthesise in required amount are called nonessential amino acids. The amino acids such as Tyrosine and Cysteine are called semi-essential amino acid because they become essential amino acid if the essential amino acids from which they are synthesised fall short.
- Part of the protein structure includes some mineral elements such as sulphur, phosphorus, copper, iron and iodine.

- Protein is present everywhere except in 100% of water, carbohydrate and/or lipids.
- Fibrous proteins are insoluble.
- Proteins provide stability to food.
- It has amphoteric properties.

## CLASSIFICATION OF PROTEINS BASED UPON AMINO ACID COMPOSITION

Proteins can be classified in many ways, such as based on nutritional quality, shape and compositions.

Protein molecule is constructed of one or more of amino acids. Protein is a vital nutrient needed for building, maintaining and repairing tissues, cells and organs of the human body.

## CLASSIFICATION OF PROTEINS ON THE BASIS OF COMPOSITION

Proteins like lipids can be classified as

- Simple protein
- Conjugated protein and
- Derived proteins

### Simple proteins

Simple proteins are those proteins which contain only amino acids. Examples include Zein in Corn, Albumin in blood etc.

## CONJUGATED PROTEINS

Conjugated proteins are those proteins which are composed of simple proteins combined with another substance. Examples include Caseins or Phosphoproteins in milk, Lipoproteins in blood, Metalloproteins (contains copper) in blood plasma.

### Derived Proteins

Derived proteins result from the partial breakdown of a native protein. Examples include Proteases, Peptones and Polypeptides are formed when digestive enzymes begin their action on the proteins.

## CLASSIFICATION OF PROTEIN ON THE BASIS OF NUTRITIONAL QUALITY

### Complete Protein

Complete Proteins are those proteins which provide all the essential amino acids in the right amount and right proportion as needed by the body. The foods which provide complete proteins are called Complete Protein foods. The example of such foods are from the animal sources only and includes Milk, eggs, cheese, curd, meat, poultry and fish.

### Incomplete Proteins

Incomplete proteins are those proteins which do not provide right amount of one or more essential amino acids. Examples include foods from plant sources such as legumes, nuts, grains, vegetables and fruits.

We can also put the foods in order of the quality of protein it provides, for example—

Egg protein is considered as the best

Next are the milk, flesh foods, legumes, nuts, grains and vegetables.

Protein from fruit is ranked lowest.

## CLASSIFICATION OF THE PROTEIN ON THE BASIS OF SHAPES

### Globular Protein

Globular proteins are the proteins in which the amino acids appear to be coiled and tightly-packed balls. Examples include Haemoglobin, insulin and Albumin.

### Fibrous Protein

Fibrous proteins are those proteins in which the amino acids appear to be layered, parallel and in linear shapes. Example includes Collagen, Myosin, Fibrin etc.

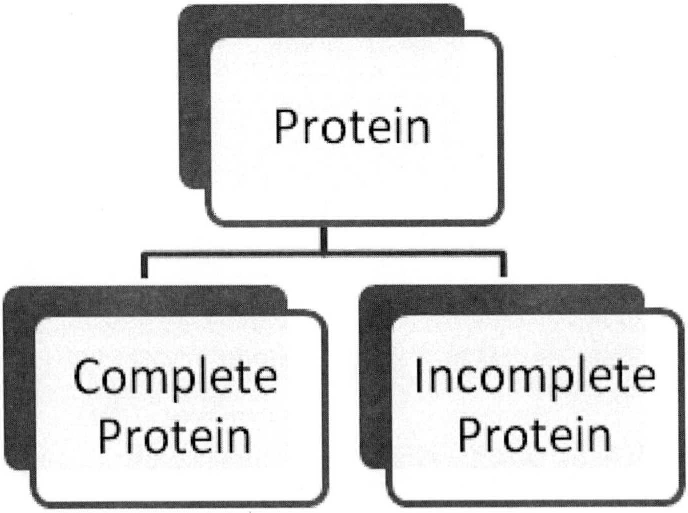


**Diag: Classification of protein on the basis of Nutritional Quality**

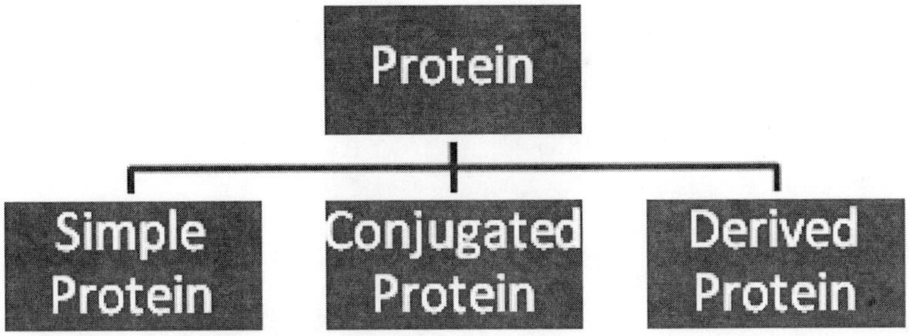


**Diag. Classification of Protein on the basis of Composition.**

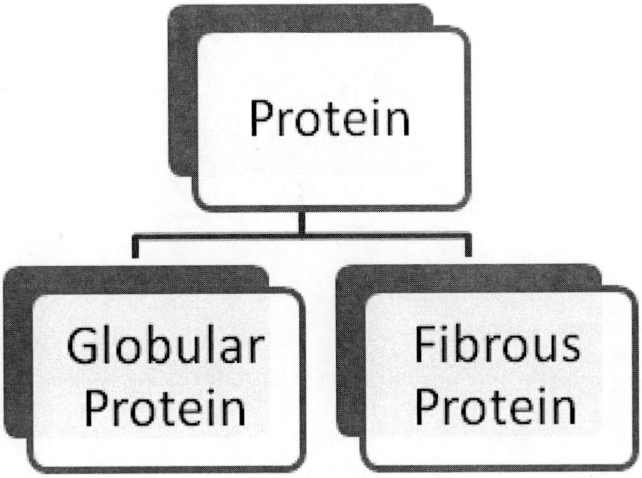


**Diag.: Classification of Protein on the Basis of Shapes.**

## DIETARY SOURCES OF PROTEIN

Dietary sources of protein include both plant and animal sources.

- Animal sources of protein include the following:
- Eggs
- Meat
- Fish and
- Milk
- One egg provides 07gms. Of Protein
- One ounce of meat provides 07gms. Of protein.
- One cup of milk provides 08gms. of protein.

The best sources of plant protein includes:

- Legumes such as Soybeans, Lentils, Chickpeas, Kidney beans, Black beans etc.
- One half cup of each of all the above legumes provides 6 to 10gms. of protein.
- Nuts and Seeds provide 10 to 14gms. of protein per cup.
- Grains such as wheat, oats and Rye are high sources of proteins.
- One half cup of each of all the grains provides 03gms.of protein.
- Vegetables and fruits contain approximately 02gms.of protein per half cup.

## FUNCTIONS OF PROTEIN

Proteins perform many different functions in the human body.

### Structural Function

- Protein is an integral part of cells.
- Skin, hair and muscles are composed of protein mainly.
- Bones and teeth are made up of protein and minerals.
- Deficiency of protein will make the muscles shorter, skin non-elastic and hair loose.

### Regulatory Function

- Protein is important in the following regulatory functions-
- Transports molecules in the blood and in cells.
- Proteins are enzymes ( lactose, pepsin etc.)
- Hormones: Insulin, growth hormones.
- Immune system molecules
- Muscle contractions
- Fluid balance
- Acid balance and nerve transmission.

### Energy Source

If the diet does not provide enough calories, protein from the diet is used to meet energy requirements. But if the diet supplies more than the body needs, excess protein is stored as fat.

Methods of improving quality of protein in food ( special emphasis on soy proteins and whey proteins)

## PROTEIN QUALITY

Protein quality is a measure to determine how useful a protein in the diet

is for the body. The factor on which this depend is the proportion of amino acids present in the protein.

## BIOLOGICAL VALUE (BV)

The Biological Value of protein is a percentage measure of how much nitrogen is retained divided by the amount absorbed in the diet.

$$\text{BIOLOGICAL VALUE} = \frac{\textit{NITROGEN RETAINED}}{\textit{NITROGEN ABSORBED}} \text{X}100$$

- Therefore to improve the quality of protein in the diet one should include the high-quality protein foods such as eggs, milk, red meat, fish, poultry etc.
- **Protein Complementation**: Protein Complementation is a technique to combine foods having different quality proteins with the diet. Examples include Corn and Beans; grains and legumes; chicken fried rice etc.
- **Soy Protein**: Soy protein concentrate is a derivative of soya beans. 'Soy protein isolates' and 'textured vegetable protein' are forms of soy protein that have been isolated from soya beans. These are available in chunks and in different shapes and flavours. These are now used as meal substitutes. These can be used in place of meat. These can also be added to the real meat dishes to increase supply of proteins.

Soya protein has become popular all over the world because of the following reasons:

- The vegetable proteins are of inferior in quality as compared to that of animal protein.
- Animal proteins are costlier than the vegetables.
- There is a shortage in supply of meat products.
- The world population is preferring the vegetarian foods more and more.
- Soya protein is the only vegetable protein which can substitute animal protein, is inexpensive and the supply is in abundance.
- The soya protein can also be processed and given the shape and look of meat products.

It is because of all the above reasons that the soya flour and other soya products are gaining popularity all over the world. The biggest challenge, however to make it acceptable to the consumers. The use of soya products had been very popular in China, Japan and USA.

The soya proteins spun into meat-like fibers, shapes and texture may be included in the diet in schools, hospitals and industrial canteens. The preparation may be in the same way as for other meat products to give it an acceptable taste.

- **Whey Proteins**; -Whey protein is the protein contained in whey, the watery portion of milk that separates from the curds when making cheese. Whey protein is a source of protein that might improve the nutrient content of the diet. Whey protein is used for protein allergy, high cholesterol, obesity etc. It may be taken as a food supplement.

- Include unsalted nuts and seeds.

## KEY TERMS

- **Protein**:-Proteins are the large, diverse and complex group of molecules. Proteins are organic compounds. The term protein means 'to take the first place' or 'of first importance'.
- **Simple proteins**:-Simple proteins are those proteins which contain only amino acids. Examples include Ze in Corn, Albumin in blood etc.
- **Conjugated Proteins:** Conjugated proteins are those proteins which are composed of simple proteins combined with another substance.
- **Derived Proteins:** Derived proteins result from the partial breakdown of a native protein. Examples include Proteases, Peptones and Polypeptides are formed when digestive enzymes begin their action on the proteins.
- **Complete Protein:** Complete Proteins are those proteins which provide all the essential amino acids in the right amount and right proportion as needed by the body.
- **Incomplete Proteins**: Incomplete proteins are those proteins which do not provide right amount of one or more essential amino acids.
- **Globular Protein**: Globular proteins are the proteins in which the amino acids appear to be coiled and tightly-packed balls. Examples include Haemoglobin, insulin and Albumin.
- **Fibrous Protein:** Fibrous proteins are those proteins in which the amino acids appear to be layered, parallel and in linear shapes. Example includes Collagen, Myosin, Fibrin etc.
- **Biological Value** (BV): The Biological Value of protein is a percentage measure of how much nitrogen is retained divided by the amount absorbed in the diet.
- Biological Value $= \frac{\textit{NITROGEN RETAINED}}{\textit{NITROGEN ABSORBED}}$ X100

**PBL:** Students may be asked to

- Find out the various food items in their daily meal that contain protein and compare them.
- Prepare a project report on Soy protein
- Make a detailed project report on the functions of protein

## IMPORTANT QUESTIONS

Q. No. 1. Define protein. Classify protein on the basis of amino acid composition.

Q.No. 2. Name the dietary sources of protein. Explain the functions of protein.

Q.No. 3. Explain the methods of improving quality of protein in food.

Chapter 18

# Vitamin

After reading this chapter, the student will be able to:

- *Define vitamin*
- *Classify vitamin*
- *Know the food sources, functions and significance of fat soluble vitamin*
- *Know the food sources, functions and significance of water soluble vitamin*

## DEFINITION

Vitamins are a group of organic, essential compound required in small amounts in the diet to perform specific functions that promote and regulate chemical reactions for growth, reproduction etc. of the body.

Some points to be remembered:

- 'Vita' means 'life' and 'amine' means 'containing Nitrogen'.
- The name vitamin was given by Polish biochemist Casimir Funk, who cured Beriberi with rice husk extract.
- Vitamins do not provide energy but help in reactions that produce energy.
- Vitamins are individual units and linked in long chains.
- Vitamin's input and requirements are measured in micrograms and milligrams.
- The availability of vitamins in the body depends on how much is provided through diet and the amount absorbed by the body.

## CLASSIFICATION OF VITAMINS

Vitamins are classified on the basis of their solubility.

1) Hydrophilic or Water-soluble Vitamins e.g. B Vitamins, Vitamin C
2) Hydrophobic or Fat-soluble Vitamins e.g. Vitamins A,D,E and K

The solubility of vitamins affects their absorption, transport, storage and excretion by the body.

The water-soluble vitamins are found in the watery compartment of food. The fat-soluble vitamins are found in the fats and oils of the food.

The water-soluble vitamins after absorption goes directly into the blood. Whereas the fat-soluble vitamins goes to the blood through lymph.

The fat-soluble vitamins need a protein-carrier to travel, whereas the water-soluble vitamins travel freely.

In the cells the water-soluble vitamins easily circulate in the water-filled compartment of the body, whereas the fat-soluble vitamins are held in the fatty tissues and the liver till required.

Water-soluble vitamins are detected and the excess amount is removed by the kidneys. Whereas the fat-soluble vitamins remain in the fat-storage sites of the body.

The water-soluble vitamins must be eaten regularly than the fat-soluble vitamins.

## FAT-SOLUBLE VITAMINS

### Vitamin A

The first fat-soluble vitamin to be recognised was the Vitamin A.

The different forms of vitamins are active in the human body, namely, Retinol, Retinol and Retinoic acids. These compounds are collectively known as Retnoids.foods from animal sources gets converted to Retinoids. Foods from plant sources contain Carotenoids, most important one is Carotene.

#### *Food Source of Vitamin A*

Fortified milk, cheese, cream, butter, fortified margarine, eggs, liver.

Spinach and other dark leafy vegetables.

Broccoli

Deep orange fruits such as Apricots, Cantaloupe etc.

Vegetables such as Squash, Carrots, Pumpkins and sweet potatoes.

#### *Functions of vitamin A*

Main functions of vitamin A in the body are:-

1) Vision
2) Maintenance of cornea, epithelial cells, mucous membranes and skin.
3) Bone and tooth growth
4) Reproduction
5) Immunity

*RDA*

Men: 1000microgram RE/Day

Women: 800microgram RE/Day

*Significance of Vitamin A*

Deficiency of vitamin A leads to

1) Night blindness
2) Infectious diseases
3) Blindness
4) Keratinisation ( keratin is a protein of hair and nails)
5) Kidney stones.

**Vitamin D**

*Food Source of Vitamin D*

- Vitamin D is synthesised in the body with the help of sunlight.
- Dietary sources include-
- Fortified milk
- Margarine
- Butter
- Cereals
- Chocolate mixes
- Veal
- Beef
- Egg yolk
- Liver
- Fatty fish ( salmon, sardines, herrings) and their oils.

*Main functions of vitamin D*

1) Mineralizations of bones raises bone calcium and phosphorus)

*Significance of vitamin D*

Deficiency of Vitamin D leads to

1) Rickets in children
2) Mal-formed, decay-prone teeth.

## Vitamin E

Vitamin E is a fat soluble component of grain. The chemical name is Tocopherol. Tocopherol is a Greek term where TOCO means 'Child birth' and PHERO means 'to bear'.

### *Food sources of vitamin E*

Vitamin E is found in almost all the foods. Most of the vitamin E comes in the diet from vegetable oils and the products made from them such as margarine, salad dressing, shortenings etc. Another major source is fruits and vegetables.

Wheat Germ oil is particularly rich source of vitamin E.

Corn and Soybean oils come second. Spinach, broccoli, tomato juice avocado shrimp cod etc provide vitamin E.

Animal fats and milk fats contain no vitamin E.

Vitamin E gets destroyed in deep-fat frying and oxidation.

### *Functions of vitamin E in the body*

1) It acts as an Antioxidant
2) Protects from ozone

### *Significance of Vitamin E*

Vitamin E, now-a-days, is advertised as a cure for infertility and fountain of youth. It is also being promoted as a protector from air pollution and an anti-scar medicine.

Deficiency of Vitamin E is very rare due to its wide spread presence in the foods.

Vitamin E deficiency leads to Anaemia ( a condition with low hemoglobin0. It may create problem with newborns with deficiency of vitamin E.

## Vitamin K

Vitamin K was previously named after a Danish word 'koagulation', meaning Coagulation or blood-clotting.

### *Food source of Vitamin K*

- It is synthesised in the small intestine by bacteria though not in required amounts.
- Fish oils
- Legumes such as dried beans and peas
- Leafy green vegetables such as spinach, broccoli, turnip greens etc.
- Liver and vegetable oils.

### *Functions of vitamin K in the body*

1) It is necessary for blood-clotting
2) It helps in regulating blood calcium levels.
3) It also helps in depositing minerals in the bone.

### *Significance of vitamin K in the body*

Deficiency may lead to

1) Abnormal blood coagulation
2) Constant use of antibiotics in adults
3) Deficiency in infants may lead to uncontrolled bleeding. Vitamin K in injected in this case.

## WATER SOLUBLE VITAMINS

### Vitamin C

### *Food source of vitamin C*

- Citrus fruits
- Cabbage type vegetables
- Dark green vegetables
- Strawberries
- Lettuce
- Tomatoes
- Potatoes
- Papaya
- Mangoes

Vitamin C is unstable and gets destroyed in the presence of oxygen.

### *Functions of Vitamin C in the body*

1) Antioxidant
2) Collagen synthesis which strengthens bones, and blood vessel walls.
3) Improves resistance to infections
4) Synthesises thyroxins
5) Amino acid metabolism
6) Helps in absorption of iron

### *Significance of vitamin C in the body*

Deficiency of Vitamin C leads to

1) Scurvy
2) Anaemia
3) Failure of wound to heal
4) Frequent infection
5) Bleeding gum
6) Rough skin and bruises

## THIAMINE

Thiamine is also known as Vitamin $B_1$

### Food source of thiamine

- Found in all nutritious foods in moderate amounts.
- Pork products, Liver, Whole grains or enriched breads and cereals, Legumes,nuts.
- It is easily destroyed by heat.

### Functions of thiamine in the body

1) Energy metabolism
2) Supports nerve functions
3) Develops normal appetite.

### *Significance of thiamine in the body*

Deficiency leads to Beriberi

## RIBOFLAVIN

It is also known as vitamin $B_2$

### Food source of riboflavin

Milk, yogurt, cottage cheese, meat, leafy green vegetables, whole grain or enriched breads and cereals.

### Functions of riboflavin in the body

1) Helps in energy metabolism
2) Supports normal vision
3) Supports skin health

### Significance of riboflavin in the body

Deficiency leads to

1) Greasy, inflammatory skin
2) Reddening of cornea and sensitivity to light
3) Cracks and redness at the corners of mouth
4) Painful, purple tongue.

## NIACIN

Also known as Vitamin $B_3$

### Food source of niacin

Significant sources of Niacin are:

Milk,eggs, meat, poultry, fish, whole grains and enriched breads and cereals, nuts and all protein containing food.

### Functions of niacin in the body

1) It is part of coenzymes used in energy metabolism
2) Supports health of skin
3) Supports nervous system
4) Supports digestive system

### Significance of niacin in the body

Deficiency leads to

1) Diarrhea
2) Abdominal pain and vomiting
3) Swollen mouth, gum and tongue
4) Depression, apathy, fatigue, loss of memory

## CYNOCOBALAMIN OR VITAMIN $B_{12}$

Cynocobalamin is a man-made form of vitamin $B_{12.}$ It is used to prevent as well as treat deficiency of this form of vitamin. In most of the cases people get adequate amount of vitamin $B_{12}$ from the daily diet. Vitamin $B_{12}$ contains approximately 4% to 5% Cobalt.

Cynocobalamin is a synthetic form of vitamin $B_{12}$.

Cobalamin and related forms are known as Vitamin $B_{12}$. Vitamin $B_{12}$ is the 'generic descriptor' name for any vitamers of $B_{12}$.

### Food source of vitamin $B_{12}$

Animal products such as meat, fish, poultry, shellfish, milk, cheese, eggs etc. The rich source is livers of goat, ox, pig and ship.

It is easily destroyed in microwave cooking.

### Functions in the body

1) Helps in new cell synthesis
2) Helps to maintain nerve cells
3) Helps to breakdown some fatty acids amino acids
4) Reforms folate co-enzymes

### Significance of Cycobalamin

Deficiency leads to-

1) Anaemia
2) Fatigue
3) Hypersensitive skin

## FOLIC ACID

Folic acid is slightly soluble in water. It is stable to heat at neutral pH.

### FOD source of folic acid

Dried yeast, hen's eggs and liver are rich sources of folic acids.

Whole cereals, legumes and green leafy vegetables are considered to fairly good source of folic acids. Nuts and oilseeds such as coconuts, groundnuts etc, tomato, goat's meat, liver of goat and sheep, mutton, milk etc also contain fair amount of folic acids.

### Functions in the body

1) Folic acid is essential for the maturation of red blood cells.
2) It as a co-enzyme in the synthesis of methionine and of purine and pyrimidine rings.

### Significance of folic acid

Deficiency of folic acid leads to

1) Nutritional Megaloblastic Anaemia in adults
2) Megaloblastic anaemia of spruce and other malabsorption syndrome.
3) Megaloblastic anaemia in infants and children

## KEY TERMS

- **Vitamin**: Vitamins are a group of organic, essential compound required in small amounts in the diet to perform specific functions that promote and regulate chemical reactions for growth, reproduction etc. of the body.
- **Folic acid:** Folic acid is slightly soluble in water. It is stable to heat at neutral pH.

## PROJECT BASED LEARNING

Students may be asked to

- Prepare a project report on the various protein supplements available in the market
- Make a report on the how the body builders fulfil their daily needs for protein
- Prepare charts on structures/functions/sources of proteins

## IMPORTANT QUESTIONS

Q. No. 1. Define vitamin. Classify vitamins.

Q. No. 2. Explain the food source, function and significance of any two fat soluble vitamin.

Q. No.3. Explain the food source, function and significance of any two water soluble vitamin.

Chapter 19

# Minerals

After reading this chapter, the students will be able to:

- *Define Mineral*
- *Classify Minerals*
- *Know about the food source, function and significance of various minerals.*

## DEFINITION

Minerals are inorganic elements needed by the body as structural components and regulators of chemical reactions and body processes.

## CLASSIFICATIONS OF MINERALS

Minerals can be classified into:

1) Major Minerals or Macro Minerals and
2) Minor minerals or Trace Minerals or Micro Minerals

## MAJOR MINERALS

Major Minerals are the essential mineral nutrients found in the human body in amounts larger than 05gms (or greater than 0.01% of body weight). Major minerals are needed in the diets in amounts greater than 100mg per day. Major minerals include calcium, phosphorus, potassium, sulphur, sodium, chloride and magnesium.

**Amount of Major ( sl.no.1 to 7) and Minor ( sl.no. 8 to 13) minerals in a 60Kg. Human body**

| Sl. No. | Name of Minerals | Amount Presnt | Human Body Weight |
|---|---|---|---|
| 01 | CALCIUM | 1150g | 60Kg. |
| 02 | PHOSPHORUS | 600g | 60Kg. |
| 03 | POTASSIUM | 210g | 60Kg. |
| 04 | SULPHER | 150 | 60Kg. |
| 05 | SODIUM | 90 | 60Kg |
| 06 | CHLORIDE | 90 | 60Kg |

| Sl. No. | Name of Minerals | Amount Presnt | Human Body Weight |
|---|---|---|---|
| 07 | MAGNESIUM | 30 | 60Kg |
| 08 | IRON | 2.4 | 60Kg |
| 09 | ZINC | 2.0 | 60Kg |
| 10 | COPPER | 0.09 | 60Kg |
| 11 | MAGNESIUM | 0.02 | 60Kg |
| 12 | IODINE | 0.02 | 60Kg |
| 13 | SELENIUM | 0.02 | 60Kg |

## MINOR MINERALS OR TRACE MINERALS OR MICRO-MINERALS

These are essential mineral nutrients found in the human body in amounts less than 05g ( or present in the body in amounts less than 0.01% of body weight). Minor Minerals are required in the diet in amounts less than 100mg per day. Minor minerals include iron, zinc, copper, magnesium, iodine, selenium.

## Calcium

### *Food source of Calcium*

**Amounts of calcium present in various food items.**

| Food source | Amount | Calcium (mg.) |
|---|---|---|
| Low fat milk | One cup | 297 |
| Curd | 08 oz | 274 |
| Cheddar Cheese | 01 oz | 204 |
| Vanilla ice-cream | 01 cup | 176 |
| Low fat paneer | 01 cup | 155 |
| Broccoli | ½ cup | 89 |
| Sardine | 03 oz | 275 |

### *Functions of Calcium*

Major functions of calcium includes-

1) Mineralization of bones and teeth
2) Muscle contraction and relaxation
3) Nerve functioning
4) Blood clotting
5) Lowering blood pressure
6) Immune defences

### *Significance of Calcium*

Calcium deficiency leads to

1) Retarded growth in children
2) Bone loss in adults ( commonly known as Osteoporosis)

## Iron

Iron's two states are Ferrous Iron and Ferric Iron. Most of the body's iron is found in two proteins-

1) Hemoglobin in the red blood cells
2) Myoglobin in the muscle cells

In both iron helps in accept, carry and release oxygen.

### *Food Source of Iron*

Significant sources of iron in the body are-

Red meats, fish, poultry, shellfish, eggs, legumes and dried fruits.

### *Functions of iron in the body*

Main functions of iron in the body are

1) Part of the protein haemoglobin, which carries oxygen from one place to the other in the body.
2) Part of the protein myoglobin, this helps in muscle contraction
3) Necessary for the utilization of energy

### *Significance of iron in the body*

1) Iron deficiency is very common in children and women all over the world. Iron deficiency causes anaemia.
2) Reduced resistance to infections
3) Weakness and fatigue
4) Pale and itching skin
5) Inability to regulate body temperature

## Sodium

### *Food Source*

Main sources of sodium are-

Table salt, soy sauce.

In moderate amount - meats, milk, breads and vegetables.

In large amounts - in processed foods.

### *Functions in the body*

Significant functions of Sodium are

1) Maintains normal fluid and electrolyte balance.
2) Helps in nerve impulse transmission
3) Helps in muscle contraction

### *Significance of sodium in the body*

Deficiency of Sodium leads to-

1) Muscle cramps
2) Mental apathy
3) Loss of appetite

## Iodine

### *Food sources of iodine*

Iodized salt, sea foods, breads, dairy products, plants grown in iodine rich soil and animals fed in those plants.

### *Functions of iodine*

Iodine is a component of two thyroid hormones that helps to regulate growth, developments and metabolic rate.

### *Significance of iodine*

Deficiency of iodine leads to Simple Goitre and Cretinism.

## Flourine

### *Food source of flourine*

Milk, eggs and fish are significant sources, fluoridation of water.

### *Functions of florine*

1) Involved in the formation of bones and teeth
2) Helps to make teeth resistant to teeth decay.

### *Signifiance of flourine*

1) Susceptibility to tooth decay.

## KEY TERMS

- **Mineral**: Minerals are inorganic elements needed by the body as structural components and regulators of chemical reactions and body processes.
- **Major Mineral**: Major Minerals are the essential mineral nutrients found in the human body in amounts larger than 05gms (or greater than 0.01% of body weight).
- **Minor Minerals**: These are essential mineral nutrients found in the human body in amounts less than 05g ( or present in the body in amounts less than 0.01% of body weight).

## PROJECT BASED LEARNING:

Students may be asked to:

- Prepare a project report on sources/functions/classification of minerals

## IMPORTANT QUESTIONS:

Q. No.1. Define minerals. Classify minerals. Explain.

Q. No. 2. Explain the food source, function and significance of any two of the following:

a) Calcium

b) Iron

c) Sodium

Chapter 20

# Water

After reading this chapter the students will be able to:

- *Define water*
- *Know the dietary source of water*
- *Explain Functions of water in the human body*
- *Learn the role of water in maintaining the health (Water Balance)*

## INTRODUCTION

Water, next to Oxygen, is most essential for life. We can survive without food and other nutrients for many weeks or for several months, but without water we cannot survive for a few days.

Water has been defined 'as the liquid forming the seas, lakes, rivers and rain', by the Oxford Dictionary.

Some points to be remembered:

- Water is a compound of Hydrogen and Oxygen
- It constitutes about 60% of an adult's body weight.
- Water is classified as Macronutrient
- Every cell of the body contains water
- It is measured in liquid volumes such as litres.

## DIETARY SOURCES OF WATER

Our body gets water in three ways:-

1) The water that we drink. It is the visible source of water. It is also the major source of water.
2) The second major source is the food in our diet. This is an invisible source of water for the body.
3) The smallest source is the metabolic water.

$$C_6H_{12}O_6 \xrightarrow{\text{Oxidation}} CO_2 + H_2O \text{ (WATER + ENERGY)}$$

Oxidation of 100g of protein yields approx.40ml. water.

Oxidation of 100g of Carbohydrate yields approx. 55ml. of water.

**Percentage of water present in some of the foods.**

| Sl. No. | Name of the Foods | % of water |
|---|---|---|
| 01 | Water | 100 |
| 02 | Non-Fat Milk,Spinach, Broccoli, Cabbage, Lettuce | 90—99 |
| 03 | Eggs | 74 |
| 04 | Bread | 35 |
| 05 | Curd, Apple,Carrots, Orange | 80—89 |
| 06 | Cooked Cereals, Pasta, Rice | 60-85 |
| 07 | Dry Cereals, Crackers | 3—7 |
| 08 | Banana, Potato, Shrimp | 70—79 |
| 09 | Oil | 0 |

Water is lost through kidney, lungs, skin and GI track. A moderate quantity of water taken half an hour before the meal aids in proper digestion. Large quantities of chilled beverage along with diet will slow down the digestion process.

Need of water for an individual varies and depends on some factors such as

1) Diet
2) Type and duration of activities
3) Humidity
4) Day's temperature

An individual who expends 2000Kcalories per day needs approximately 2 to 3 litres of water.

## FUNCTIONS OF WATER

The entire life process of the body is dependent on water. The functions water performs in the body are as follows:

1) The ingested food gets moistened by saliva and digested with gastric juices.
2) Water carries nutrients and waste products throughout the body.
3) Maintains the structure of proteins and glycogen
4) Many chemical reactions in the body require water
5) Water acts as a solvent for minerals, vitamins and many other molecules.
6) Water acts as a lubricant and cushion for bone joints, spinal chord and inside the eyes.

7) It helps in regulating the body temperature
8) It helps maintaining blood volume.
9) It quenches thirst.

## ROLE OF WATER IN MAINTAINING HEALTH (WATER BALANCE)

The role of water in maintaining health cannot be over-emphasised. The 60% of body weight is made up by water only. Water helps in transporting all the nutrients throughout the body, carries $CO_2$ and waste products away from the cells, carries urea and Ketones away from the body, participates in chemical reactions, acts as an ideal solvent, acts as an ideal shock-absorber, maintains body temperature.

## WATER BALANCE

Water Balance may be defined as the equalisation between water intake and water output of the body.

Water Balance = water intake – water output

Or

Ingested water+ water in food + metabolic water = loss of water from (Kidney + skin +lungs +faces)

The 'I & O' or Input and Output chart has been given below.

**Typical 'I & O' or Input and Output of water of an adult.**

| Sources of water | Quantity | Losses of water | Quantity |
|---|---|---|---|
| Ingested water | 1500 | Kidneys | 1450 |
| Ingested food | 700 | Skin | 450 |
| Metabolic water | 200 | Lungs | 300 |
| | | Gi track | 200 |
| Total | 2400 | Total | 2400 |

## DEHYDRATION

Dehydration occurs in extreme shortage of water in the body. The result of dehydration is thirst, fatigue, reduced blood volume, headache, nausea, less urine, faint etc. Dehydration may result in due to diarrhoea, vomiting, excessive sweating, uncontrolled blood sugar, hot and humid weather condition etc.

The person should be given Electoral dissolved in water. ORT or Oral Rehydration Therapy is technique of treating dehydration.

## WATER INTOXICATION

Water Intoxication results in excess intake of water. It may lead to headache, nausea, vomiting, convulsion etc.

## KEY TERMS

- **Water**: Water has been defined 'as the liquid forming the seas, lakes, rivers and rain', by the Oxford Dictionary.
- **Water Balance:** Water Balance may be defined as the equalisation between water intake and water output of the body.

  Water Balance = water intake – water output

  Or

  Ingested water+ water in food + metabolic water = loss of water from (Kidney + skin +lungs +faces)

  The 'I & O' or Input and Output chart has been given below.
- **Dehydration**: Dehydration occurs in extreme shortage of water in the body. The result of dehydration is thirst, fatigue, reduced blood volume, headache, nausea, less urine, faint etc. Dehydration may result in due to diarrhoea, vomiting, excessive sweating, uncontrolled blood sugar, hot and humid weather condition etc.
- **Water Intoxication**: Water Intoxication results in excess intake of water. It may lead to headache, nausea, vomiting, convulsion etc.

## PROJECT BASED LEARNING

Students may be asked to –

- Prepare a project report on the sources of water in your city
- Prepare a project on common pollutants of water
- How water is wasted in your institute and solution for the same
- Mineral water and spring water bottles sold in your city market
- How water is treated in your college

## IMPORTANT QUESTIONS

Q. No. 1. Define water. Give the dietary source of water. Explain the functions of water.

Q. No. 2. Explain the following:

a) Water balance

b) Water intoxication

c) Dehydration

Chapter 21

# Balanced Diet

After reading this chapter, the student will be able to:

- *Define balanced diet*
- *Explain the importance of balanced diet*
- *Know the RDA for various nutrients as per age, gender and physiological state.*

## INTRODUCTION

A Balanced Diet may be defined as a diet that provides all the nutrients in ideal proportion or in enough amounts to meet the needs of healthy people.

A well-planned balanced diet will ensure the following guidelines:

a) An adequate diet which provides enough energy and nutrients to remain healthy.

b) A diet that uses enough of each type of food.

c) A diet that controls energy.

d) A nutrient dense diet

e) Selecting foods that are low in fat and sugar

f) A diet that includes variety.

Nutrient Density: Nutrient Density is defined as 'a measure of the nutrients relative to the energy a food provides'. A nutrient dense food will have more nutrients and fewer Kcalories.

## IMPORTANCE OF BALANCED DIET

A balanced diet is important because of the following reasons: -

- It prevents and reduces the risk of diseases and infections: since a balanced diet provides all different types micro-and-macronutrients to the body in proper proportion, it is highly likely that an individual will be able to develop enough immunity to fight all types of diseases.

- It helps control and manages a desired body weight: A balanced diet is one that prevents weight gains and maintains the desired weight of an individual. Though the best approach to weight management is to combine diet with physical activity.
- It helps to promote and maintain healthy growth of the body: Growth directly reflects nutrient intake and is considered to be an important parameter in judging the nutrition status. A balanced diet during childhood and at the onset of adolescence will ensure proper growth pattern.
- It helps to promote mental health: To function properly , the enzymes involved in neurotransmitter synthesis require nutrients in adequate amounts. A balanced will only ensure that there is no degenerative disease such as memory loss or Alzheimer's disease.
- It enhances external beauty: A balanced diet coupled with physical activity will lead to fitness. Fitness improves the skin health other than many associated benefits. It helps in building strong self-image.

## RDA FOR VARIOUS NUTRIENTS--AGE, GENDER, PHYSIOLOGICAL STATE

The full form of RDA is Recommended Dietary Allowance. The calorie requirements depend on various factors such as age, sex, weight, physical activities, climatic condition, digestive abilities etc. The protein requirements of the boys aged 12-14 years are more than the men. In order to maintain optimum health, the daily diet should provide adequate amounts of all nutrients. The Recommended Dietary Allowance is decided by Nutrition Expert Committee ICMR (Indian Council of Medical Research).

## KEY TERMS:

- Balanced Diet: A Balanced Diet may be defined as a diet that provides all the nutrients in ideal proportion or in enough amounts to meet the needs of healthy people.
- Nutrient Density: Nutrient Density is defined as 'a measure of the nutrients relative to the energy a food provides'. A nutrient dense food will have more nutrients and fewer Kcalories.
- RDA: The full form of RDA is Recommended Dietary Allowance

## PROJECT BASED LEARNING OR PBL:

Students may be asked to: -

- Prepare a balanced B/F, Lunch and Dinner menu for their mess

## IMPORTANT QUESTIONS

Q. No. 1. Explain what do you understand by :Balanced Diet".

Q. No. 2. Explain the importance of balanced diet. What is meant by Nutrient Density?

Q. No. 3. "Balanced diet is important to live a healthy life". Do you agree with this statement? Why?

**Table 1: RDA for Indian Men of various works groups.**

| Target Group | Characteristics | Appr. Body Weight (in Kg.) | Energy Require- ments (Kcal/D) | Protein (g/d) | Fat (g/d) | Calcium (mg/d) | Iron (mg/d) | Vitamin Retinol b- Carotene A (μg/d) | Vit. $B_{12}$ (μg/d) | Folic acid (μg/d) | Ascor- bic Acid (mg/d) | Pyrid oxin (mg/d) | Nico tinic acid (mg/d) | Ribo Flavin (mg/d) | Thia- min (mg/d) |
|---|---|---|---|---|---|---|---|---|---|---|---|---|---|---|---|
| Indian Men | Sedentary Lifestyle | 60Kg | 2425 | 60 | 20 | 400 | 28 | 600/2400 | 1 | 100 | 40 | 2.0 | 16 | 1.4 | 1.2 |
| | Medi-UmWorkGroup | 60Kg | 2875 | 60 | 20 | 400 | 28 | 600/2400 | 1 | 100 | 40 | 2.0 | 18 | 1.6 | 1.4 |
| | Heavy WorkGroup | 60Kg | 3800 | 60 | 20 | 400 | 28 | 600/2400 | 1 | 100 | 40 | 2.0 | 21 | 1.9 | 1.6 |

**Table 2: RDA for Indian ladies of various works groups.**

| Target Group | Characteristics | Appr. Body Weight (in Kg.) | Energy Require- ments (Kcal/D) | Protein (g/d) | Fat (g/d) | Calcium (mg/d) | Iron (mg/d) | Vitamin Retinol b- Carotene A (μg/d) | Vit. $B_{12}$ (μg/d) | Folic acid (μg/d) | Ascor- bic Acid (mg/d) | Pyrid oxin (mg/d) | Nico tinic acid (mg/d) | Ribo Flavin (mg/d) | Thia- min (mg/d) |
|---|---|---|---|---|---|---|---|---|---|---|---|---|---|---|---|
| Indian | SedenTaryLifeStyle | 50Kg | 1875 | 50 | 20 | 400 | 30 | 600/2400 | 1 | 100 | 40 | 2.0 | 12 | 1.1 | 0.9 |
| Ladies | Medi-UmWorkgroup | 50Kg | 2225 | 50 | 20 | 400 | 30 | 600/2400 | 1 | 100 | 40 | 2.0 | 14 | 1.3 | 1.1 |
| | Heavy Workgroup | 50Kg | 2925 | 50 | 20 | 400 | 30 | 600/2400 | 1 | 100 | 40 | 2.0 | 16 | 1.5 | 1.2 |

**Table 3: RDA for Indian Pregnant ladies and Lactating mothers**

| Target Group | Characteristics | Appr. Body Weight (in Kg.) | Energy Require- ments (Kcal/D) | Protein (g/d) | Fat (g/d) | Calcium (mg/d) | Iron (mg/d) | Vitamin Retinol b- Carotene A (μg/d) | Vit. $B_{12}$ (μg/d) | Folic acid (μg/d) | Ascor- bic Acid (mg/d) | Pyrid oxin (mg/d) | Nico tinic acid (mg/d) | Ribo Flavin (mg/d) | Thia- min (mg/d) |
|---|---|---|---|---|---|---|---|---|---|---|---|---|---|---|---|
| Pregnant | SedentaryLifestyle | 50Kg | 2175 | 65 | 30 | 1000 | 38 | 600/2400 | 1 | 100 | 40 | 2.0 | 14 | 1.3 | 1.1 |
| Indian | MediUmWorkgroup | 50Kg | 2525 | 65 | 30 | 1000 | 38 | 600/2400 | 1 | | | | 16 | 1.5 | 1.3 |
| Ladies | Heavy Workgroup | 50Kg | 3225 | 65 | 30 | 1000 | 38 | 600/2400 | 1 | 100 | 40 | | 18 | 1.7 | 1.5 |
| | Lactation | | 50Kg | | | 45 | 1000 | 30 | 950/3800 | 1.5 | 150 | 80 | 2.5 | | |

**Table 4: RDA for Indian Infants from the birth to one year olds.**

| Target Group | Characteristics | Appr. Body Weight (in Kg.) | Energy Require-ments (Kcal/D) | Protein (g/d) | Fat (g/d) | Calcium (mg/d) | Iron (mg/d) | Vitamin A Retinol b-Carotene (µg/d) | Vit. $B_{12}$ (µg/d) | Folic acid (µg/d) | Ascor-bic Acid (mg/d) | Pyrid oxin (mg/d) | Nico tinic acid (mg/d) | Ribo Flavin (mg/d) | Thia-min (mg/d) |
|---|---|---|---|---|---|---|---|---|---|---|---|---|---|---|---|
| Indian Infants | Upt o Six months | 5.4 | 583.2 | 11.7 | | 500 | | 350/1200 | 0.2 | 25 | 25 | 0.1 | 710 µg/kg | 65 µg/kg | 55 µg/kg |
| | Six Months to 1 year | 8.6 | 842.8 | 14.19 | | | | | | | | 0.4 | 650 µg/kg | 60 µg/kg | 50 µg/kg |

**Table 5: RDA for the Indian infants aged between one year to nine years.**

| Target Group | Characteristics | Appr. Body Weight (in Kg.) | Energy Require-ments (Kcal/D) | Protein (g/d) | Fat (g/d) | Calcium (mg/d) | Iron (mg/d) | Vitamin A Retinol b-Carotene (µg/d) | Vit. $B_{12}$ (µg/d) | Folic acid (µg/d) | Ascor-bic Acid (mg/d) | Pyrid oxin (mg/d) | Nico tinic acid (mg/d) | Ribo Flavin (mg/d) | Thia-min (mg/d) |
|---|---|---|---|---|---|---|---|---|---|---|---|---|---|---|---|
| Indian | 01 Yr. To 03 Yrs. | 12.2 | 1250 | 22 | 25 | 400 | 12 | 400/1600 | | 30 | 40 | 0.9 | 8 | 0.7 | 0.6 |
| Children | 04 Yrs.To 06 Yrs | 19 | 1700 | 30 | | | 20 | 400/1600 | 0.2To01 | 40 | | 0.9 | 11 | 1 | 0.9 |
| | 07 Yrs To 09 Yrs. | 27 | 1950 | 40 | | | 26 | 600/2400 | | 60 | | 1.6 | 13 | 1.2 | |

**Table 6: RDA for Indian boys aged between ten years to eighteen years.**

| Target Group | Characteristics | Appr. Body Weight (in Kg.) | Energy Require-ments (Kcal/D) | Protein (g/d) | Fat (g/d) | Calcium (mg/d) | Iron (mg/d) | Vitamin A Retinol b-Carotene (μg/d) | Vit. $B_{12}$ (μg/d) | Folic acid (μg/d) | Ascor-bic Acid (mg/d) | Pyrid oxin (mg/d) | Nico tinic acid (mg/d) | Ribo Flavin (mg/d) | Thia-min (mg/d) |
|---|---|---|---|---|---|---|---|---|---|---|---|---|---|---|---|
| Indian Boys | 10 Yrs. To 12 Yrs. | 35.4 | 2200 | 55 | 22 | 600 | 35 | 600/2400 | 0.2To01 | 70 | 40 | 1.6 | 15 | 1.3 | 1.1 |
| | 13 Yrs. To 15 Yrs | 47.8 | 2500 | 70 | 22 | 600 | 40 | 600/2400 | 0.2To01 | 100 | 40 | 2 | 16 | 1.5 | 1.2 |
| | 16 Yrs. To 18 Yrs. | 57 | 2640 | 80 | 22 | 500 | 50 | 600/2400 | 0.2To01 | 100 | 40 | 2 | 17 | 1.6 | 1.3 |

**Table 7: RDA for Indian girls aged between ten years to eighteen years.**

| Target Group | Characteristics | Appr. Body Weight (in Kg.) | Energy Require-ments (Kcal/D) | Protein (g/d) | Fat (g/d) | Calcium (mg/d) | Iron (mg/d) | Vitamin A Retinol b-Carotene (μg/d) | Vit. $B_{12}$ (μg/d) | Folic acid (μg/d) | Ascor-bic Acid (mg/d) | Pyrid oxin (mg/d) | Nico tinic acid (mg/d) | Ribo Flavin (mg/d) | Thia-min (mg/d) |
|---|---|---|---|---|---|---|---|---|---|---|---|---|---|---|---|
| Indian Girls | 10 Yr. To 12 Yrs. | 31.4 | 1900 | 57 | 22 | | 19 | | | | | | 13 | 1.2 | 1 |
| | 13 Yrs. To 15 Yrs | 46.8 | 2000 | 65 | 22 | | 28 | | | | | | 14 | 1.2 | 1 |
| | 16 Yrs To 18 Yrs. | 50 | 2000 | 65 | 22 | | 30 | | | | | | 14 | 1.2 | 1 |

Chapter 22

# Menu Planning

After reading this chapter, the learner will be able to:

- *Plan nutritionally balanced meal based on the three food group system*
- *Learn the factors affecting meal planning*
- *Conduct critical evaluation of a few meals served at the Institutes/Hotels based on the principle of meal planning*
- *Calculate the nutritive values of dishes/meals.*

## INTRODUCTION

Menu planning may be defined as an important process of developing an attractive, palatable at the same time nutritionally balanced meals. Menu planning calls for the thorough knowledge of the food habits, liking and disliking, nutrients etc.

The aims and objectives of menu planning include-

- To provide nutritionally balanced meals
- To provide an attractive and palatable meal
- To ensure profit by controlling expenditures effectively
- To ensure timely ordering and receiving of raw materials in right quantity
- To maintain desirable food cost
- To ensure ease in timely preparation and storage of right quantity of meals
- To minimize wastage and pilferage.

## PLANNING NUTRITIONALLY BALANCED MEAL BASED ON THE THREE FOOD GROUP SYSTEM

Simply put, a balanced meal is the one that provide all the nutrients required to maintain a healthy body. The food acts as a "fuel" in our body. It supplies chemical energy to perform daily activities and also synthesize required chemicals within the body.

The three main functions of food in our body are:

- To supply energy
- To supply building blocks for growth and maintenance
- To provide defence against diseases as well as regulate body processes.

A food group may be defined simply as the food items sharing some common characteristics. A number of food items help us to perform each of the above specific functions. On the basis of this characteristics we can categorize a number of food items into three basic groups.

### The basic three food groups are:

1) **Energy-providing food group**: The foods in this group supplies carbohydrates, fats and proteins. Theirs conversion to energy is the fundamental important function. The fats are the most concentrated source of energy, whereas the carbohydrates are the cheapest and proteins are the most expensive source of energy. The food items belonging to this group are:

   Cereals, millets, roots and tubers

   Sugars and Jaggery

   Lipids

2) **Body-building food groups**: The foods in this group are mainly rich in proteins. Proteins provide chemical building materials for the synthesis of body tissues and other constituents of life. The foods included in this group are

   All animal proteins with high Biological Value(BV), such as those found in fish, meat, poultry, eggs and milk.

   Pulses, nuts and oilseeds etc.

3) **Regulatory or Protective food group**: All the fruits and vegetables are included in this food group. Botanically, the parts of a plant that contain seeds are called fruits. Therefore, the tomatoes, cucumber, okra, eggplants are considered as fruits. But, as far as usage is concerned the plant item eaten with the main course are vegetable and those eaten alone or as a dessert are termed as fruits. Vegetables and fruits, when fresh, contain 70% to 85% water, 3.5% protein and 0.5% fat. The examples of this food group include:

   All green leafy vegetables.

   Fruits and vegetable of all different colours.

   All citrus fruits.

Therefore, it is clear that to plan a nutritionally balanced meal, we need to include foods from each of the above three groups.

## FACTORS AFFECTING MEAL PLANNING

Following are the factors to be kept in mind while planning a meal:

- Nutritional aspect: the nutritional aspect of the meal is of utmost importance while planning a meal. The meal must provide all the nutrients as per Recommended Dietary Amounts or RDA to maintain an optimum health. As discussed above the food items from all the basic food groups must be added to make it a balanced meal. Special needs such as pregnancy; lactation etc must also be taken into account.
- Budget: The meal planner must take the budget into account. The food cost and the economic state of the target market segment must be considered while planning a meal. The low cost nutritious substitutes need to be explored for the low budget clients.
- Types of service and the type of meal: The type of meal includes meal for Breakfast, lunch, Brunch, Snacks, Dinner etc. the meal items should be according to the type of meals for which meal is being planned. The type of service includes Self service, assisted service, Silver service; buffet service, Gueridon service etc. meal should be planned according to the service to be provided to the clients.
- Equipments and space: The meal should include such items for which the equipments are available. For example, if sizzlers are included in the meal then adequate number of sizzler dishes must be available. The space for proper service and the space for keeping the equipments in both kitchen and restaurant must be kept in mind.
- Skill of the staff: the restaurant and the kitchen staff should be trained properly to produce and serve all the dishes included in the meal.
- Liking and disliking of the clients: The food habit of the customers is of prime importance. The meal must include all the dishes which are acceptable to the customers. The religious beliefs, type of community, liking and disliking of the clients must be kept in mind while planning a meal.
- Season: Seasonal vegetables and fruits must be included in the meal. Seasonal fruits and vegetables will be cheaper, easily available and fresh. This will in turn ensure more margin of profit, more satisfied clients, better nutritional quality and more tasty foods.
- Customer profile, meal frequency and meal pattern: The customer profile such as age, gender, sex, activity level, religion, physiological state, economic power etc are to kept in mind while planning a menu. The number of times the meal is going to be consumed by the customer should be considered. The meal pattern such packing or table service need to be also considered.
- Variety: The dishes in the meal should include variety and not be repetitive. The ingredients, seasoning, methods of cooking, colour, texture, taste, garnish, presentation etc should be different.

## HOW TO PLAN A BALANCED MEAL

Following are the steps in planning a balanced meal:

**Fig: Three Groups of Food**

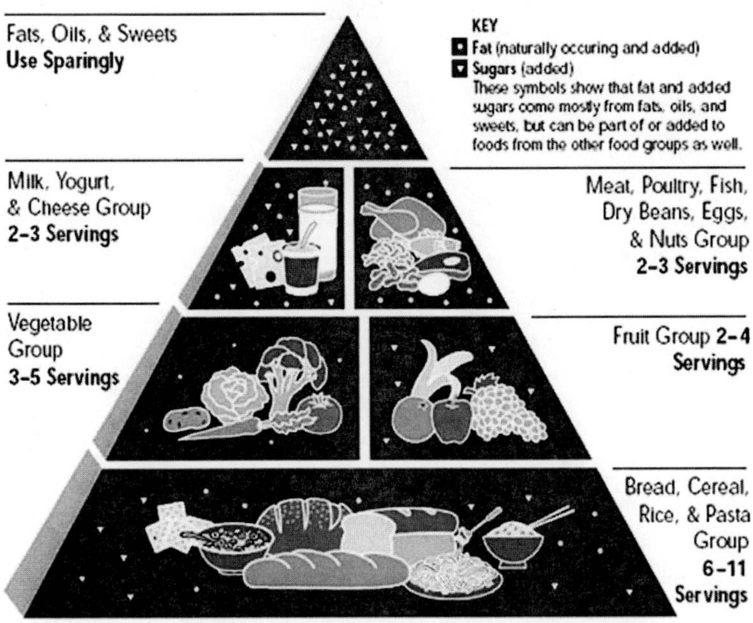


**Fig. Five Groups of Foods**

- Gather customer profile:

  Gather following information of the potential customer—

  Age,

  Sex,

  Religion,

  Liking and disliking of foods,

  Activity level,

  Social status,

  Economic standard etc.

- Keep the Recommended Dietary Allowance chart ready.
- Decide on meal frequency,
- Prepare a food plan,
- Choose foods from each group, size of serving.
- Chat out a menu now,
- Cross check to ensure all factors are taken into account.

**Table 1: Portion size and nutrient contents of various food items required for Meal Planning.**

| Food Items | Gm./Portion | Energy (Kcal) | Protein (Gm.) | Carbohydrate (Gm.) | Fat (G) |
|---|---|---|---|---|---|
| Cereals & Millets | 30 | 100 | 3.0 | 20 | o.8 |
| Pulses | 30 | 100 | 6 | 15 | 0.7 |
| Meat/chicken/Fish | 50 | 100 | 9.0 | - | 7.0 |
| Egg | 50 | 85 | 7.0 | - | 7.0 |
| Milk (ml.)& Milk Products | 100 | 70 | 3.0 | 5.0 | 3.0 |
| Roots & Tubers | 100 | 80 | 1.3 | 18 | - |
| Green leafy vegetables | 100 | 46 | 3.6 | - | 0.4 |
| Othervegetables | 100 | 28 | 1.7 | - | 0.2 |
| Fruits | 100 | 40 | - | 10 | - |
| Sugar | 05 | 20 | - | 5.0 | - |
| Fats & Oils | 05 | 45 | - | - | 5.0 |

**Table 2: Nutrient contents of some more food items.**

| Nutrient Type | Food groups | Food items belonging to the group | Nutrient amounts per100 gms. Portion |
|---|---|---|---|
| Energy | Cereals & Tubes | Rice, wheat & Tapioca | 340 Kcal |
| | Nuts and Oilseeds | Almonds, Cashewnuts, | 600 Kcal. |
| | Veg. Oil, Vanaspati, Desi Ghee | ground nuts, Coconut(dry). Vegetable oil,Vanaspati, Desi Ghee | 900 Kcal |
| Proteins | Pulses, Legumes | Blackgram, Greengram, Bengalgram, Redgram, Lentil etc. | 22 gm. |
| | Nuts and Oilseeds | Groudnuts, Cashewnuts, Almonds | 23 gms. |
| | Fish Meat and Poultry | Fish<br>Egg white,<br>Meat | 20 gms.<br>11 gms.<br>22 gms. |
| | Milk Products | Skimmed cow milk powder, Whole milk powder, Cheese, Khoa | 30 gms. |

The below given Tables contain some of the most common items found in the menu planning. The table should be kept handy while planning a nutritionally balanced menu.

## DETAILED CALCULATION OF NUTRITIVE VALUE OF A BREAKFAST MENU

Besan ka paratha,

Curd,

Coffee

| Sl. No. | Ingredients | Quantity |
|---|---|---|
| 01 | Wheat flour | 100 g |
| 02 | Besan | 20 g |
| 03 | Onion | 25 g |
| 04 | Fat | 15 g |
| 05 | Curds | 100 g |
| 06 | Milk | 50 g |
| 07 | Sugar | 10 g |

**Table 3: Nutrient contents of cereal, grains, pulses and legumes.**

| Food Items | Energy (Kcal) | Protein (g) | Fat (g) | Vit C (mg) | Calcium (mg) | Iron (mg) | Carbohydrate (g) | Fibre (g) |
|---|---|---|---|---|---|---|---|---|
| **Cereals and Grains** | | | | | | | | |
| Rice | 345 | 7 | 0.5 | 0 | 10 | 0.7 | 78 | 0.2 |
| Refined flour | 348 | 11 | 0.9 | 0 | 23 | 2.7 | 74 | 0.3 |
| Whole wheat flour | 341 | 12 | 1.7 | 0 | 10 | 0.7 | 78 | 0.2 |
| **Pulses and legumes** | | | | | | | | |
| Lentils | 343 | 25 | 0.7 | 0 | 69 | 7.6 | 59 | 0.7 |
| Bengal gram ( whole) | 360 | 17 | 5 | 3 | 202 | 4.6 | 61 | 4 |

**Table 4: Nutrient content of vegetables.**

| Food Items | Energy (Kcal) | Protein (g) | Fat (g) | Vit C (mg) | Calcium (mg) | Iron (mg) | Carbohydrate (g) | Fibre (g) |
|---|---|---|---|---|---|---|---|---|
| **Green Leafy Vegetables** | | | | | | | | |
| Spinach | 26 | 2 | 0.7 | 28 | 73 | 1.1 | 3 | 0.6 |
| Roots and Tuber | | | | | | | | |
| Potato | 97 | 1.6 | 0.1 | 17 | 10 | 0.5 | 23 | 0.4 |
| Carrot | 48 | 0.9 | 0.2 | 3 | 80 | 01 | 11 | 1.2 |
| **Other vegetables** | | | | | | | | |
| Lady's Finger | 35 | 2 | 0.2 | 1 | 66 | 0.4 | 06 | 1.2 |

**Table 5: Nutrient content of common fruits and nuts**

| Food Items | Energy (Kcal) | Protein (g) | Fat (g) | Vit C (mg) | Calcium (mg) | Iron (mg) | Carbohydrate (g) | Fibre (g) |
|---|---|---|---|---|---|---|---|---|
| **Fruits** | | | | | | | | |
| Apple | 59 | 0.2 | 0.5 | 1 | 10 | 0.7 | 13 | 1 |
| Orange | 48 | 0.7 | 0.2 | 30 | 26 | 0.3 | 11 | 0.3 |
| Banana | 116 | 1 | 0.3 | 7 | 17 | 0.4 | 27 | 0.4 |
| Papaya | 32 | 0.6 | 0.1 | 57 | 17 | 0.5 | 07 | 0.8 |
| **Nuts** | | | | | | | | |
| groundnuts | 567 | 25 | 40 | 00 | 90 | 2.5 | 26 | 3.1 |

**Table 6: Nutrient contents of meat, poultry and fish**

| Food Items | Energy (Kcal) | Protein (g) | Fat (g) | Vit C (mg) | Calcium (mg) | Iron (mg) | Carbohydrate (g) | Fibre (g) |
|---|---|---|---|---|---|---|---|---|
| **Meat and poultry** | | | | | | | | |
| Mutton | 194 | 18.5 | 13.3 | - | 150 | 2.5 | - | - |
| Egg | 173 | 13.3 | 13.3 | 0 | 60 | 2.1 | - | - |
| Sheep liver | 150 | 19 | 7.5 | 20 | 10 | 6.3 | 1.3 | - |
| **Fish** | | | | | | | | |
| Pomfret | 87 | 17 | 1.3 | — | 200 | 0.9 | 1.8 | - |

**Table 7: Nutrient contents of milk & milk products and Fats & oils**

| Food Items | Energy (Kcal) | Protein (g) | Fat (g) | Vit C (mg) | Calcium (mg) | Iron (mg) | Carbohydrate (g) | Fibre (g) |
|---|---|---|---|---|---|---|---|---|
| **Milk & milk products; Fats & Oils** | | | | | | | | |
| Cow milk | 67 | 3.2 | 4.1 | 2 | 120 | 0.2 | 4.4 | - |
| Paneer | 265 | 18.3 | 20.8 | 3 | 208 | - | 1.2 | - |
| Butter | 729 | - | 81 | - | - | - | - | - |
| Cooking oil | 900 | - | 100 | 0 | - | - | - | - |
| Ghee | 900 | - | 100 | - | - | - | - | - |

**Table 8: Nutrient contents of sweet ingredients.**

| Food | Serving | Calories | Protein (g) | Calcium (g) | Iron (mg) | Vitamins A (IU) | C (MG) | D (IU) | Thia-min (µg) | Ribo-flavin (µg) | Niacin (mg) | Water (%) |
|---|---|---|---|---|---|---|---|---|---|---|---|---|
| Beans Green, cooked | 1 cup | 27 | 1.8 | 45 | 0.9 | 830 | 18 | 0 | 90 | 120 | 0.6 | 92 |
| Brocoli, cooked | 2/3cup | 29 | 3.3 | 130 | 1.3 | 3400 | 74 | 0 | 70 | 150 | 0.8 | 90 |
| Cabbage, cooked | ½ cup | 20 | 1.2 | 39 | 0.4 | 75 | 27 | 0 | 40 | 40 | 0.3 | 92 |
| Cheese, cheddar | 1 Oz | 113 | 7.1 | 206 | 0.3 | 400 | 0 | 0 | 10 | 120 | Tr. | 36 |
| Chicken, fried | ½ breast | 232 | 26.8 | 19 | 1.3 | 460 | 0 | 0 | 67 | 101 | 10.2 | 53 |
| Oatmeal, cooked | 1 cup | 148 | 5.4 | 21 | 1.7 | 0 | 0 | 0 | 220 | 50 | 0.4 | 85 |
| Tomato, raw | 1 large | 40 | 2 | 22 | 1.2 | 2200 | 46 | 0 | 120 | 80 | 1 | 94 |

**Source**: The World Encyclopaedia, 1 Cup=237ml., 1 ounce= 28g, 1 Tablespoon= 15ml.

**Table 9: Detailed calculation of a B/F menu**

| Food Items | Protein (g) | Fat (g) | Fiber (g) | Carbohydrate (g) | Energy (kcal) | Calcium (mg) | Iron (mg) | Carotene µg | Vit. C Mg |
|---|---|---|---|---|---|---|---|---|---|
| Whole wheatFlour | 12 | 1.7 | 1. | 69 | 341 | 48 | 4.9 | 29 | 00 |
| Besan | 21 | 6.5 | 10.2 | 54 | 77 | 42 | 5 | | 00 |
| Onion | 0.3 | 0.02 | 0.15 | 2.75 | 12 | 11.75 | 0.15 | 00 | 2.75 |
| Fat | - | 15.4 | - | - | 135 | - | - | 90 | |
| Curds | 3.1 | 3.3 | | 4.7 | 61 | 121 | | 27 | 0.14 |
| Milk | 1.6 | 2.1 | - | 2.2 | 34 | 60 | 0.1 | 26 | 1 |
| Sugar | - | - | - | 10 | 40 | 1.2 | 0.1 | - | - |
| Total | 38 | 29.02 | 11.17 | 142 | 700 | 284 | 10.25 | 172 | 3.89 |

| | Qty. | Energy(Kcal) | Protein(g) | Fat(g) | Carb.(g) | Calcium(g) | Iron(mg) | Vit. A | Vit. C |
|---|---|---|---|---|---|---|---|---|---|
| Plain rice | 100 | 118 | 2.4 | 0.2 | 26.8 | 0.004 | 1 | - | - |
| Idli | 100 | 96 | 3.4 | 0.15 | 20.3 | 0.02 | 0.6 | 6 | - |
| Chappati | 100 | 339 | 8.8 | 9.6 | 54.0 | 0.04 | 5.3 | 224 | - |
| Puris | 100 | 425 | 6.9 | 26.3 | 40.6 | 0.03 | 4.1 | 15 | - |
| Plain paratha | 100 | 461 | 6.8 | 29.7 | 41.4 | 0.015 | 4.1 | 707 | - |
| Lucchi | 100 | 487 | 5.6 | 33.8 | 39.4 | 0.01 | 0.56 | 821 | - |
| CookedBeng.GramDal | 100 | 188 | 6 | 10.9 | 16.7 | 0.05 | 2.5 | 242 | 1.2 |
| CookedGr. GramDal | 100 | 120 | 4.9 | 5.4 | 12.9 | 0.06 | 1.9 | 23 | 1.1 |
| Cooked Red GramDal | 100 | 115 | 6.7 | 2.1 | 17.1 | 0.05 | 2.7 | 67 | - |
| Amaranth Curry | 100 | 168 | 5.6 | 8.2 | 17.6 | 0.14 | 23.6 | 6934 | 182.2 |
| Gobi & gajar kiSabzi | 100 | 145 | 2.7 | 10.0 | 10.9 | 0.07 | 1.6 | 1835 | 67.9 |
| Coffee | 200 | 104 | 3.8 | 3.4 | 14.4 | 0.10 | 1.20 | 154 | 1.4 |

## SAMPLE MENU FOR A LADY TEACHER HAVING LIGHT PHYSICAL ACTIVITIES

Life Style: Sedentary, Energy Needed: 1812, Protein Needed: 59.8, Iron Needed: 30mg,

| | Meal Time | Menu | Ingredients |
|---|---|---|---|
| 01 | Bed Tea | Tea | Milk |
| | | | Sugar |
| 02 | Breakfast | Mushroom Omelette | Egg |
| | | | Mushroom |
| | | | Onions |
| | | | Fat |
| | | Toasts with butter | Breads |
| | | | Butter |
| | | Tea | Milk |
| | | | Sugar |
| 03 | Lunch | Minced meat (dry) | Meat |
| | | | Onion |
| | | | Tomato |
| | | | Fat |
| | | Methi Paratha | Wheat flour |
| | | | Methi |
| | | | Fat |
| | | Salad + Apple + Papaya | Cucumber |
| | | | Capsicum |
| | | | Tomato |
| | | Rice | Rice |
| 04 | High Tea | Biscuits | Biscuits |
| | | Tea | Milk |
| | | | Sugar |
| 05 | Dinner | Aloo Palak | Aloo |
| | | | Palak |
| | | | Onion |
| | | | Fat |
| | | Dal | Arhar |
| | | | Onion |
| | | Rice | Rice |
| | | Roti | Wheat flour |
| | | Curd | Curd |
| | | Kheer | Rice |
| | | | Milk |
| | | | Sugar |

| Ingredients | Quantity (gm) | Protein (g) | Fat (g) | Fibre (g) | Carbo-Hydrate (g) | Energy (kcal) | Calcium (Mg) | Iron (Mg) | CaroTene (µg) | Vit. C (mg) |
|---|---|---|---|---|---|---|---|---|---|---|
| Milk | 25 | 0.8 | 1.0 | - | 1.1 | 1.7 | 30 | 0.05 | 13 | 0.5 |
| Sugar | 05 | - | - | - | 5 | 20 | 0.6 | - | - | - |
| Egg | 40 | 5.3 | 5.3 | - | - | 68 | 24 | 0.8 | 168 | 0 |
| Mushroom | 25 | 7 | 0.07 | 0.25 | 0.8 | 6 | - | 0.5 | - | 0.75 |
| Onions | 50 | 0.6 | 0.5 | 0.3 | 6 | 25 | 24 | 0.3 | 0 | 6 |
| Fat | 10 | - | 10 | - | - | 90 | - | - | 00 | 00 |
| Breads | 40 | 3.5 | 1.2 | 1.2 | 21 | 103 | 10.4 | 7.2 | 00 | 00 |
| Butter | 10 | - | 8.1 | - | - | 73 | - | - | 96 | - |
| Milk | 25 | 4 | 5 | - | 5.5 | 8.5 | 30 | 0.25 | 65 | 2.5 |
| Sugar | 05 | - | - | - | 5 | 20 | 0.6 | - | - | - |
| Meat | 50 | 9.25 | 6.7 | - | - | 90 | 120 | 2.5 | 9 | - |
| Onion | 25 | 0.3 | 0.25 | 0.15 | 3 | 12.5 | 12 | 0.15 | 0 | 3 |
| Tomato | 25 | 0.2 | 0.05 | 0.3 | 1 | 5 | 3.8 | 0.01 | 300 | 4.8 |
| Fat | 05 | - | 5 | - | - | 45 | - | - | 00 | 00 |
| Wheat flour | 30 | 3.6 | 0.51 | 0.52 | 21 | 102 | 16 | 1.5 | 12 | 00 |
| Methi | 25 | 1.1 | 0.25 | 0.3 | 1.5 | 12 | 9.8 | 0.5 | 590 | 13 |
| Fat | 05 | - | 05 | - | - | 45 | - | - | 00 | 00 |
| Cucumber | 25 | 0.2 | 0.25 | 0.12 | 0.9 | 4 | 0.25 | 0.25 | 0.05 | 1 |
| Capsicum | 30 | 0.5 | 0.05 | 0.35 | 2.2 | 10 | 0.25 | 0.15 | 0.6 | 101 |
| Tomato | 25 | 0.2 | 0.05 | 0.3 | 1 | 5 | 3.8 | 0.01 | 300 | 4.8 |
| Rice | 50 | 3.5 | 0.25 | 0.1 | 39 | 173 | 5 | 0.35 | 00 | 00 |
| Apple | 100 | 0.2 | 0.5 | 1 | 13 | 59 | 10 | 0.7 | 00 | 1 |
| Papaya | 100 | 0.6 | 0.1 | 0.8 | 7 | 32 | 17 | .5 | 666 | 57 |

| Ingredients | Quantity (gm) | Protein (g) | Fat (g) | Fibre (g) | Carbo-Hydrate (g) | Energy (kcal) | Calcium (Mg) | Iron (Mg) | CaroTene (µg) | Vit. C (mg) |
|---|---|---|---|---|---|---|---|---|---|---|
| Biscuits | 25 | 1.7 | 4 | 0.35 | 11 | 70 | 6 | 4 | - | - |
| Milk | 25 | 0.8 | 1.0 | - | 1.1 | 1.7 | 30 | 0.05 | 13 | 0.5 |
| Sugar | 05 | - | - | - | 5 | 20 | 0.6 | - | - | - |
| Aloo | 100 | 1.6 | 0.1 | 0.4 | 23 | 97 | 10 | 0.5 | 24 | 17 |
| Palak | 100 | 2 | 0.7 | 0.6 | 3 | 26 | 50 | 1.1 | 5580 | 28 |
| Onion | 50 | 0.6 | 0.5 | 0.3 | 6 | 25 | 24 | 0.3 | 0 | 6 |
| Fat | 05 | - | 5 | - | - | 45 | - | - | 00 | 00 |
| Arhar | 30 | 6.6 | 0.3 | 3 | 19 | 102 | 3 | 7 | 00 | 00 |
| Onion | 25 | 0.3 | 0.25 | 0.15 | 3 | 12.5 | 12 | 0.15 | 0 | 3 |
| Rice | 30 | 2.1 | 0.15 | 0.06 | 22 | 102 | 3 | 0.02 | 00 | 00 |
| Wheat flour | 30 | 3.6 | 0.51 | 0.52 | 21 | 102 | 16 | 1.5 | 12 | 00 |
| Sugar | 15 | - | - | - | 15 | 60 | 1.8 | 0.01 | - | - |
| Rice | 25 | 1.8 | 0.12 | 0.05 | 20 | 86 | 2.5 | 0.17 | 00 | 00 |
| Milk | 200 | 8 | 10 | - | 11 | 17 | 240 | 0.5 | 130 | 5 |

Critical Evaluation of the Menu:

In order to critically evaluate a menu following points must be kept in mind-

- The menu should include food items from all the food groups
- The RDA must be kept in mind
- Salads and fruits must be included in the menu
- Ensure adequate supply of milk to provide calcium
- Cereals should not supply more than seventy five percent of total calories required.

In the above menu-

- The total calories are provided as per the RDA i.e. approximately 1800 kcal required for Indian ladies having sedentary life style.
- The protein requirement has been met in the above menu. The protein is part of the food items of the body building group and is very essential.
- The iron requirement is another important factor for the menu prepared for the ladies. Adequate supply of iron is kept in mind in planning the above menu.
- Raw vegetables in the form of salads has been included in the menu,
- The fruits are supplied in the menu, which are part of the Protective food groups.
- Adequate supply of milk has been kept in mind to ensure provision of enough calcium.
- The food items included in the menu are based on the general liking and disliking of the consumer.
- All major meals along with bed tea and high tea has been taken care of.

## KEY TERMS

- Menu Planning: Menu planning may be defined as an important process of developing an attractive, palatable at the same time nutritionally balanced meals.
- Energy-providing food group: The foods in this group supplies carbohydrates, fats and proteins.
- Body-building food groups: The foods in this group are mainly rich in proteins.
- Regulatory or Protective food group: All the fruits and vegetables are included in this food group.

## PROJECT BASED LEARNING:

Students may be asked to plan a menu for someone in their family keeping in mind his/her age, lifestyle etc.

## IMPORTANT QUESTION

Q. No. 1. What are the various factors involved in menu planning in relation to nutrition?

Chapter 23

# Mass Food Production

## EFFECT OF COOKING ON NUTRITIVE VALUE OF FOOD (QFP)

It is the responsibility of the chef/Food Scientist to retain as much nutrients as possible during cooking. This is possible only when he/she has a good knowledge about the stability of different nutrients during preparation.

- Vegetables contain vitamin A and Vitamin C.
- Carotene is insoluble in water and is not much affected by heat/cooking.
- The vitamin C content of cabbage is affected as it gets oxidised in the presence of air.
- Using utensils made of iron may damage the vitamin content. Therefore, to retain maximum vitamin in vegetables such as Cabbage the below-mentioned practices need to be followed:
  a) Less water should be used for cooking as vitamin C is highly water-soluble.
  b) Cook at high temperature to destroy enzymes.
  c) Large pieces of cabbage will reduce cooking water loss.
  d) Use HTST method.
  e) The cooking water should be used in soup/stock/gravy.
- Vitamin A is very much unstable to heat, air, light and acid.
- It is obvious from the table given below that the loss is more than 75% for many nutrients.
- The modern technique in modern food processing units has been able to successfully reduce the loss of nutrients and it is below 25%.
- However, if the loss of nutrient is very high, the food should be enriched with the addition of essential nutrients. Many of the flours are now fortified with nutrients.
- The extent of loss of nutrients during bulk cooking also depends on the genetics of the plants. The animals eating these plant will also fall into that category.
- The pre-cooking process such as the washing and trimming also affect the nutritional value of the food during quantity food preparations.
- The other cooking procedures used in bulk cooking such as Canning,

evaporating, drying and freezing affect the nutritional value of the food.

- The improper packaging and storing of the processed food are also important factors to be taken care of. Improper packaging and storing can affect the nutritive value of the food.
- The steam can also destroy much of the nutrients.

**Table: The stability of nutrients**

| Nutrients | Neutral pH 7 | Acid <pH7 | Alkaline >pH 7 | Air or Oxygen | Light | Heat | Coking Losses % |
|---|---|---|---|---|---|---|---|
| VITAMINS | | | | | | | |
| Vitamin A | S | U | S | U | U | U | 0—40 |
| Ascorbic acid (C) | U | S | U | U | U | U | 0-100 |
| Biotin | S | S | S | S | S | U | 0-60 |
| Carotenes(pro -A) | S | U | S | U | U | U | 0-30 |
| Choline | S | S | S | U | S | S | 0-5 |
| Cobalamin | S | S | S | U | U | S | 0-10 |
| Vitamin D | S | - | U | U | U | U | 0-40 |
| Essential fatty acids | S | S | U | U | U | S | 0-10 |
| Folic acid | U | U | S | U | U | U | 0-100 |
| Inositol | S | S | S | S | S | U | 0-95 |
| Vitamin K | S | U | U | S | U | S | 0-5 |
| Niacin(PP) | S | S | S | S | S | S | 0-75 |
| Panthothenic acid | S | U | U | S | S | U | 0-50 |
| p-Amino benzoic acid | S | S | S | U | S | S | 0-5 |
| Vitamin B6 | S | S | S | S | U | U | 0-40 |
| Riboflavin (B2) | S | S | U | S | U | U | 0-75 |
| Thiamin (B1) | U | S | U | U | S | U | 0-80 |
| Tocopherols(E) | S | S | S | U | U | U | 0-55 |
| Essential Amino Acids | | | | | | | |
| Isoleucine | S | S | S | S | S | S | 0-10 |
| Leucine | S | S | S | S | S | S | 0-10 |
| Lysine | S | S | S | S | S | U | 0-40 |
| Methionine | S | S | S | S | S | S | 0-10 |
| Phenylalaline | S | S | S | S | S | S | 0-5 |
| Threonine | S | U | U | S | S | U | 0-20 |
| Tryptophan | S | U | S | S | U | S | 0-15 |
| Valine | S | S | S | S | S | S | 0-10 |
| Mineral Salts | S | S | S | S | S | S | 0-3 |

Source: Harris,R.S. and Kamas, E. 1975. Nutritional Evaluation of Food Processing, 2nd ed. AVI Publishing Westport, CT.

S = Stable. U = Unstable

Blanching of fruit causes loss of turgor, because of which the fruits become soggy and loses juice. The best way is to use them without cooking. Calcium salt is added for blanching and then put the fruits in the freezer.

For white meats the method of cooking and the cut make a lot of difference to the composition of the edible parts.

Roasted white meat without the skin contains about 64% water, 32% protein and 64% fat.

Roasted dark meat without the skin contains about 65% water, 28% protein and 6% fat.

The nutritional value of cooked meat generally remains very high. Normal cooking methods has hardly any effect on the nutritional value of meat proteins. The mineral content of the meat remain unchanged. When meat is cooked in water the calcium partly gets dissolved in the water and thus enriching the stock. The well-done meat will have the vitamin B destroyed to nearly 10%.

## PBL:

Students may be asked to visit a place and prepare a report where bulk cooking is done such as Mid Day Meal Project.

## IMPORTANT QUESTION:

Q. No. 1. Discuss the effect of cooking on nutritive value of food.

Chapter 24

# Newer Trends in Food Service Industry in Relevance to Nutrition and Health

After reading this chapter the student will be able to:

- Understand the need for introducing nutritionally balanced meals
- Learn about various health specific meals
- Evaluate fast foods
- Know about the new products being launched in the market (nutritional evaluation)

## NEED FOR INTRODUCING NUTRITIONALLY BALANCED AND HEALTH SPECIFIC MEALS

Food is required for good and optimum health. We need proper diet for energy, growth and disease-free health. This is possible only when we provide required amount of nutrients through diet to the body. These nutrients include carbohydrates, lipids, proteins, vitamins, minerals and water. Deficiency or over consumption of any of these may result in complications and diseases. Therefore we need to have knowledge of nutrition to ensure intake of a balanced meal to remain healthy. Knowledge of nutrition helps us to maintain the balance of foods and nutrients. A balanced diet develops a combination of different food items which provide adequate amount of all nutrients to maintain good health.

A balanced diet is therefore, required to—

- To ensure supply of adequate energy to satisfy—
  a) Basal metabolic needs
  b) Physical activities and
  c) Dietary Thermo genesis (refers to the energy required to digest, absorb, transport and store foods and its nutrients).
- To ensure proper growth rate

- To ensure strong immune system to fight against the disease-causing pathogens
- To maintain reproduction process
- To avoid over weight and under-weight
- To increase the consumption of complex carbohydrates and naturally occurring sugars ( from 28% to approximately 48% of energy intake).
- To reduce the consumption of refined and processed sugar (to approximately 10% of total calories).
- To reduce overall lipid consumption, mainly, the consumption of saturated fats.
- To reduce cholesterol consumption.
- To limit consumption of salt.

All the above can be done by carefully planning a balanced diet. A balanced diet takes care of some dietary guidelines such as

- Inclusion of food items from each food groups
- Limits saturated fat intake
- Considers an individual's age, gender, weight, life-style, food habits, liking & disliking, religion etc.
- Includes food with adequate amount of dietary fibre
- Avoids too much sugar and sodium

A planned introduction of nutrition programme through educating the population about balanced diet will help eradicating malnutrition, ensure proper supply of dietary essentials to the most vulnerable strata of population and help build a healthy society free from deficiency diseases.

While introducing nutritious balanced menu, following factors need to be considered:

- The existing popular items may just be modified to make it more nutritious. Since these items are well known and liked by the guests, they will be more marketable. Modifications may include minimising use of fat or butter, changing cooking method from frying to broiling, reducing sodium content, changing the garnish etc.
- Adding new creative dishes to meet the nutritional goal will be another good idea.

However, while introducing the balanced menu following factors need to be kept in mind—

- The dishes should be delicious in taste.
- The dishes must be attractive. An eye appeal is an important factor for repeat orders and repeat customers.

- It should be nutritious.
- Creativity in the preparation will be an added advantage. This will give an edge over the competitors.
- The menu must portray an acceptable image. The description of the dishes must portray an agreeable image.
- Quantity, quality and price must match. Both the low-cost and high-cost balanced meals must be included in the menu.
- The items must be profit-yielding (proper costing must be done to decide on the pricing). No commercial restaurant will continue to sell such dishes if the menu does not sell well or not profit yielding.
- A separate section on the menu may be made for the nutritionally balanced and health specific dishes.
- The waiting staff should be trained well to explain and recommend the menu items.
- The menu must be advertised through different media to ensure that potential customers are well-aware about the introduction of the menu/dishes.

## HEALTH SPECIFIC MEALS

Health specific meals in the menu may include some or all of the following:

1) **Balanced diet at low cost**: The dishes in this diet include all the ingredients which are nutritious as well as available at a low cost such as cereals, millets, green leafy vegetables etc.
2) **Balanced diet at high cost**: This diet includes various ingredients from each food groups such as milk, eggs, meat, fish, cereals, legumes, leafy vegetables etc.
3) **Kempner's rice diet**: Kempner's , in 1948, had given a strict rice-fruit-sugar diet (2000 Kcal) for individuals having high BP.
4) **High protein diet**: A diet with double the amount of RDA protein content with restrictions of other nutrients are developed for individuals having specific health complications such as Peptic ulcer, Protein-calorie malnutrition, cirrhosis of liver etc.
5) **Low protein diet**: A Low-protein or Protein Free diet may be developed for individuals suffering from Uraemia, Hepatic coma etc.
6) **High Fat diet**: == High fat menu is meant for individuals suffering from acute undernutrition.
7) **Low Fat diet**: This is meant for people suffering from liver disease etc.
8) **High fibre and Low Fibre diets**: High fibre diets are recommended to individuals suffering from constipation. Low fibre diets are for the people suffering from various gastrointestinal problems.

9) **Liquid diets**: These diets are based on milk mainly.

10) **High calcium diet**: these type of menu may be made for people having rickets etc.

11) **Gluten-free diet**: This is for people having problem in digesting gluten containing items.

12) **High calorie and low calorie diets**: High calorie diet is for people having malnutrition, Hyperthyroidism, Mal-absorption problem etc. Whereas, low-calorie diet is required by persons suffering from obesity, heart problems etc.

13) **High and low Carbohydrate diets**: High carbohydrate diet is required for those suffering from Addison's disease, liver disease etc. The low carbohydrate diet is meant for people suffering from Diabetes Mellitus.

14) **Modified Vitamin diet**: Synthetic vitamins maybe added to increase the vitamin content.

## CRITICAL EVALUATION OF FAST FOODS

Fast food consumption on regular basis can create an adverse effect on our body. Fast food may not be very bad, but it is loaded with high amounts of carbohydrates, added sugar, unhealthy fats, and salt (sodium). It has been noticed that regular consumption of fast foods can lead to various health complications because -

- It provides excess calories
- Develops resistance to insulin
- Raises blood pressure
- causes respiratory troubles such as shortness of breath
- causes Dental decay
- may cause mental depression
- Raises blood sugar
- Leads to obesity
- Raises cholesterol level
- Creates heart problem
- May lead to acne and head ache
- Nutrient deficiency related problems

Food is called the fuel of the body. If nutritious food is provided to the body it will help us to maintain a good health. On the other hand food lacking in nutritive value will lead to poor health.

### Effect of fast foods on digestive system

Fast food loads of calories through carbohydrates is provided to the digestive system Digestive system breaks carbohydrates down into sugar (glucose) sugar is released into bloodstream pancreas responds by releasing insulin( which is needed to transport sugar to cells throughout body) As the sugar is absorbed, blood sugar levels drop pancreas releases another hormone called glucagon Glucagon directs the liver to start making use of stored sugars.

Thus, when one takes in high amounts of carbohydrate, it increases blood sugar. That can change the normal insulin response. If the blood sugar level goes up frequently then it can lead to type 2 diabetes.

### Effect on Cardiovascular system

High cholesterol and high blood pressure are among the top risk factors for heart disease and stroke.

### Effect of Sugar and Fat in fast foods on the health

Added sugars are basically empty calories. It has no nutritional value. The fast foods and soft drinks are loaded with sugar double the RDA. All these empty calories add up to contribute weight gain or obesity and leads to heart trouble.

The Trans fat present in fast foods also has no nutritive values. This trans fat increases the LDL or bad cholesterol and reduces the HDL or good cholesterol. This again contributes to type 2 diabetes, obesity, high BP and heart problem.

### Effect of high Salt (or Sodium) content in fast foods

Fast foods are liked by people because of high sodium contents. This high sodium content increases water retention level making one feel bloated and puffy. High sodium content in foods can cause high BP or enlarged heart muscle, kidney stones, kidney disease, and stomach cancer.

### Effect of fast foods on Respiratory System

Being overweight increases the risk of respiratory problems. An overweight individual may have shortness of breath and development of sleep disorder, asthma (prevalent in children mainly) and running nose ( also prevalent mainly in children).

### Psychological effects

It has been found that the children who consume fast often, suffers from mental depression. It has been noted in a study published in Public Health Nutrition Journal that consumption of fast foods and commercial baked products are associated to mental depression the study in the journal concluded that an individual is 51% more likely to suffer from depression in comparison to the individual not exposed to fast foods the study also revealed that more a person consumed fast foods the more he is prone to develop depression..

### Effect fast food consumption on Skin

It has been found that those who consume fast foods thrice a week or more develop acne and Eczema.

### Effect of fast foods on bones

Consumption of too much salt or sodium may lead to Osteoporosis.

### Effect on teeth

Consumption of fast foods which are high on fats, carbohydrates and sugar may lead to tooth decay. The greasy fast food items, chocolates etc. help the micro-organisms in the mouth to produce acids, which is the cause for dental decay and bad breath.

### Effects of fast food consumption on Society

Most of the European countries are fighting the battle of bulge. The obesity among the children in these countries is increasing day by day. The fast food outlets are also multiplying all over the world. This is a very dangerous sign for any country. Double income couples are having less time and more disposable income. So, they go out to eat in fast food joints. The children grown up eating fast food items are not ready to eat nutritive home-made foods. The complication is doubled up with consumption of fast foods and less physical activities. India is fast becoming the diabetic capital of the world. Therefore obesity, diabetes, cardiovascular diseases are becoming very common in the population of all the countries. The medical costs are also increasing tremendously.

## NEW PRODUCTS BEING LAUNCHED IN THE MARKET (NUTRITIONAL EVALUATION)

Following are some of the new products launched in the market:

### Probiotics

The World Health Organization (WHO), 2001, defined Probiotics as "live micro-organisms which, when administered in adequate amounts, confer a health benefit on the host." The idea was first introduced by noble laureate Elie Metchnikoff in 1907.

So, probiotics are good and beneficial live bacteria. These are good for health, mainly beneficial for the digestive system. Therefore,-

- Probiotics can replace the lost beneficial bacteria. We may lose good bacteria after consuming antibiotics.
- Probiotics can maintain a balance of good and bad bacteria to keep us in optimal health.

There are many types of bacteria which bare beneficial or probiotics as is found in the curd and fermented food items. The most common probiotics are Bifidobacterium and Lactobacillus. The probiotics help in IBS or Irritable Bowel Syndrome, IBD or Inflammatory bowel disease, Infectious Diarrhea, Antibiotic-induced diarrhea.

The FDA regulates Probiotics as food item.

### Prebiotics

Prebiotics are non-digestible substances that help the growth of bacteria and fungi, which are beneficial to the host. Roberfroid , 2007, defined Prebiotics as "A prebiotic is a selectively fermented ingredient that allows specific changes, both in the composition and/or activity in the gastrointestinal microflora that confers benefits upon host well-being and health." In diet, prebiotics are non-digestible fibre compound that pass undigested through the upper part of the gastrointestinal tract and stimulates the growth of beneficial bacteria habituating in the large intestine.

Prebiotics are found in the following foods-Raw, dry garlic, Raw, dry onions, Raw Asparagus, Raw banana, Raw, wheat bran.

### Antioxidants

An antioxidant may be defined as a molecule that stops the oxidation of other molecules. An antioxidant such as Thiols or Ascorbic acid stops the chain reaction of oxidation which damages cells by producing free radicals.

Antioxidant dietary supplements such as Vitamin A, Vitamin E, Betacarotene etc. do not reduce the risk of CVD or improve health. Industrial antioxidants are used as food preservatives.

### Phyto-chemicals

Many new products contain phytochemical. Phytochemicals may be defined as chemical compounds produced by plants through metabolism and play a role in plant growth and defence against competitors. Pathogens or predators. It has not yet been proved that phytochemicals have any health effects. Non-digestible dietary fibers from plant foods, are considered as a phytochemical, are now considered as nutrient group having approved health claims for reducing the risk of Cancers and coronary heart disease.

## DIETARY SUPPLEMENTS

A dietary supplement is consumed to receive nutrients which are not received in adequate amounts by the body through diets. The dietary supplements include vitamins, minerals, fibres, amino acids etc. there are more than fifty thousands dietary supplements available for the consumers. In some countries are regarded as foods whereas in other countries they are considered as drugs or other products.

### Bodybuilding supplements

Bodybuilding supplements are dietary supplements used by bodybuilders and athletics. These are used to gain weight, reduce weight, replace meals, improve athletic performance etc.

### Nutraceutical

A nutraceutical is a pharmaceutical-grade and standardized nutrient. Nutraceuticals are products extracted from food sources that are purported to provide extra health benefits, in addition to the basic nutritional value found in foods. These products claim to prevent chronic diseases, improve health, delay ageing process, increase life expectancy or support the structure or the function of the body.

## FUNCTIONAL FOODS

Functional foods are ordinary foods, enriched or fortified through Nutrification and are designed to deliver an enriched food close to the natural form. This helps consumer to get a food similar in nutrient content before it was processed.

Haarlem oil

Haarlem oil or Medicamentum Gratia Probatum is a dietary supplement. The potion is a produced in Haarlem of Netherlands and is a mixture of sulphur, herbs and Terebinth oil.

## MEGAVITAMIN THERAPY

Megavitamin therapy is the use of large amount of vitamins, much more than RDA to prevent or treat diseases. It is mainly used in Alternative medicine.

### Nutritional Evaluation

The food labels must contain information about the nutrient content of the product.

The required information that a label should carry are -

- The name of the item: The container must carry the name of the product so that the customer is aware about the product he/she is purchasing.
- The actual weight of the product: The actual weight of the product must be mentioned. This weight is the net weight of the food item in which the weight of the packaging is not included.
- The list of ingredients used: A list of ingredients must be mentioned. The quantity of the ingredients used should be in the decreasing order. The ingredient that has been used maximum should be mentioned first and then the other ingredients in the decreasing manner.
- The name of the manufacturing company: The name of the manufacturing company with address and contact number should be mentioned on the packaging.
- The name of the packaging company or the distributor: The name of the packaging company or distributor should also be mentioned.
- Serving size : Serving size should be mentioned
- Number of portions: The number of portioned that can be served from each container must be mentioned.
- Calories, protein, fat, carbohydrate, sodium, vitamin, calcium, iron etc. per portion must also be mentioned.
- The storage instructions should be mentioned.
- The date of packaging/manufacturing should be mentioned
- "The Date of Expiry" or "Best Before" information should be mentioned.

Some of the terms used on the food labels are given below:

Enrichment: It means that the nutrients lost during processing has been replaced

Fortification: It means that the food contains some nutrients more than it's natural content.

Supplement: If the fortification crosses more than 50% of the Recommended Daily Allowance then

The item is termed as supplement.

Low Calorie: It means that the calorie content is less than 40% per portion.

Low Sodium: It means that the sodium content is 140 mg or less per portion.

PBL: Students may be asked to prepare a project report on the various new food items launched in the market.

**IMPORTANT QUESTIONS**

Q. No. 1. What is the need for introducing nutritionally balanced meals?

Q. No. 2. How will you evaluate fast foods?

Q. No. 3. Discuss about new nutritional food items being launched in the market.

Q. No. 4. What do you understand by health specific meals?

Chapter 25

# Glossary

**Biological Value**: The Biological Value of protein is a measure of how much nitrogen is retained by the to the amount absorbed in the diet

Carbohydrates: Carbohydrates may be defined as chemical compounds containing carbon (hence 'Carbo') as well as hydrogen and oxygen in the same proportion as found in water ( hence 'hydrate').They may also be referred to as hydrates of carbon.

**Cholesterol:** Cholesterol may be defined as liquid consisting of multiple chemical rings that is only made by animal cells. Cholesterol is the best known sterol. cholesterol is found in animal foods but not in plant foods. There is no cholesterol in white of eggs and all plant foods. High in cholesterol are egg yolks, liver, brains, kidney, fish roe, shrimp etc.

**Complete Protein:** Complete Proteins are those proteins which provide all the essential amino acids in the right amount and right proportion as needed by the body. The foods which provide complete proteins are called Complete Protein foods. The example of such foods are from the animal sources only and includes Milk, eggs, cheese, curd, meat, poultry and fish.

*COMPLEX* **CARBOHYDRATES** which include polysaccharides. 'Poly' means 'many'.

**Compound lipids**: Compound lipids are the lipids in which at least one of the fatty acids is replaced by another chemical group such as nitrogen, phosphate, carbohydrate or protein. The glycerol is replaced sometimes by another alcohol. Examples include phospholipids, lipoprotein, glycolipids etc.

**Conjugated Proteins:** Conjugated proteins are those proteins which are composed of simple proteins combined with another substance. Examples include Caseins or Phosphoproteins in milk, Lipoproteins in bloof, Metalloproteins ( contains copper) in blood plasma.

**Crude Fibres**: Crude fibre is a fibre that remains after a food has been treated with acids and base.

**Derived lipids**: Derived lipids are fatlike compounds that contain carbon in the shape of ring structures.

**Derived Proteins:** Derived proteins result from the partial breakdown of a native protein.

Examples include Proteoses, Peptones and Polypeptides are formed when digestive enzymes begin their action on the proteins.

**Dietary Fibre**: Dietary fibres consist of substances which cannot be digested in stomach and small intestine because humans do not have enzymes which will break the bond. Fibres are of two types: **Insoluble fibre and soluble fibre**

**EFA OR ESSENTIAL FATTY ACIDS**: Fatty acids that are essential for the body but cannot be synthesised in required quantity are known as Essential fatty acids.

**Fatty acids**: high in saturated fatty acids are whole milk, cream, ice cream, fatty meats, lamb, pork, ham, butter, coconut oil, palm oil, shortenings etc. Cakes, cookies, chocolates etc.

**Fibre** is a mixture of substances, mainly polysaccharides; fibres cannot be digested by the human stomach.

**Fibrous Protein:** Fibrous proteins are those proteins in which the amino acids appear to be layered, parallel and in linear shapes. Example includes Collagen, Myosin, Fibrin etc.

**Globular Protein**: Globular proteins are the proteins in which the amino acids appear to be coiled and tightly-packed balls. Examples include Haemoglobin, insulin and Albumin.

**Glycogen** is the storage form of carbohydrates in animals.

**HDL**: High Density Lipoprotein. High in protein. Commonly known as good cholesterol. Probably reduces the risk of heart diseases.

High **in essential fatty acids** are vegetable oils, fatty fish etc.

**High in omega 3 fatty acids** are fish (salmon, herring, carp etc).

**Incomplete Proteins**: Incomplete proteins are those proteins which do not provide right amount of one or more essential amino acids. Examples include foods from plant sources such as legumes, nuts, grains, vegetables and fruits.

**Invisible fats are** in whole milk, cheese, egg yolk, cake, candy, pie etc.

is for the body. The factor on which this depend is the proportion of amino acids present in the protein.

**LDL**: Low Density Lipoproteins. Synthesised by liver. Main carrier of Cholesterol. High-fat diet increases the level.

**Lipids**: Lipids may be defined as organic molecules, most of which are insoluble in water. This class of macronutrients are commonly called fats and oils.

**Major Minerals**: Major Minerals are the essential mineral nutrients found in the human body in amounts larger than 05gms (or greater than 0.01% of body weight).

**Minerals:** Minerals are inorganic elements needed by the body as structural components and regulators of chemical reactions and body processes.

**Minor Minerals**: These are essential mineral nutrients found in the human body in amounts less than 5g (or present in the body in amounts less than 0.01% of body weight)

**Mono saturated** fatty acids are high in olives, olive oil, cashew nuts, peanut oil etc.

**MUFA OR MONOUNSATURATED FATTY ACIDS**: MUFA are those with one double bond.

**Protein Quality:** Protein quality is a measure to determine how useful a protein in the diet

**Protein-sparing effect**: Body derives all its energy requirements from carbohydrates instead of using proteins from diet or body tissues. Therefore carbohydrates spare proteins.

**Protein:** Proteins are the large, diverse and complex group of molecules. Proteins are organic compounds. The term protein means 'to take the first place' or 'of first importance'.

**PUFA or polyunsaturated fatty acids**: PUFA are those with two or more double bonds.

**Saturated Fatty Acids**: Saturated fatty acids may be defined as a fat or fatty acid in which the carbon atoms are bonded to as many hydrogen as possible ( hence Saturated ) and contains no carbon-carbon bonds in its chemical structure. We can also say that when each carbon in the middle of the chain has two hydrogen bonds to it, the fatty acid may be termed as 'Saturated'.

**SIMPLE CARBOHYDRATES** which includes monosaccharide and disaccharides. 'Mono' means 'one' and 'di' means 'two'.

**Simple lipids**: Simple lipids are commonly known as fats and oils. Fats and oils differ in their composition and properties and a few similarities.

**Simple proteins**:-Simple proteins are those proteins which contain only amino acids. Examples include Zein in Corn, Albumin in blood etc.

the diet to perform specific functions that promote and regulate chemical reactions for growth, reproduction etc. of the body.

**Total fats**:_Total fats are clearly visible fats are butter,margarine, shortenings, oil.

**UFA or Unsaturated fatty acids:** Unsaturated fatty acids are those fatty acids that contain one or more carbon-carbon double bonds. Such fatty acids can take ip more hydrogen ( hence Unsaturated).

**Vitamin:** Vitamins are a group of organic, essential compound required in small amounts in

**VLDL**: Very Low Density Lipoproteins. It consists of mainly Triglycerides.

**Water Balance**: Water Balance may be defined as the equalisation between water intake and water output of the body.

**Water Intoxication**: Water Intoxication results in excess intake of water. It may lead to headache, nausea, vomiting, convulsion etc.

**Water:** Water has been defined 'as the liquid forming the seas, lakes, rivers and rain', by the Oxford Dictionary.

Chapter 26

# Question Bank

**NATIONAL COUNCIL FOR HOTEL MANAGEMENT AND CATERING TECHNOLOGY**

**NUTRITION**

**ACADEMIC YEAR - 2016-2017**

TIME ALLOWED—03 HOURS MAX. MARKS—100

Q.1. DISCUSS THE IMPORTANCE OF FOOD IN MAINTAINING THE GOOD HEALTH.

OR

CLASSIFY NUTRIENTS AND DISCUSS THEM BRIEFLY. (10)

Q.2. DEFINE ENERGY. DISCUSS THE VARIOUS FACTORS AFFECTING THE REQUREMENTS OF ENERGY. (10)

Q.3. WHAT ARE THE FUNCTIONS OF CARBOHYDRATES IN OUR BODY?

OR

ILLUSTRATE THE ROLE OF DIETARY FIBRE IN HUMAN DIET. (10)

Q.4. CLASSIFY VITAMINS AND EXPLAIN THE SIGNIFICANCE OF VITAMIN A AND D.

OR

DEFINE AND CLASSIFY PROTEINS. SUGGEST METHODS TO IMPROVE THEIR QUALITY. (10)

Q.5. ENLIST THE VARIOUS FUNCTIONS OF WATER IN MAINTAINING GOOD HEALTH.

OR

DEFINE INVISIBLE SOURCE OF WATER. HOW WATER BALANCE IS MAINTAINED IN OUR BODY? (10)

Q.6. 'BALANCED DIET IS IMPORTANT TO LIVE A HEALTHY LIFE". HOW FAR DO YOU AGREE WITH THIS STATEMENT? (10)

Q.7. WHAT ARE THE VARIOUS FACTORS INVOLVED IN MENU PLANNING IN RELATION TO NUTRITION? (10)

Q.8. DISCUSS THE FAST FOOD TREND IN THE FOOD SERVICE INDUSTRY, WITH REFERENCE TO NUTRITION AND HEALTH. (10)

Q.9. WHAT MEASURES SHOULD BE TAKEN IN THE MASS FOOD PRODUCTIONTO RETAIN MAXIMUM NUTRITIVE VALUE OF FOOD? (10)

Q.10. STATE TRUE OR FALSE:

A) ANOTHER NAME OF VITAMIN-A IS THIAMINE

B) ENERGY IS DEFINED AS THE CAPACITY FOR DOING WORK.

C) COFFEE IS AN INVISIBLE SOURCE OF WATER.

D) LACTOSE SUGAR IS FOUND IN MILK.

E) 1-GRAM OF PROTEIN GIVES 4-KCAL WHEN OXIDISED IN THE BODY.

F) PYRIDOXINE DEFICIENCY CAUSES PELLAGRA.

G) AMLA IS A GOOD SOURCE OF VITAMIN-C.

H) DEFICIENCY OF IODINE CAUSES GOITRE.

I) FATS ARE CLASSIFIED UNDER MICRONUTRIENTS.

J) VITAMIN-B IS SOLUBLE IN WATER.

# NATIONAL COUNCIL FOR HOTEL MANAGEMENT AND CATERING TECHNOLOGY

## NUTRITION

## ACADEMIC YEAR - 2015—2016

TIME ALLOWED—03 HOURS MAX. MARKS—100

Q.1. Nutritive meal is important for maintaining good health. Discuss the principles of meal planning. (10)

Q.2. a) Briefly explain the role of water in the body.

b) Define balance diet and list the importance of it.

OR

a) Draw flow chart showing classification of minerals.

b) Draw a flowchart showing classification of vitamins. (5+5=10)

Q.3. Suggest methods to improve quality of protein for a sports person. (10)

Q.4. Define the following terms (any five) (5x2=10)

a) Health

b) Energy

c) Malnutrition

d) Polysaccharides

e) Anaemia

f) Cholesterol

g) Beriberi

Q.5. Define carbohydrate and mention its function in our diet. (10)

Q.6. Mention the food sources of following nutrients (any five) (5x2=10)

a) Vitamin $B_1$

b) Iron

c) Vitamin A

d) Vitamin K

e) Iodine

f) Sodium

g) Vitamin C

Q.7. Nutritive value of food gets reduced by certain faulty practices. Suggest procedures to improve nutritive value of foods. (10)

Q.8. Explain BMR as part of energy metabolism and the factors affecting them. (10)

Q.9. Differentiate between the following (any five) (5x2=10)

a) Unsaturated fat and Saturated fat

b) Insoluble fibre and soluble fibre.

c) Visible fat and hidden fat

d) Night blindness and rickets

e) Water soluble vitamin and fat soluble vitamin

f) Body building foods and protective foods

g) Sprouting and fermentation.

Q.10. Match the following: (10x1=10)

| | |
|---|---|
| a) Nutrient | i) Linolenic Acid |
| b) Insoluble fibre | ii) 9Kcal/g. |
| c) Hormone | iii) Vitamin A |
| d) Building block of protein | iv) Carrots |
| e) Cholesterol | v) Protein |
| f) Essential fatty acid | vi) 4Kcal/g |
| g) Ascorbic acid | vii)Osteoporosis |
| h) Calcium | viii) Cellulose |
| i) Iodine | ix) Amla |
| j) Fat | x) Insulin |
| | xi) Amino acid |
| | xii) Animal foods |
| | xiii) Goitre |

## NATIONAL COUNCIL FOR HOTEL MANAGEMENT AND CATERING TECHNOLOGY

## NUTRITION

## ACADEMIC YEAR - 2014—2015

TIME ALLOWED—03 HOURS MAX. MARKS—100

Q.1. Define energy and discuss the factors affecting energy requirements.

OR

Classify lipids with suitable examples (10)

Q.2. Food is incomplete without nutrients. Discuss.

OR

Critically evaluate the growth of fast foods in India. (10)

Q.3. Classify menu planning according to three food group system and discuss any five factors Affecting meal planning.

OR

Signify the role of calcium and iron in the body. (10)

Q.4. Balance Diet is essential for wellbeing. Define and discuss the factors responsible for Making a balanced diet.

OR

What are the health hazards associated with energy balance? (10)

Q.5. a) Discuss the importance of food in maintaining good health.

b) Signify the role of dietary fibre in our diet. (5+5=10)

Q.6. Enlist the methods to improve the quality of protein in food. (10)

Q.7. Cooking affects the nutritive value of food. Suggest methods of nutrient conservation. (10)

Q.8. Give two food sources and three functions each of the following nutrients; -

a) Vitamin A

b)Vitamin $B_2$

c)Vitamin C

d) Vitamin D

e) Vitamin K (10)

Q.9. Water balance is important for maintaining good health. Discuss. (10)

Q.10. Match the following: - (10x1=10)

| | |
|---|---|
| a) Good cholesterol | i) Energy unit |
| b) W-3 | ii) Thiamine |
| c) Kcal | iii) Goitre |
| d) Lactose | iv) 22 |
| e) Vit D | v) HDL |
| f) Vit $B_1$ | vi) 1.5 g/kg. Body weight |
| g) Iodine | vii) Hypertension |
| h) Amino acid | viii) Disaccharide |
| i) Protein requirement | ix) EFA |
| j) Sodium | x) Rickets |
| | xi) Night blindness |

# NATIONAL COUNCIL FOR HOTEL MANAGEMENT AND CATERING TECHNOLOGY

## NUTRITION

## ACADEMIC YEAR - 2013—2014

TIME ALLOWED—03 HOURS MAX. MARKS—100

Q.1. How would you classify carbohydrate? Explain giving examples of each. What are effects of Deficiencies and excess of carbohydrates in diet?

OR

Define and classify proteins, Suggest methods to improve their quality. (10)

Q.2. Define the term cholesterol. Give the sources and functions of cholesterol. Why they need to be maintained?

OR

How water balance is maintained in the body? Give the functions of water. (10)

Q.3. Define the terms fats and fatty acids. Explain the types of fatty acids and give the functions of fats. (10)

OR

Define the following terms: (5x2=10)

a) Nutrition

b) Health

c) Malnutrition

d) Obesity

e) SDA

Q.4. What is BMR and explain the facts affecting it.

OR

What are the fibres? Give their significance in the diet along with dietary sources. (10)

Q.5. Classify vitamins and explain the functions and sources of Vitamin D and C. (10)

Q.6. What are nutrients? Classify them. (10)

Q.7. What is balanced diet? Classify foods into various groups. (10)

Q.8. Explain the concepts of RDA and the factors that influence it. (10)

Q.9. a) Name the conditions that lead to obesity,

b) Explain the factors affecting the meal plan. (5+5=10)

Q.10. Fill in the blanks: - (10x1=10)

a) Protein requirements of adults is —- gm./kg of body weight (1/3/7)

b) Loss of water and electrolyte leads to— (dehydration/Rehydration/Obesity)

c) — are the building blocks of proteins (Fatty acids/Amino acids/ Glucose)

d) Night blindness is caused by deficiency of — (Vit. B/E/A)

e) Niacin deficiency causes — (Beriberi/Scurvy/Pellagra)

f) Each gram of fat supplies — Kcal (4/6/9)

g) Simple lipids are — and — (Fats & oils/Amino acids & Proteins/ MUFA & PUFA0

h) — sugar is found in milk (Maltose/Fructose/Lactose)

i) Iodine deficiency leads to — (Rickets/Goitre/Anaemia)

j) — is called the reference protein (Meat/Milk/Egg).

## NATIONAL COUNCIL FOR HOTEL MANAGEMENT AND CATERING TECHNOLOGY

## NUTRITION

## ACADEMIC YEAR - 2012—2013

TIME ALLOWED—03 HOURS MAX. MARKS—100

Q1. Discuss in detail the need for food groups. Also classify foods into food groups based on the five food group method. How is it used in menu planning?

OR

How would you classify carbohydrates? Explain giving examples of each classification. What are effects of deficiency and excess of carbohydrates in diet? (10)

Q.2. Define the following terms: (5x2=10)

i) Health

ii) Calorie

iii) SDA

iv) Lipid

v) Nutrition

OR

Explain the concept of BMR. What factors are responsible for the energy requirements of an Individual? (10)

Q.3. Define and classify proteins. Suggest methods to improve quality of proteins.

OR

What are the uses of water in the body? Describe the effects of excess and deficiency of water in the body and methods to improve balance. (10)

Q.4. Discuss the psychological, physiological, and social functions of food in maintaining good health.

OR

Discuss the role of cholesterol in our body discussing the reasons to control its level. (10)

Q.5. Food, nutrition and health are interrelated. Discuss. (10)

Q.6. What are nutrients? Classify nutrients and briefly discuss the functions of each. (10)

Q.7. Explain the concept of balanced diet. Explain the importance and meaning of RDA in our diet and the factors which influence the RDA in the body. (10)

Q.8. Classify Vitamins and enumerate the functions of Vit A in the body along with its important sources. (10)

Q.9. Explain briefly:

a) Significance of fibre in the body.

b) Factors influencing meal planning. (5+5=10)

Q.10. Fill in the blanks:

a) Energy is measured in —- (Kcal/joules/c).

b) —— sugar is found in honey (lactose/fructose/maltose).

c) —— are the building blocks of proteins (fatty acids/cellulose/amino acids).

d) Being overweight is known scientifically as being —-(bulky/hyperactive/obese).

e) A diet complete in all the essential and nonessential nutrients is known as —- (rich diet/complete diet/balanced diet).

f) Vitamin is gained through — (water/air/sun).

g) RDA of protein is —- (6g/kg body weight/3g/kg body weight/ 1g/kg body weight)

h) Thiamine deficiency causes — (beri-beri/scurvy/pellagra).

i) Rickets is caused by deficiency of — (fluorine/calcium/magnesium).

j) Each gram of protein supplies —— Kcal (4/6/9). (10x1=10)

PART THREE

# Food Safety and Quality

Chapter 27

# Basic Introduction to Food Safety, Food Hazards and Risks, Contaminants and Food Hygiene

## INTRODUCTION TO FOOD SAFETY

Food safety may be defined as a branch of scientific knowledge teaches proper way of handling, transporting, storing, cooking and serving food with the goal of preventing food borne diseases. In order to achieve these lots of tasks must be followed to bring food safe from farm to fork. These activities may be divided into three basic areas such as from farm to industry, from industry to market and from market to consumers. To bring food safe from farm to industry, one should ensure that the food is free from soil, free from pesticides, harvested at the right time, free from foreign materials, transported in proper way etc.

To ensure safety from industry to market, following points must be kept in mind:

- Proper food labeling
- Good food hygiene practices (GHP) are followed
- Use of permitted food additives
- Absence of pesticide residues
- All food laws and regulations are followed under careful observations and inspections

To ensure safety of food from market to consumers, one need to keep the following points in mind: -

- Keeping the food in proper conditions as specified by the manufacturers
- No damage in packages
- Delivery in proper conditions

One of the major concern in almost all developing and under developed countries is the safe water.

The five key principles of food hygiene according to WHO or World Health Organisation are:

1) Prevention of contamination of foods by pathogens from human to human as well as from pests, pets and chemicals.
2) Cooking foods properly i.e. right temperature and right time.
3) Storing foods at right temperature.
4) Use of safe water and safe commodities.

The food safety issues include, Good Hygiene Practices, Good Manufacturing Practices, Food Additives, Genetically Modified Foods, Novel Foods, Prevention of Food Adulteration Act, Essential Commodities Act etc. ISO 22000 is a standard developed by the International Organization for standardization concerning food safety. Codex Alimentarius Committee has also laid down guidelines to food safety. The national and local authorities also ensure that the food business operators follow all th laws and regulations relating to food.

## HAZARD AND RISK ANALYSIS

HACCP may be defined as a statement of a preventive system of controls on the basis of identification and analysis of hazards and critical control points. This may be internal inspection of chemical or microbiological or physical hazards.

### Hazard Identification

Hazard Identification, therefore, may be defined as the identification of chemical, biological and physical agents which may be present in a food and cause detrimental effect on health.

Hazard identification is an important first step in a risk analysis. If this is not identified at the initial stage may cause a fatal effect latter on.

Chemical hazards may include insecticide, pesticides, food allergens, food additives, toxic plant materials etc.

The Biological Hazards may include Bacteria, Molds, Yeasts, Parasites, Mycotoxins, pests etc.

The Physical Hazards may include glass, wood, metal, packaging materials, stones etc.

### Risk

Risk in relation to food means the probability of an adverse effect on the health of consumers of such food and the severity of that effect, consequential to a food hazard.

### Risk Analysis

Risk Analysis, in relation to food means a process consisting of the following steps

- Risk Assessment: Risk Assessment may be defined as a scientific process which includes Hazard Identification, Hazard characterization, Exposure Assessment and Risk Characterization.
- Risk management: Risk Management may be defined as the process of evaluating policy alternatives considering all relevant factors, to protect public health and fair trade practices through prevention and control.
- Risk Communication: Risk Communication may be defined as exchange of information and opinions relating risks among all the stake holders. These stake holders include the risk managers, industry, consumers etc.

Risk Analysis should be based on scientific data. The risk analysis and assessment should be through, accurate, unbiased and transparent. WHO or World Health Organization has developed scientific risk assessments to define safe exposure levels which form the basis for the development of national and international food safety standards to protect the health of the consumers and ensure fair trade practices.

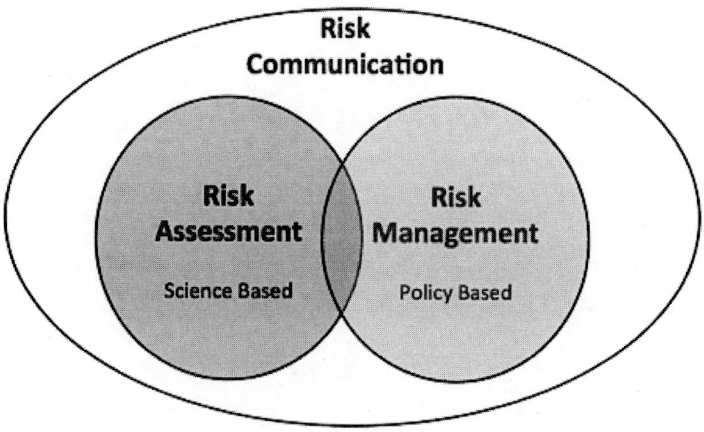


## CONTAMINANTS

Contaminant may be defined as any substance, whether or not added to food, but which is present in such food as a result of the production, manufacture, processing, preparation, treatment, packing, packaging, transport or holding of such food or as a result of environmental contamination and does not include extraneous matters. Extraneous matter refers to such matter which does not render the food unsafe for human consumption.

The sources of food contamination includes-

**Pesticide residues**: Pesticide may be defined as a substance which is used on the crops to destroy the organisms which may damage the crops. There are various types of pesticides such as insecticides, fungicides, herbicides and nematocide (a substance that kills nematode worms). Pesticide Residues may be defined as the pesticides that remain on or in the food after they are used on the food crops.

**Bacterial toxins**: Bacterial toxins may be defined as toxic substances that are produced by their activities and released to target other bacteria and host cells. Bacterial toxins are Endotoxins and Exotoxins.

**Mycotoxins:** The word mycotoxin has been derived from the Greek word, Mykes means Fungus and Toxikon means Poison. Mycotoxins are toxic secondary metabolite produce by fungus, which can lead to diseases and death in human if ingested through contaminated food.

Mycotoxicosis is a disease which is caused due to natural toxin produced by fungus

Seafood toxins: Sea food toxins cause seafood intoxication, which a food borne disease is caused by the ingestion of shellfish that contain toxins.

**Metallic contaminants**: Food may get contaminated by toxic metals such as lead, mercury, arsenic, cadmium, etc. through water, soil, temperature, etc.

**Residues from packaging materials** - Packaging may become a dangerous source of contamination such as recycled paperboards, plastic foil etc. It may be thin coating of food grade wax or multilayered system of paper-plastic-metallic component-adhesive. Packaging material becomes a source of contamination when it leaches undesirable compounds into the food.

The unprotected surface of food may get contaminated by pathogens from soil, air, water, animals, sewage etc.

## GENERAL PRINCIPLES OF FOOD HYGIENE

Food hygiene may be defined as all conditions and measures necessary to ensure the safety and suitability of food at all the stages of the food chain.

### Codex General Principles of Food Hygiene

#### *Primary production*

a) Managing primary production in a way that ensures that food is safe and suitable for its intended use.

b) Reduction of likelihood of introducing a hazard which may adversely affect the safety of food, or its suitability for consumption, at later stages of food chain.

#### *Establishment: design and facilities*

a) Premises, equipment and facilities should be located, designed and constructed according to the nature of operations and associated risks.

b) Control of hazards through good hygiene design and construction, appropriate location and provision of adequate facilities.

#### *Control of Operation*

**a)** Production of food which is safe and suitable for human consumption.

b) Reduction of risk of unsafe food by taking preventive measures to assure the safety and suitability of food at an appropriate stage in the operation by controlling food hazards.

*Establishment: maintenance and sanitation*

a) Establishment of effective systems

b) Facilitation of continuing effective control of food hazards, pests, and other agents likely to contaminate food.

*Establishment: Personal hygiene*

a) Reduction of food contamination by people with direct or indirect contact with food.

b) Food contamination and illness transmission by people who do not maintain an appropriate degree of personal cleanliness, who have certain illness or conditions or who behave inappropriately.

*Transportation*

a) Taking of necessary measures to prevent food contamination, damage and growth of pathogens.

b) Effective control measures during transport prevent food contamination and assure that the food reaches its destination in suitable condition for consumption.

*Production information and consumer awareness*

a) Products should bear appropriate information.

b) Consumers should have enough knowledge to make informed choices.

c) Avoidance of mishandling of product at later stages in the food chain.

*Training*

a) Those engaged in food operations should be trained in food hygiene.

b) Training is fundamental in any food hygiene system.

c) Inadequate trained personnel poses a potential threat to the safety of food and its suitability for consumption.

In 1963, Codex Alimentarius Commission was formed by FAO or Food Agriculture Organization and WHO or World Health Organization to formulate food standards and guidelines regarding codes of practice under FAO/WHO Joint Food Programme. The principle objective of this programme was to safeguard public health, ensure fair trade practices and to develop international food standards.

Chapter 28

# Microorganisms in Food

After reading this chapter, the student will be able to:

- *Know the general characteristics of Microorganisms based on their occurrence and structure.*
- *Understand the factors affecting their growth in food (intrinsic and extrinsic)*
- *Learn about common food borne microorganisms e.g. Bacteria, Virus, Fungi and Parasites.*

## INTRODUCTION

A microorganism or microbe is a microscopic organism, which may be single-celled or multi-cellular. The study of microorganism is called Microbiology. It was Antonie Van Leeuwenhoke, who discovered microorganism in 1670. Louis Pasteur found out, that it was microorganisms which are responsible for the spoilage of food. Mr. Robert Koch, latter, found out that microorganisms are responsible for causing diseases also. Microorganisms include Bacteria, virus, protozoa, Algae, Fungi etc. it does not include some other microscopic organisms such as Eelworm and Rotifiers.

## GENERAL CHARACTERISTICS OF MICROORGANISMS

Following are the general characteristics of microorganisms:

1) All microorganisms are minute and cannot be seen by the naked eyes. They can only be seen by electron microscope.
2) Microorganisms may be harmful or beneficial.
3) They are spread all over the biosphere. They are ubiquitous
4) The microorganisms and the humans have simultaneously gone through the process of evolution.
5) It is considered the oxygen in the atmosphere was produced by the microorganisms only.
6) Microorganisms belong to both Prokaryotic species and Eukaryotic species. The Prokaryotic species has no nucleous, no membrane-bound organells and

has cell wall. The Eukaryotic species on the contrary has nucleous and membrane-based organel but no cell-wall except Fungi.

7) Microorganisms belong to Monera, protista and fungi kingdom. A few algae and all viruses are also included under microbes.

8) All microorganisms need temperature, right pH, $O_2$, and micronutrients for their growth.

9) Microorganisms are highly adaptable and can survive in severe conditions such as hot springs, icy water, desserts etc.

The main factors affecting the growth of microorganisms in food

The factors affecting the growth of microorganisms in food may be divided under two categories e.g.

1) **Intrinsic factors**: Intrinsic factors are the ones which are essential.

2) **Extrinsic factors**: Extrinsic factors are the ones which exerts outward influences

The Intrinsic factors include:

a) Nutrient content: The growth of microorganisms depend largely on the supply of nutrients. Microorganisms need nutrients for reproduction.

b) Water activity: This is very essential for the microorganisms. The growth of microorganisms depends heavily on the availability of moisture. In general the microorganisms grow well with a water activity ($a_w$) 1.00.

c) The pH value: Microorganisms need right amount of pH value (Hydrogen-ion concentration) for their growth The microorganisms cannot adjust their own pH , therefore, each type has a maximum-minimum-optimal pH content for their growth.

d) Redox potential: The presence of high free oxygen will help the aerobic microorganisms whereas the absence of free oxygen will help the anaerobic microorganisms.

e) Presence of anti-microbial substances: The presence of antimicrobial substances will inhibit the growth of microorganisms. This substance may be part of the food or added intentionally.

**The Extrinsic factors include** all the conditions in which foods are kept:

a) Storage temperature: The chances of spoilage of food becomes more at the temperature between $-5^0$ C to $70^0$C. at different temperature different type of microorganisms grow well.

b) Gases present: The presence of germicidal vapours or $SO_2$ gas or ozone will reduce the growth and presence of microorganisms.

c) Relative humidity: Decreasing temperature and relative humidity produces a lesser hospitable environment for the growth of the microorganisms.

## COMMON FOOD-BORNE MICROORGANISMS

The common food borne microorganisms which are of interest to the catering industry are bacteria, virus, fungi and parasites. Knowledge about all these microorganism is of utmost importance for a person dealing with food.

### Bacteria

Following facts must be kept in mind about bacteria: -

- The study of bacteria is known as Bacteriology
- The term ''bacteria' is the plural form of Bacterium, which means a single organism.
- Bacteria are single-celled microorganism.
- This unicellular plant does not contain chlorophyll.
- It was Anton Van Leeuwenhock, an amateur scientist, who first observed bacteria and coined a term "animalcule", for them.
- Bacteria belong to the Prokaryotic cells. The prokaryotic cells do not contain nucleous.
- Presence of Bacteria is the most common cause of human illness due to food poisoning.

#### *Occurrence of bacteria*

Bacteria are present everywhere in the nature. Bacteria are transmitted by air, water, animals and humans from one place to another.

Reproduction of bacteria:

Bacteria reproduce by dividing from cell to two and then from two to four and so on. This process reproduction is called Binary Fission.

**Shape and size of bacteria**:

Bacteria are so minute that they can only be seen by a microscope. This unicellular plant has a size of $\frac{1}{25000}$ th an inch.

Bacteria are classified according to their shapes e.g.

**Cocci:** These are round-shaped bacteria.

**Bacilli**: These are in the shapes of rods and tubes. The Bacilli can change into **spores**. These spores protect them from unfavourable conditions such as heat and cold. They remain inactive and do not grow at this stage. When in **spores** they cannot be destroyed by heat and cold which otherwise will kill them. This spore formation helps Clostridium Botulinum withstand severe conditions. When the condition becomes congenial again they become active and starts reproducing.

**Spirilla:** These bacteria are spiral in shape. These bacteria are not harmful to humans.

*Some important terms:*

**Capsule:** The capsule is a jelly-like layer that protects the bacteria during unfavourable conditions such as heat and cold. This acts as a thick protective layer.

**Binary Fission**: Binary Fission is a type of reproduction by which a cell divides into two cells and then into four and so on.

**Flagella:** This is like a thread which is found on the outer surface of bacteria that helps bacteria in movement.

### Virus

Following facts should be kept in mind:

- The study of virus is called Virology.
- A single virus is called a Virion.
- Viruses are minute infectious living particles. Virus can only be seen under an Electron Microscope.
- It replicates only in a living cell of another organism.
- Antibiotic has no effect on virus as they do not have any metabolism of their own.
- Virus can infect any living beings including even bacteria.
- Viruses that attack bacteria are called Bacteriophages.
- Out of millions of virus species, we properly know only about 5000 ,
- Virus can be crystallised and stored.
- Plant viruses are with RNA as their genetic materials. Animal and Bacteriphages are with DNA as their genetic materials. Only exception is Human Immunodeficiency Virus (HIV), which has got RNA. (DNA: Deoxyribonucleic acid. RNA: Ribonucleic acid. RNA translates genetic information from DNA into proteins.)

*Occurrence of virus:*

Virus is present all over the eco-system on earth.

*Structure, Size and shape:*

Size of a virion is so small that it cannot be seen even under an optical microscope. One virion is approximately $\frac{1}{100}$th of a bacterium. The size of a virion ranges from 0.015 micron to 0.2 micron.

1 micron = $\frac{1}{1000}$ milimeter.

Viruses have a wide variety of shapes and sizes e.g. Helical, Icosahedral, Prolate, Envelope.

The virion have three parts:

- Either DNA/RNA
- A protein coat, called Capsid around DNA/RNA
- An envelope of lipids around the protein coat.

Viruses can spread by

- By insects from one plant to another.
- By blood sucking insects like mosquitoes in animals and humans.
- By coughing and sneezing through oral route.
- Through infected blood.
- By sexual contact.

### *Reproduction of virus*

Viruses need a cell of another organism for their own metabolism they therefore, reproduce in this host –cell. Accepted forms of life use cell division to reproduce, whereas viruses spontaneously assemble within cells.

## Fungi

- Study of fungi is called mycology
- Fungus is the plural form of fungi.
- It belongs to the eukaryotic group of organisms.
- Examples included: yeasts, mushrooms, moulds.
- Fungi have chitin in their cell walls, this characteristic puts fungi in a different kingdom

### *Metabolism*

- Fungi are heterotrophic.
- It does not photosynthesise.
- They get food by absorbing dissolved molecules.

### *Occurrence*

- Abundantly distributed world wide.

### *Structure*

- Thread like structure 2-10 μm in diameter to several centimeters in length

*Reproduction:*

- Reproduction is complex.

**Parasites**

- Parasitology is the study of parasites.
- Parasites live in or on the body of another living organism. It harms and eats up the nutrients of the host.
- Parasites include some bacteria, fungi, protozoa, worms etc.
- They enter the body through liquid, food, contact etc.

*Digestive system*

- They have no digestive system of their own. They absorb partially digested food through their skin from the host.

*Life cycle of a parasite*

- The life goes through two or more changes in their body structure.

*Vector*

- Dead or living agent that carries parasites.

*Ectoparasites*

- These parasites live on a host's body surface to feed.

*Endoparasites*

- These parasites remain inside a host's body

*Types of parasites*

- The main types include protozoa, helminths, or worms. There are 45000 species of protozoa.

*Prokaryotic cells*

- It does not have a well defined nucleus with nuclear membrane.
- The only cell organelle is ribosome.

*Eukaryotic cells*

- It has a well defined nucleus and membrane bound cell organelles.

*Kingdom*

- The five kingdom classification of whittaker included monera, protista, fungi, plantae, and animalia.

### *Monera*

- It includes all bacteria, cyanobacteria(blue green algae) and mycoplasma. Monera is characterised by a prokaryotic and unicellular condition.

### *Protista*

- Protista are eukaryotic and unicellular.

### *Plantae*

- Includes all the plants which are multi-cellular eukaryotic with cell walls.

### *Animalia*

- Includes eukaryotic, multi-cellular, and heterotrophic organisms.

## KEY TERMS

- Microorganism/microbe: A microorganism or microbe is a microscopic organism, which may be single-celled or multi-cellular. The study of microorganism is called Microbiology. It was Antonie Van Leeuwenhoke , who discovered microorganism in 1670. Louis Pasteur found out, that it was microorganisms which are responsible for the spoilage of food. Mr. Robert Koch, latter, found out that microorganisms are responsible for causing diseases also. Microorganisms include Bacteria, virus, protozoa, Algae, Fungi etc. it does not include some other microscopic organisms such as Eelworm and Rotifiers.
- **Cocci:** These are round-shaped bacteria.
- **Bacilli**: These are in the shapes of rods and tubes. The Bacilli can change into **spores**. These spores protect them from unfavourable conditions such as heat and cold. They remain inactive and do not grow at this stage. When in **spores** they cannot be destroyed by heat and cold which otherwise will kill them. This spore formation helps Clostridium Botulinum withstand severe conditions. When the condition becomes congenial again they become active and starts reproducing.
- **Spirilla:** These bacteria are spiral in shape. These bacteria are not harmful to humans.
- **Capsule:** The capsule is a jelly-like layer that protects the bacteria during unfavourable conditions such as heat and cold. This acts as a thick protective layer.
- **Binary Fission**: Binary Fission is a type of reproduction by which a cell divides into two cells and then into four and so on.
- **Flagella:** This is like a thread which is found on the outer surface of bacteria that helps bacteria in movement.
- **Virology**: The study of virus is called Virology.

- **Virion**: A single virus is called a Virion.
- **Bacteriophages**: Viruses that attack bacteria are called Bacteriophages
- **DNA**: Deoxyribonucleic acid.
- **RNA**: Ribonucleic acid. RNA translates genetic information from DNA into proteins.
- **Mycology**: Study of fungi is called mycology
- **Fungi**: Fungus is the plural form of fungi
- **Parasitology**: Parasitology is the study of parasites.

## PROJECT BASED LEARNING OR PBL:

Students may be asked to –

- Prepare a project report on the factors that affect the growth of microbes
- Prepare a project report on the common diseases caused by bacteria/virus/parasites/fungi

## IMPORTANT QUESTIONS:

Q.1. Explain the extrinsic and intrinsic factors that affect the growth of microorganisms in the foods.

Q.2. Write short notes on any three:

a) Bacteria

b) Virus

c) Fungi

d) Parasites.

Chapter 29

# Food Spoilage and Food Preservation

After reading this chapter, the student will be able to:

- *Know the types and causes of spoilage*
- *Learn the sources of contamination*
- *Understand about the spoilage of different products*
- *Know the basic principles of food preservation*
- *Learn methods of preservation*

Food spoilage may be defined as a process in which food deteriorates to the point in which it is no longer safe or becomes unfit for human consumption.

Every food item has a natural life period, after which it starts deteriorating or the quality is reduced. On keeping natural shelf life of food items, we can broadly divide them into following categories:-

1. Perishable or Highly Perishable Food items: All the foods that get spoiled fast are included in this category. Examples include fish, meat, poultry, milk, eggs, majority of the fruits and vegetables.
2. Semi-Perishable Food Items: This group includes all the food items which have comparatively longer shelf life if they are stored properly. This group includes potatoes, onion, apples, etc.
3. Non-Perishable Food items : These are the food items which has a much longer shelf life such as rice, atta, sugar, etc.

## TYPES AND CAUSES OF FOOD SPOILAGE

There are different types of food spoilage. If we analyze the causes of food spoilage we can find that their mainly

Three types of food spoilages, such as

1. Physical Spoilage

2. Chemical Spoilage
3. Microbial Spoilage

The Physical spoilage includes the damage of the outer surface and dryness of the food item.

The Chemical type of spoilage includes chemical toxicity, enzyme spoilage, rancidity, non-enzyme browning etc.

The microbial spoilage is due to the growth of microorganism in or on the food items.

## CAUSES OF FOOD SPOILAGE

Whenever a food items is unfit for human consumption, it is called 'spoiled'. This spoilage of food may be due to any one or combination of the following reasons:-

1. ***Food Spoilage due to Physical Damage***: This physical damage may take place due to wrong harvesting, bad packaging, faulty handling, presence of insects, etc.
2. ***Food Spoilage due to improper moisture content:*** Food item may get spoil due to absorbing atmospheric moisture as is evident in sogginess and subsequent growth of moulds on biscuits. Food may get spoil due to dryness by loosing water content to the atmosphere.
3. ***Food Spoilage due to presence of Chemical***: Food gets spoiled due to presence of disinfectant, insecticides, cleaning materials, etc.
4. ***Food Spoilage due to Enzymes***: Most of the microorganisms use the nutrients of the food to grow in number and produce enzymatic changes, making the food off-flavour.
5. ***Rancidity:*** - Rancidity is spoilage of fats and oils. Fats and oils may get spoiled if stored near strong smelling chemicals (Absorption Rancidity) or conversation of Triglycerol into glycerol and fatty acids (Hydrolytic rancidity) or Oxidation (Oxidative rancidity).

### Food Spoilage due to Maillard Reaction:

Unwanted Maillard reaction or Non-enzymatic Browning can spoil food items such as fruit juice, vegetables etc. This reaction is between reducing sugar and amino acid groups.

### Food spoilage due to Microbial Growth

Microbial spoilage takes place due to improper storage or poor sanitary conditions. Microorganisms produce enzymes to breakdown the food to sugar ( from carbohydrates), amino acids (from proteins) for their own consumption. This causes deterioration of the food.

Removal of the above-mentioned causes, good sanitary practice will ensure that the food being served to the guests are in good condition.

## SOURCES OF CONTAMINATION

The fruits and vegetables are prone to get contaminated from the time these are harvested. Likewise the meat, poultry, fish are also have a high chance of contamination at the time of slaughtering and thereafter till served to the guests. There are various ways the food items get contaminated. The major sources of their contaminations are listed below:

- **Humans**: Poor personal hygiene of the food handler is one of the common source of food contamination. Dirty clothes, hands, unhygienic habits etc, can cause contamination of food items.
- **Pets and Pests**: The commonly found domestic pets such as dogs and cats may become a source of contamination. Similarly, the pests such as flies, cockroaches, rodents etc. can be a potential source of food contamination.
- **Plants and Animals**: The flora of microorganisms on the surface of the plants may cause contamination. Similarly, the flora of microorganisms on the skins of animals, on their digestive tract and respiratory tract can be a potential cause of contaminations.
- **Water**: The water used for drinking, washing utensils, rinsing the fruits and vegetables or cooking may cause contamination.
- **Soil**: Soil is yet another source of spore-forming bacteria which is carried on the surface of plants and animals and a great cause of contamination.
- **Air**: A large number of disease-causing microorganisms may cause contamination to the food items.
- **Sewage**: when the dirty untreated water or night soil is used as manure in the field for growing crops, contamination is a huge possibility.
- **Processing of food**: Food goes through different stages while processing such as gathering, handling etc. Contamination can easily take place during these stages if proper care is not taken.
- **Equipments:** Food may get contaminated by the equipments used which has not been properly sanitized.
- **Packaging**: Improper packaging will contaminate the food packed in it.
- **Storage container**: If the food is not stored in clean containers, the food kept in it may get contaminated.
- **Serving utensils**: the server must ensure that the serving equipments used in the food and beverage serving outlets such as the service gears, chafing dishes etc. are properly cleaned. Otherwise it will become a source of contamination.

## SPOILAGE OF DIFFERENT PRODUCTS

As has been discussed earlier, different types of food groups have different shelf lives. Here, we will discuss about the spoilage of some of these foods and their products.

## Spoilage of milk and milk products

Milk is considered to almost pure when freshly taken out from the udder of a disease-free cow. But the chance of contamination becomes more as it comes in contact with the utensils used in the dairy. The milking machine, the storage container, the transporting pipe-line, the strainers etc. all contribute to the chance of contaminations. Milk provides a congenial atmosphere for the Lactic Streptococci, coliform bacteria. The growth of microorganism and chances of contamination in milk is huge due to the following factors:

- Large amount of moister content
- Presence of Lactose, the energy food
- Presence of citrate and
- Nitrogenous compounds etc.

When milk turns sour or curdles, it is considered to be spoilt.

***Cream:*** The sources of contamination in cream are water, utensils etc. The spoilage imparts ropiness or sliminess to the cream.

***Butter:*** The chances of spoilage in butter is reduced due to the reasons that

- The moisture content in butter is very low
- Butter is generally kept in the refrigerated condition

However, butter may get spoilt by Lactic acid bacteria if present in the cream from which it was produced.

***Dry milk:*** Dry milk is very low in moisture content , because of which the chances of its contamination is also very low.

***Ice-cream:*** Chances of spoilage is very low as it remains refrigerated all the time. However the contamination may take place from the ingredients used in the preparation.

***Custard:*** Again the chances of spoilage are very low but may get contaminated from the ingredients used for the preparation such as eggs.

## Spoilage of cereals and cereal products

***Grains:*** The chances of grains getting contaminated arise from the soil, pesticides, insecticides etc. The grains may get contaminated during the process of blending and packaging also. However the chances of spoilage are very low due to very low moisture content. However as soon as the cereal grains are moistened. It will attract the microbial growth.

***Flour:*** The moistening of flour will attract microbial growth and will become the reason for spoilage by molds.

***Breakfast Cereals:*** Again when these are moistened, there is a possibility of microbial growth.

***Macaroni and Pasta:*** Moist macaroni is a cause of concern for microbial growth. But the pasta generally does not get spoilt.

## Spoilage of meat and meat products

Usually, mutton, poultry and fish are used in large quantities in the catering industry. These items are found mostly fresh, but the processed, cured and dried form are also used.

The uncooked flesh of a healthy animal is expected to have minimal or no microorganisms in it. But, if stored for longer period of time, the autolytic enzymes will enhance spoilage of meat and meat products. In general, the causes of spoilage of meat and meat products are due to microorganisms such as Staphylococci, Streptococci, Salmonella which enters into the meat and meat products in various ways such as:-

- Intestinal tract of the animal
- Respiratory tract of the animal
- From the outer surface such as from skin of the animal
- Equipments used during the slaughtering or dressing or in the butchery
- Unhygienic handling of meat and meat product by anybody from slaughtering till consumed
- Contaminated air of the atmosphere
- Dirty protective clothes of the food handler
- Unsanitary storage containers.

The changes that occurs, when the meat and meat products get spoilt are-

- Unacceptable odour
- Undesirable colour
- Stickiness on the surface
- Undesirable taste
- Unpleasant spots, patches etc.

**Sausage** may develop microorganisms such as yeast or micrococci.

**Hams** may get sour by Lactobacillus, Clostridium etc.

## Spoilage of eggs

The eggs freshly laid by a healthy hen (hen is an adult female, chicken is a young female), will be free from microorganisms. But it may get contaminated and spoilt due to:

- Cracks or breakage of the shells as the microorganisms will get a chance to enter
- Excretory product of the bird
- Dirty dwelling unit of the bird
- Water in which the eggs are washed

- Improper handling of the eggs by the workers
- Unsanitary packaging of the eggs
- Improper storage

Spoilage of eggs is more often by bacteria. But a variety of molds and fungi can also play a role in the spoilage of the eggs.

### Spoilage of fruits and vegetables

The fruits and vegetables used in the catering industry are supplied in various forms such as—

- Fresh
- Frozen and
- Canned

The spoilage of fruits and vegetables are due to one or combination of the following causes:

- Contact with already spoilt fruits and vegetables
- Improper environmental conditions at the time of plucking
- During transport
- By the action of birds, animals, pests, insects
- Presence of germicidal or pesticides
- Mishandling by food handlers/workers
- Improper storing and storage containers

Therefore any one or combination of the above-mentioned causes may render fruits and vegetables unfit for consumption.

### Spoilage of canned products

Canned products are widely used in the catering industry to reduce cooking time, to dish out a standardized product, easier portion control and for convenience. It is now become indispensable at home also due to busy life style.

Canning may be defined as the process of food preservation by mainly heat treatment in an air-tight container to prevent spoilage. The containers used for this purpose may be tin-coated steel, glass jars. Aluminium containers, plastic containers/pouches etc. In recent times the term 'hermetically sealed container' is widely used. It is good to know that Nicolas Appert is called 'father of canning'.

## CAUSES OF SPOILAGE OF CANNED PRODUCTS

The causes of spoilage of canned products can be divided into two groups:

1) ***Biological Spoilage***: The factors for biological spoilage of canned products are due the microbial attack. This may take place mainly by the following two

ways— a) The biological spoilage may be because of the microorganisms which could withstand the heat treatment that the can was subjected to. b) The biological spoilage of canned products may be due to the leakage of the container through which the microorganisms got an entry into the food items after the heat treatment.

2) *Chemical Spoilage*: The Chemical Spoilage of the canned products is basically due to the production of Hydrogen gas in the container. The Hydrogen gas is produced inside the container by the reaction of iron (Fe) of the can and acid present or developed in the food. This process is known as Hydrogen Swell. Hydrogen Swell may occur due to the following reasons: a) If the food is highly acidic. b) If the Cans are stored in a hot atmosphere c) Defective Cans are used etc.

The spoilage of canned products will result in the food being:

- Off-colour,
- Bad odour,
- Haziness in the preserving liquor,
- Flat and sour,
- Growth of molds or yeasts etc.

## PRINCIPLES OF FOOD PRESERVATION

The aim of food preservation is to increase the shelf-life without decomposition. This can be achieved by following three basic principles of food preservation. The three basic principles and how they can be achieved are discussed below:

1) Preservation by delaying microbial deterioration: This is achieved by the following ways— a)By the removal of microorganisms. This can be achieved by filtration b) By keeping the microbes out or Asepsis c) By minimising or stopping the growth of microorganisms. This can be done by subjecting to low temperature or by adding chemicals d) By destroying the microorganisms. This is done by radiation or high heat.

2) Preservation by delaying self-decomposition: This can be achieved in the following ways-a) By controlling food enzymes b) By delaying the chemical reactions. Enzyme spoilage can be obstructed by low temperature or by changing the $O_2$ and $CO_2$ ratio.

3) Preservation by safe guarding the food from pests, pets, mechanical damage etc.

So, foods can be preserved or deterioration can be delayed by employing one or a combination of a few methods mentioned above.

## METHODS OF FOOD PRESERVATION

### Preservation of food at high temperature

The treatment of food with high temperature delays the decomposition because of the following two reasons—

a) High temperature causes the Denaturation of proteins

b) High temperature inactivates the enzymes required for the metabolisms of the microorganisms.

Preservation by using high temperature causes destruction of microorganisms partially. The degree of temperature and the time will vary according to

- The type of microorganism present in the food e.g. heat resistant microbes
- The state, the microbes are in e.g. growing or in spore
- The environment, the microorganisms are in e.g. pH value.

The heat treatment subjected to the food may be wet or dry heat. The TDT or Thermal Death Time may be defined as the time or duration required, at a particular temperature to destroy a concentration of microorganisms'

### Pasteurization

Pasteurisation may be defined as a heat treatment method by which the microorganisms present can be partly destroyed by heating at below 100°C. pasteurization process is best employed when the food contains lesser number of heat-resistant microbes and the food is also subjected to another preservative process e.g. Chilling.

The HTST method or High Temperature Short Time method. As the name suggests, food is subjected to high temperature for a shorter period of time. Where as, in LTH method or Low Temperature Holding method, food is subjected to low temperature for a longer period of time. The UHTS or Ultra High Temperature Sterilization method, foods are subjected at above $135^0$ C for only 02 seconds.

### Canning

Canning may defined as a method of preservation of food in an air-tight containers which is subjected to heat treatment to destroy the spoilage microbes.

### Baking

Baking is a heat treatment process used to hinder spoilage of food. The temperature , generally , do not exceed $100^0$C. The baking of breads, cakes etc. use this heat treatment method. Ropiness in bread is caused by the bacteria which do not get killed by the heat-treatment.

### Simmering

This is a cooking method in which food is cooked by gentle heat. The temperature is below $100^0$ C.

### Roasting

Another heat treatment method to prevent spoilage of food. The temperature used is about $60^0$ C to $80^0$ C.

### Frying

The outer part of the food gets hotter whereas the inner part of the food gets cooked at a temperature below $100^0$ C.

### Preservation of food by low temperature

Food items can be preserved by the use of low temperature because:

a) Lower the temperature, slower the chemical reactions.

b) Low temperature slows down the rate of enzyme reactions of microorganisms which in turn slows down their metabolic reactions.

c) Low temperature slows down the metabolic reactions of microorganisms which in turn slows down their growth and activities.

- ***Cold Storage:*** In the catering industry all perishable food items such as eggs, meats, vegetables, fruits are stored in cold storage before use in the kitchen. The temperature is above freezing point and thus the growth and activities of spoilage microbes are arrested.
- ***Frozen Storagel Freezing***: By this method the growth and activities of spoilage microorganisms are completely stopped and the fod enzyme reactions are hampered. However, it is recommended to blanch the vegetables, whenever possible, before freezing to get better results.
- ***Cook Chill:*** This is another method of preservation in which cooked food is subjected to rapid chilling and then stored at a temperature ranging between $0^0$C to $03^0$ C. in this method food is cooked first to kill the flora of vegetative bacteria present in the food. Food must be reheated at above $70^0$ C, served and consumed within an hour otherwise discarded.
- ***Cook Freeze***: As the name suggests, the food is cooked and then subjected to blast freezing at around –20$^0$C, and subsequently, stored at the same temperature. Food must be reheated at 75$^o$C, served, consumed or discarded.

## PRESERVATION OF FOOD BY DRYING

The method of drying for the preservation of food is probably one of the oldest methods of preservation. The reason why drying delays the spoilage of food is that the microorganisms do not get enough moisture which is crucial for their growth. Drying of food may be done by solar drying or by using mechanical dryers.

### Sun-drying/Solar Drying

Sun drying is a method of drying in which temperature cannot be controlled. Various fruits such as figs, apricots, grapes, pears, peaches and prunes are dried in the Sun. fish is another food item which is Sun-dried.

### Mechanical Drier

Drying by Mechanical dryer can be done in any of the following two ways:

a) Food is passed on conveyer belt through hot air. Relative Humidity or RH must be controlled during the process.

b) The controlled hot air is passed over the food to be dried. Relative humidity must be controlled in this case also.

After drying process of the food is over, the food should be packed in a sealed container, the earliest possible.

## PRESERVATION OF FOOD BY PRESERVATIVES

A preservative may be defined as a substance which is intentionally added to the food or beverage to prevent the microbial decomposition by microbial growth.

### Class I Preservative

No legal restrictions are imposed on the use of Class I Preservatives. The Class I Preservatives include the items such as sugar, salt, glucose, fructose, alcohol, spices, vinegar, honey, wood smoke ( wood smoke is used for giving flavour to the food as well as preservation). The addition of either sugar or salt dehydrates the food, thus the growth of microorganisms is prevented due to lack of moisture content.

### Class II Preservatives

The use of Class II Preservatives is restricted by law. The Class II Preservatives are chemicals added to some of the foods in a definite quantity to prevent the growth of microorganisms. Whenever these are used, it must be mentioned on the label. This preservative includes the salt of fumaric acid, sulphurous acid, propionic acid, acetic acid, benzoic acid etc. These preservatives are commonly used in Tomato sauce ( Benzoic acid and its salts), meat items (nitrates and nitrites of sodium and potassium). Sorbic acid and its salts are used for the preservation of various fruit juices, jams, sauces, margarine etc.

## PRESERVATION BY IRRADIATION

Irradiation is a process by which an item is exposed to radiation.

In the quest to find better methods of food preservation, scientists have come up with ultraviolet radiation, Ionizing radiation and Microwave heating. It has been observed that the "high-frequency with shorter-wavelength radiations" are effective in killing microorganisms in the food and also food temperature remains normal.

### Ultraviolet Irradiation

Ultraviolet irradiation for food preservation is used extensively in the catering industry. However, ultraviolet rays can only kill the flora of microorganisms found on the surface of the food items. Therefore, this method is used for the following activities only- a) to destroy microorganisms on the surface of the food b) To preserve meat c) To sterilize utensils and equipments used in food industries d) To treat water etc.

### Microwave Oven

The microwaves are electromagnetic waves which fall in between infrared and radio waves. Microwave ovens has become extremely popular now-a-days. The microwaves create highly rapid oscillation of the food molecules. This movement of the food molecules generate heat due to frictions amongst them. This heat, in turn, kills the microorganisms present in the food.

Ionizing Radiation: Foods are treated with irradiation to inhibit sprouting, sterilization, delay spoilages and destroy insects etc. though this process is sparingly used.

## KEY TERMS

- Food spoilage: Food spoilage may be defined as a process in which food deteriorates to the point in which it is no longer safe or becomes unfit for human consumption.
- Perishable or Highly Perishable Food items: All the foods that get spoiled fast are included in this category. Examples include fish, meat, poultry, milk, eggs, majority of the fruits and vegetables.
- Semi-Perishable Food Items: This group includes all the food items which have comparatively longer shelf life if they are stored properly. This group includes potatoes, onion, apples, etc.
- Non-Perishable Food items :- These are the food items which has a much longer shelf life such as rice, atta, sugar, etc.
- Physical spoilage: The Physical spoilage includes the damage of the outer surface and dryness of the food item.
- Chemical spoilage: The Chemical type of spoilage includes chemical toxicity, enzyme spoilage, rancidity, non-enzyme browning etc.
- Microbial spoilage: The microbial spoilage is due to the growth of microorganism in or on the food items.
- Pasteurization: Pasteurisation may be defined as a heat treatment method by which the microorganisms present can be partly destroyed by heating at below 100°C. pasteurization process is best employed when the food contains lesser number of heat-resistant microbes and the food is also subjected to another preservative process e.g. Chilling.
- The HTST method: HTST or High Temperature Short Time method. As the name suggests, food is subjected to high temperature for a shorter period of time.
- LTH: LTH method or Low Temperature Holding method, food is subjected to low temperature for a longer period of time.
- UHTS: The UHTS or Ultra High Temperature Sterilization method, foods are subjected at above $135^0$ C for only 02 seconds.

- Canning: Canning may defined as a method of preservation of food in an air-tight containers which is subjected to heat treatment to destroy the spoilage microbes.

- Baking: -Baking is a heat treatment process used to hinder spoilage of food. The temperature , generally , do not exceed 100°C. The baking of breads, cakes etc. use this heat treatment method. Ropiness in bread is caused by the bacteria which do not get killed by the heat-treatment.

- Simmering*:* This is a cooking method in which food is cooked by gentle heat. The temperature is below $100^0$ C.

- Roasting*:* Another heat treatment method to prevent spoilage of food. The temperature used is about $60^0$ C to $80^0$ C.

- Frying*:* The outer part of the food gets hotter whereas the inner part of the food gets cooked at a temperature below $100^0$ C.

- Cold Storage*:* In the catering industry all perishable food items such as eggs, meats, vegetables, fruits are stored in cold storage before use in the kitchen. The temperature is above freezing point and thus the growth and activities of spoilage microbes are arrested.

- Frozen Storage/ Freezing: By this method the growth and activities of spoilage microorganisms are completely stopped and the food enzyme reactions are hampered. However, it is recommended to blanch the vegetables, whenever possible, before freezing to get better results.

- Cook Chill*:* This is another method of preservation in which cooked food is subjected to rapid chilling and then stored at a temperature ranging between $0^0$ C to $03^0$ C. in this method food is cooked first to kill the flora of vegetative bacteria present in the food. Food must be reheated at above $70^0$ C, served and consumed within an hour otherwise discarded.

- Cook Freeze: As the name suggests, the food is cooked and then subjected to blast freezing at around –20°C, and subsequently, stored at the same temperature. Food must be reheated at 75°C, served, consumed or discarded.

- Class I Preservative: No legal restrictions are imposed on the use of Class I Preservatives. The Class I Preservatives include the items such as sugar, salt, glucose, fructose, alcohol, spices, vinegar, honey, wood smoke ( wood smoke is used for giving flavour to the food as well as preservation). The addition of either sugar or salt dehydrates the food, thus the growth of microorganisms is prevented due to lack of moisture content.

- Class II Preservatives: The use of Class II Preservatives is restricted by law. The Class II Preservatives are chemicals added to some of the foods in a definite quantity to prevent the growth of microorganisms. Whenever these are used, it must be mentioned on the label. This preservative includes the salt of fumaric acid, sulphurous acid, propionic acid, acetic acid, benzoic acid etc. These preservatives are commonly used in Tomato sauce ( Benzoic acid and its salts), meat items (nitrates and nitrites of sodium and potassium). Sorbic acid and its salts are used for the preservation of various fruit juices, jams, sauces, margarine etc.

- IRRADIATION: Irradiation is a process by which an item is exposed to radiation.

## PROJECT BASED LEARNING

Students may be asked to visit a dairy plant and prepare a report on it.

## IMPORTANT QUESTIONS—

Q. 1. Explain the types and causes of spoilages.

Q. 2. What are the various sources of contaminations?

Q. 3. Explain the basic principles of food preservations.

Q. 4. Briefly explain various methods of food preservation.

Q. 5. Explain how milk and milk products get spoilt.

Chapter 30

# Beneficial Roles of Microorganisms

After reading this chapter, the learner will be able to:

- *Understand Fermentation & role of Lactic acid bacteria*
- *Learn about the Fermentation in foods (Dairy foods, vegetables, Indian foods, Bakery products and alcoholic beverages)*
- *Learn about the role of microorganisms in Vinegar and Antibiotics.*

## INTRODUCTION

There are many microorganisms which play a beneficial role for the humans. The microorganisms are used by the humans for the following purposes:

a) To manufacture medicines such as antibiotics

b) To prepare various food items

c) To produce commercial acids, pigments and enzymes

d) To produce bio-fertilizers, bio-pesticides etc, in agriculture

e) Useful for degeneration of toxic wastes

f) Production of bio-fuels by algae

g) For treatment of waste materials etc.

In this chapter we will concentrate on the beneficial role of microorganisms in the food industry in particular.

## FERMENTATION AND ROLE OF LACTIC ACID BACTERIA

### Fermentation

Fermentation may be defined as a process in which a substance goes through chemical breakdown by the action of microorganisms (e.g. bacteria, fungi, yeast etc.), also produces heat and gases. Therefore, fermentation is a metabolic process in which yeasts and bacteria consumes sugar in the absence of oxygen and produces alcohol or organic acids and gases. So, this is an energy-releasing metabolic process that takes place under anaerobic conditions. But if the sugars are available, the presence or absence of oxygen has little effect. A chemical representation of fermentation is given below in which glucose is broken down by the action of yeasts to produce Ethyl alcohol or Ethanol—

$$C_6H_{12}O_6 \xrightarrow{\text{By the action of yeast}} 2C_2H_5OH + 2CO_2$$

The process of fermentations is helpful for the production breads, cheese, wine, beer etc. To start the process of fermentation sometimes the cultured yeasts are added as in the case of producing wine or beer. But in some cases naturally present flora of microbes bring about the desirable change. This is evident in the case of fermentation of rice and black gram while making Idli. The bacteria such as Streptococcus, Leuconostoc present on the grains start the fermentation.

## ROLE OF LACTIC ACID BACTERIA

The Lactic Acid bacteria or Lactics or Lactic acid-forming bacteria include Lactobacillus, streptococcus, Leuconostoc and Pediococcus. These bacteria are very much important in catering industry. The reasons which make the lactic acid bacteria so much important in the catering industry are-

a) The ability of lactic acid bacteria to convert sugar by fermentation to lactic acid
b) They form acid faster and in appreciable quantity
c) Lactobacillus grow only in foods which do not have vitamins in it, so are helpful in determining for the vitamin content of foods.

The above-mentioned characteristics of lactic acid bacteria helps us to produce various food items such as cheese, Sauerkraut etc. However, it may not a desirable characteristic in certain cases such as spoilage of wines.

***Homo-lactic Fermentations*** (producing only lactic acid) is the simplest type of fermentation. Some bacteria produce only lactic acid during fermentation, so is termed as Homo-lactic Fermentation.

$$C_6H_{12}O_6 \xrightarrow{\text{By the action of Homolactic bacteria e.g. Lactobacilli}} CH_3CHOHCOOH$$

**Hetero-lactic Fermentation** are the fermentations in which some lactate is metabolized further and results in Ethyl alcohol, carbon-di-oxide, Acetate or other metabolic products. Therefore, some bacteria produce a mixture of acid plus neutral products and are termed as Hetero-lactic Fermentation. Chemical representation would be:

$$C_6H_{12}O_6 \xrightarrow{\text{By the action of Hetero-lactic bacteria}} CH_3CHOHCOOH + C_2H_5OH + CO_2$$

In case of yogurts and cheese, lactose is fermented into glucose first.

$$C_{12}H_{22}O_{11} + H_2O \longrightarrow 2C_6H_{12}O_6$$

## FERMENTATION IN FOODS

### Fermentation in dairy foods

There are various dairy products which are prepared through fermentation in which Lactic Acid bacteria produce lactic acid. Most common dairy products which are prepared by using the process of fermentation are:

a) Cheese, of many varieties

b) Fermented milk e.g. buttermilk, yogurts, kefir etc.

**Cheese**: Producing cheese is a process by which milk is converted into a very nutritious product. It also helps in increasing the shelf life of milk. Lactic acid bacteria play a beneficial role in producing cheese.

Emmental cheese is produced with the help of Propionibacterium freudenreichi.

Cheddar cheese is produced with the help of Streptococcous thermophilus

Cottage cheese is produced with the help of S.Lactis Subsp. Lactis

Hard cheese is produced with the help of Lactobacillus

**Yogurts:** Yogurts is very popular and widely consumed fermented milk from Western Asia and Eastern Europe. Yogurt can be prepared from both skimmed milk or full-fat milk or a mixture of both. The microorganism used for fermentation are Lactobacillus Bulgaricus and Streptococcus thermophillus. They produce lactic acid in appreciable quantities. It is acetaldehyde which is also produced during fermentation and gives yogurts its distinct flavour.

**Butter:** Butter is produced from separated cream. Bacteria, in some cases, are added to the cream to make it sour. If added, it produces acid as well as Diacetyl. This diacetyl imparts a distinct flavour in butter. It is because of this flavour that a sour cream butter can be easily distinguished from a sweet cream butter.

### Fermentation in vegetables

Vegetables are fermented chiefly because of two reasons:

a) Fermentation in vegetables delays the spoilage

b) Fermentation in vegetables develops a distinct flavour in it

**Sauerkraut**: Sauerkraut is obtained by the process of fermentation of shredded cabbage. The salt content is restricted from 2 to 3% by weight. The microorganism used is Enterobactor.

**Pickles:** pickles can be prepared from vegetables such as cucumber by the process of full fermentation or semi-fermentation method. Microorganisms used are Pediococcus Cerevisiae.

**Spinach**: Spinach can be fermented as is done in the case of Sauerkraut from cabbage.

**Lettuce Kraut:** It is also prepared in the same way as Sauerkraut.

Fermented Green Tomato: Prepared in the similar style as Sauerkraut.

### ermentation in Indian foods

Fermentation plays an important role in Indian foods. Almost every state of India has food items prepared with the help of fermentation process. Some prominent ones are discussed below-

**Idli:** Idli is prepared by the fermented mixture of rice and black gram paste. The fermentation takes place without the addition of cultured microorganisms. The natural flora of microorganisms present on the grain brings about the desired change.

**Dahi or Curd**: Curd is prepared by the fermentation of milk. The microorganisms responsible are Streptococcus Lactis, Streptococcus Cremoris and Leuconostoc cremoris.

**Kinema**: Kinema is prepared by the fermentation of soyabeans. The microorganism responsible for the fermentation is E. faecium. This dish is from Sikkim and Darjeeling.

**Dhokla**: Dhokla is a Gujrati delicacy produced by the fermentation of Bengal gram dhal, rice and leafy vegetables. The microorganism responsible are L. fermentum, L. mesenteroids and E. faecalls.

**Rabdi or Rabadi**: A dish originated in Rajasthan, prepared by fermentation from barley flour, corn pearl millet and country buttermilk. The microorganism responsible are Bacillus and Micrococcus Sp.

**Kullu:** A dish from H.P. prepared from wheat flour and butter milk. Microorganism responsible are Lactobacillus Sp.

**Bakery products**

**Bread:** The role of microorganisms in bread making is -

a) Fermentation by microorganisms produce gas to leaven

b) Fermentation by microorganisms produce desirable flavouring substances

c) It helps in conditioning the dough.

5) Alcoholic Beverages

The alcoholic beverages produced by fermentation are discussed below-

**Beer:** Beer is an alcoholic beverage manufactured by a long process in which the sugar in Wort is converted by yeasts to alcohol and carbon dioxide. The strain of yeasts used is Saccharomyces Carlbergensis.

**Wines**: Wines are alcoholic beverages produced by the fermentation of freshly gathered grape's juice, at the place of their origin, according to the local tradition and custom. Nothing artificial is added to it. The fermentation starts by the addition of yeasts. Wines are also produced by fermenting juice of Rhubarb, berries, dandelions etc.

**Sake**: Sake is a Japanese yellow rice wine or beer.

**Ale**: Ale is a fermented beverage made from malted barley.

**Cider**: Fermented beverages made from apples.

**Ginger Beer**: Less alcoholic, made from fermentation ginger and sugar solution.

**Pulque**: American alcoholic beverage just like beer, produced by natural fermentation by yeast of Agave juice.

## Miscellaneous

**Vinegar**: Vinegars are of different types such as-

- Fruit vinegars e.g. apples, oranges, grapes etc.
- Vegetable vinegars e.g. sweet potatoes
- Cereals vinegars e.g. Barleys, rye, corn
- Sugar vinegars e.g. molasses, honey
- Alcohol vinegars e.g. denaturated etanol

Vinegar production involves two steps-

a) Sugar is fermented to produce Ethyl alcohol

b) Ethyl alcohol is oxidised to acetic acid

The first step is carried out by Saccharomyces cerevisiae var.ellipsoideus by anaerobic process.

$C_6H_{12}O_6 2C_2H_5OH + 2CO_2$

Oxidation of alcohol is aerobic reaction by the acetic acid bacteria-

$C_2H_5OH + O_2$——$CH_3COOH + H_2O$

ALCOHOL + OXYGEN—-ACETIC ACID + WATER

Bacteria which oxidises the alcohol are Acetobactor aceti and Gluconobacter.

**Anti-biotic**: - The word antibiotic has been derived from the Greek word Antiviotika. It is also called antibacterials. It either kills or inhibits the growth of bacteria. The term antibiotic means 'opposing life'. In 1928, Sir Alexander Fleming identified Penicillium , a molecule produced by certain molds that kills or stops the growth of certain kinds of bacteria. Penicillin is produced by fungi in the genus Penicillium. The production of the active compounds is carried out using fermentation. Producing antibiotics can be done by three methods e.g. natural fermentation, semi-synthetic and synthetic. Industrial microbiology can be used to produce antibiotics via the process of fermentation, where the source microorganism is grown in large containers. Some antibiotics are produced naturally by fungi e.g. Acremonium chrysogenum. Other microorganisms used are Streptomyces Hygroscopicus, Streptomyces griseus, Streptomyces Aureofaciens, Streptomyces Orientalis etc.

## KEY TERMS

- Fermentation: Fermentation may be defined as a process in which a substance goes through chemical breakdown by the action of microorganisms (e.g. bacteria, fungi, yeast etc.), also produces heat and gases. Therefore, fermentation is a metabolic process in which yeasts and bacteria consumes sugar in the absence of oxygen and produces alcohol or organic acids and gases. So, this is an energy-releasing metabolic process that takes place under anaerobic conditions. But if the sugars are available, the presence or absence of oxygen has little effect. A chemical representation of fermentation is given below in which glucose is broken down by the action of yeasts to produce Ethyl alcohol or Ethanol—

$C_6H_{12}O_6 2C_2H_5OH + 2CO_2$

Homo-lactic Fermentation: ***Homo-lactic Fermentations*** (producing only lactic acid) is the simplest type of fermentation. Some bacteria produce only lactic acid during fermentation, so is termed as Homo-lactic Fermentation.

$C_6H_{12}O_6 CH_3CHOHCOOH$

Hetero-lactic-Fermentation: **Hetero-lactic Fermentation** are the fermentations in which some lactate is metabolized further and results in Ethyl alcohol, carbon-di-oxide, Acetate or other metabolic products. Therefore, some bacteria produce a mixture of acid plus neutral products and are termed as Hetero-lactic Fermentation. Chemical representation would be—

$C_6H_{12}O_6 CH_3CHOHCOOH + C_2H_5OH + CO_2$

In case of yogurts and cheese, lactose is fermented into glucose first.

$C_{12}H_{22}O_{11} + H_2O$——$2C_6H_{12}O_6$

- **Beer:** Beer is an alcoholic beverage manufactured by a long process in which the sugar in Wort is converted by yeasts to alcohol and carbon dioxide. The strain of yeasts used is Saccharomyces Carlbergensis.
- **Wines**: Wines are alcoholic beverages produced by the fermentation of freshly gathered grape's juice, at the place of their origin, according to the local tradition and custom. Nothing artificial is added to it. The fermentation starts by the addition of yeasts. Wines are also produced by fermenting juice of Rhubarb, berries, dandelions etc.
- **Sake**: Sake is a Japanese yellow rice wine or beer.
- **Ale**: Ale is a fermented beverage made from malted barley.
- **Cider**: Fermented beverages made from apples.
- **Ginger Beer**: Less alcoholic, made from fermentation ginger and sugar solution.
- **Pulque**: American alcoholic beverage just like beer, produced by natural fermentation by yeast of Agave juice.
- **Anti-biotic**: - The word antibiotic has been derived from the Greek word Antiviotika. It is also called antibacterials. It either kills or inhibits the growth of bacteria. The term antibiotic means 'opposing life'. In 1928, Sir Alexander Fleming identified Penicillium , a molecule produced by certain molds that kills or stops the growth of certain kinds of bacteria. Penicillin is produced by fungi in the genus Penicillium. The production of the active compounds is carried out using fermentation. Producing antibiotics can be done by three methods e.g. natural fermentation, semi-synthetic and synthetic. Industrial microbiology can be used to produce antibiotics via the process of fermentation, where the source microorganism is grown in large containers.

## PROJECT BASED LEARNING:

Students may be asked to prepare a project report on how breads are prepared in a bakery through fermentation.

They may be asked to prepare curd and make a report on it.

## IMPORTANT QUESTIONS

Q. 1. What is fermentation? Explain the role of Lactic Acid Bacteria

Q. 2. Explain the fermentation in Indian foods and dairy foods.

Q. 3. Write short notes on Vinegar and Anti-biotic.

Chapter 31

# Food Borne Diseases

After reading this chapter, the learner will be able to:

- *Learn types of food borne diseases*
- *Understand common diseases caused by food borne pathogens*
- *Learn preventive measures for food borne diseases*

## INTRODUCTION

Food borne diseases include wide varieties of illness caused by the ingestion of food items contaminated with microorganisms or chemicals. This contamination of food may take place at any stage from 'firm to fork'. Food borne diseases are also commonly called Food Borne Illness or Food Poisoning. The contamination of food may take place due to any one or combination of the following reasons:

- Pollution of water
- Pollution of soil
- Pollution of air
- Improper handling of food
- Due to improper cooking
- Improper storage of food etc.
- From insects, pests, pets or rodents
- From chemicals e.g. pesticides, insecticides etc.
- Natural toxic substances such as poisonous mushrooms or reef fish
- Food spoilages due to pathogenic bacteria, virus or parasites.

Food borne diseases commonly cause stomach pain, stomach upset, vomiting, dehydration etc.

## TYPES OF FOOD BORNE DISEASES

The food borne diseases are commonly divided into Chemical, Intoxications and Infectious.

### Intoxications

Intoxications are the food borne diseases caused by the presence of toxins in the food items. The toxicants may come from some plants or animals or from a toxic metabolic product excreted by a microorganism. Therefore, a bacterial intoxication will mean a food borne disease caused by bacterial toxin which has contaminated the food. The bacteria which cause food borne diseases are Clostridium botulinum, Staphylococcus aureus, Clostridium perfringens and Bacillus cereus. There is a possibility of intoxication from chemicals e.g. pesticides, cleaning agents, sanitizers and metals. Plants and mushroom can also cause intoxications. Some fish and shell fish toxins too can cause intoxications. Therefore, intoxication takes place only when a person eats the food which contains the toxins.

### Infections

Infections will refer to food borne diseases caused by the entrance of microorganisms into the body through the ingestion of contaminated food items. Therefore, infection occurs when live bacterial cells are ingested via food. These bacterial cells can grow in the digestive tract and cause symptoms e.g. Salmonella infection. Infections are caused by certain bacteria, all types of virus as well as all parasites. The bacteria responsible for food borne diseases are Salmonella spp., Listeria monocytogenes, Campylobacter jejuni etc. the most common virus are Hepatitis A, norovirus and rotavirus. Most common parasites are Trichinella spiralis, Anisakis simplex, Cyclospora cayetanesis.

A classification of food borne diseases is given below:

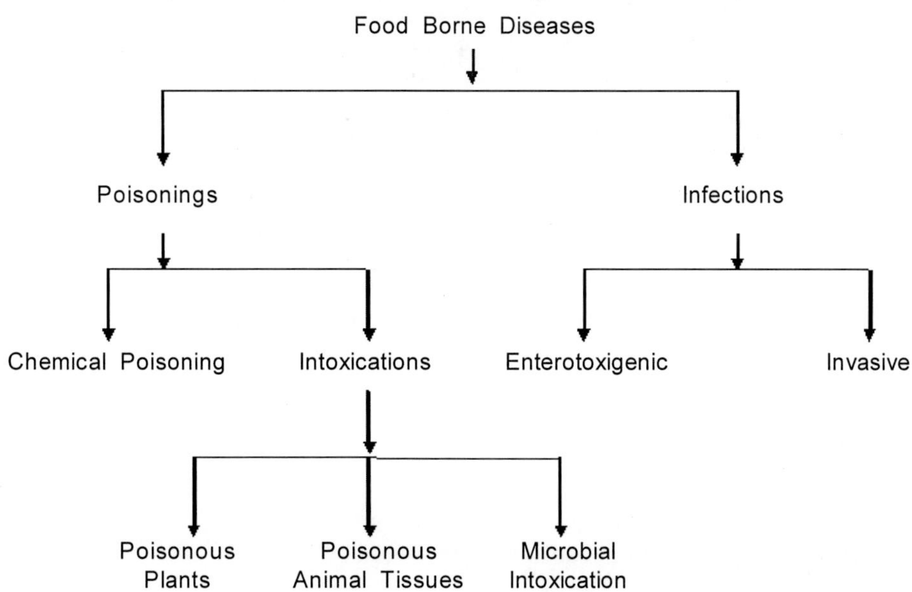


**A Classification Of Food Borne Diseases.**

Differences between food poisoning and infection are-

There are various differences between food poisoning or food intoxication and food infections. The differences between the two are given below.

| Sl. No. | Food infection | Sl. No. | Food poisoning or food intoxication |
|---|---|---|---|
| 01 | This is a disease that is caused due to consumption of food which contains living bacteria. | 01. | This is caused due to ingestion of contaminated food which contains toxins. |
| 02 | This is caused by parasitic micro-organisms in which food acts just as a vehicle. | 02. | This is caused by the ingestion of food which is<br>a) Naturally poisonous<br>b) Having toxic chemicals<br>c) Contaminated by microorganisms. |
| 03 | Incubation period is from 12 hours to a day/ to several weeks. | 03. | Incubation period is very fast e.g. within two hours from the ingestion of food. |
| 04 | It turns very severe | 04. | Generally not so severe |
| 05 | It can spread to all over the body starting from the gut. | 05. | Usually confined to the gut only. |
| 06. | It is associated with fever and abdominal pain along with other symptoms. | 06. | Usually no fever and abdominal pain but other symptoms are same. |
| 07. | Cannot be prevented by the refrigeration of food. | 07. | Can be prevented by storing the food at low temperature which inhibits the growth of food poisoning bacteria. |

## COMMON DISEASES CAUSED BY FOOD BORNE PATHOGENS

Following are the common diseases caused by food borne pathogens--

### Botulism

This is caused by **Clostridium botulinum**. This disease is caused if food contaminated with neurotoxin produced by C. Botulinum is ingested. Even a very tiny amount of toxin can cause death. The symptom starts showing within 12 to 36 hours after the consumption of food. The symptoms include fatigue, diarrhoea, dizziness, double vision, nausea, headache etc.

*Prevention:*

- The heat process used for canned items should be the approved one.
- the puffed up cans should not be used.
- The rusty, leaky or damaged cans should not be used.

- As a tiny amount can cause severe infection, so doubtful food items should not be tasted at all.
- Stored food must be reheated properly (at 100$^0$C for15 minutes).

### Staphylococcus Food Intoxication

This is a very common type of food borne illness. It is caused by bacteria called **Staphylococcus aureus.** The bacteria contaminate the food with enterotxin, a simple protein. When food contaminated with heat-resistant enterotoxin, is consumed, food poisoning occurs. The incubation period is 2 to 4 hours. The symptoms include nausea, vomiting, diarrhoea, salvation, abdominal cramps etc. the duration ranges from 24hrs. to 48hrs. it is found in throats, nose, nasal discharge, skin etc.

*Prevention:*

* Not to ingest contaminated food.
* Stop the growth of bacteria in the food.
* Destroying the bacteria by heat treatment e.g. pasteurization.
* Maintain proper hygiene.

### Salmonelosis

This is the commonest bacterial food borne infection. This is caused by the consumption of viable cells of a member **Salmonella**. This is a non-spore-forming bacteria. The incubation period is 5 to 72 hours. The symptoms include diarrhoea, fever, abdominal pain, dehydration, vomiting etc. The sources of these bacteria are the faces of infected animals and humans. Salmonella infection may occur from foods such as sausages, meat, poultry etc.

*Preventions:*

* Stay away from Salmonella infected food e.g. contaminated eggs.
* Proper heat treatment e.g. cooking, pasteurization etc. will destroy Salmonella.
* Low temperature such as refrigeration of food items will retard the growth of Salmonella bacteria.
* Hygienic food handling is a must.
* Proper food preparation technique will ensure the elimination of the bacteria.
* Pets, pests and insects must be kept away from the food preparation areas.
* Left-over foods should be properly reheated, served, consumed otherwise discarded.

### Typhoid

Typhoid is caused by **Salmonella typhi**. Incubation period is about two weeks. The disease lasts for two months. The symptoms include high fever, headache, cough, vomiting, bleeding from the bowel etc.

*Prevention:*

* The patint must be kept away from the food preparation and service areas.
* Treated water should be used.
* Pasteurized milk should be used.
* Pests and insects must be eliminated.
* Vaccination gives protection.

**Paratyphoid**

This is caused by bacteria called Vibrio Cholerae. The incubation period is from a day to one week. The symptoms include diarrhoea, cramps in the legs, vomiting, dehydration, abdominal pain etc. the sources include fish and shellfish from polluted water, drinks prepared from untreated water, contaminated food items.

*Prevention: -*

* Maintain hygiene.
* Control pests and insects. *Use properly treated water.
* Stay away from contaminated food items.
* Eat foods which have been cooked properly.

**Cholera**

This disease is caused by bacteria called **Vibrio Cholerea**. The incubation period is from a day to one week. The symptoms include diarrhoea, cramps in legs, vomiting, dehydration, abdominal pain etc. The sources include fish and shellfish from polluted water, beverages prepared from untreated water, contaminated food items.

*Prevention:*

* Maintain hygiene,
* Control pests and insects.
* Use only properly treated water.
* Stay away from contaminated food items.
* Eat foods which have been cooked properly.

**Enteropathogenic Escherichia Coli**

The organism, which causes the diarrhoeal disease Traveller's Diarrhoea, is known as enteropathogenic E. Coli, and are normally present in our intestinal tract. But, some strains present in heavy dose may cause illness. The incubation period is about 12 hours to a few days. The source is raw contaminated foods, cross contamination, improper storage of foods, unhygienic food handling etc. Raw meat, poultry, vegetables etc, may get contaminated by excreta. Symptoms are same as of Cholera.

*Prevention*

* Food should be cooked well.
* Maintain hygiene
* Raw vegetables, meat, poultry should be washed thoroughly.
* Use only treated water.
* Dispose sewage properly.

## Infectious Hepatitis

This is caused by Infectious Hepatitis Virus. The incubation period of Hepatitis A virus is about 25 days. The foods commonly involved are milk, shellfish, various beverages, untreated water, infected food items etc. Symptoms include Jaundice, lack of appetite, dehydration, vomiting etc.

*Prevention*

* Maintain proper hygiene.
* Use treated water.
* Eliminate house flies.
* Shellfish must be properly cooked.
* Use pasteurized milk.

## Trichinosis

This is caused by a worm called **Trichinella Spiralis**. The possible cause of infection is the consumption of pork which has not been subjected to proper heat treatment (> 59$^0$C). The incubation period is 24 hours to a few weeks. Symptoms include nausea, vomiting, diarrhoea, lack of appetite, colic etc.

*Prevention:*

* pork must be cooked properly.
* The pork product must be subjected to proper and approved processing.
* Storage should be at –18$^0$C or lower.

## Perfringens Food Poisoning

This is caused by spore-forming ***Clostridium perfringens***. This is found in our intestinal tract, soil, dried food items, contaminated meat/poultry etc. The illness is caused when there is a heavy dose of these microorganisms are present. The disease is caused due to wrong food handling, unhygienic conditions prevailing in the kitchen, service or stores etc. The vehicle could be the sauces, gravies, cooked meat and poultry etc. The usual symptoms include nausea, abdominal pain etc.

*Prevention:*

* Food especially the meat and meat products must be cooked properly.
* Food should be stored low temperature as early as possible. *Avoid cross-contamination.
* Maintain personal hygiene.
* Use treated water.
* All raw vegetables, meats and fruits must be cleaned before using.

## PREVENTIVE MEASURES FOR FOOD BORNE DISEASES

Food may get contaminated by pathogens or chemicals at any stage from 'firm to fork'. Therefore, following preventive measure must be taken in order to stop the vector (a carrier of contamination):

1. The supplier should be chosen carefully. Foods should be purchased from a vendor who supplies meat, poultry, vegetables, fruits etc. in a clean refrigerated delivery van. The manager must ensure that the supplier follows food safety guidelines.
2. All items should be stored at the right temperature after the delivery till these are issued to various outlets. The storage area should be free from rodents, insects and must be kept clean at all times. Proper care should be taken for ventilation, moisture, lighting etc.
3. Proper hygiene and sanitation guidelines must be followed in the food preparation areas. The chefs must ensure that they clean their hands frequently in $KMNO_4$ solutions.
4. Chefs must ensure that the dishes are cooked properly. A through and proper cooking will destroy all the pathogenic microorganisms.
5. All service equipments must be cleaned properly. The chafing dishes, service bowls, service gears, cruet sets, menu etc. must be free from dust, chemicals etc. used for cleaning.
6. All food handlers must ensure high standard personal hygiene. The in-charge of the respective areas should practice daily frequent checking of the hygiene and sanitation in their departments.
7. There should be proper ventilation, lighting etc. in the store, kitchen and service areas. Care should be taken for proper garbage disposals.
8. Measures must be taken to eliminate rodents and insects from storage, kitchen and service areas.
9. All left-over foods should be under refrigeration. It should be properly thawed, reheated, served for consumption or discarded.
10. All foods suspected to be contaminated must be discarded.
11. Ensure the use of treated water.

12. Adequate facilities such as toilets, hand wash etc. should be provided to the staff

All the above-mentioned points must be kept in mind to ensure elimination/ prevention of food borne diseases. The manager must train the staff to ensure high standard of hygiene is practised at every phases of the food handling.

## KEY TERMS

- **Intoxications** are the food borne diseases caused by the presence of toxins in the food items. The toxicants may come from some plants or animals or from a toxic metabolic product excreted by a microorganism.
- ***Infections*** will refer to food borne diseases caused by the entrance of microorganisms into the body through the ingestion of contaminated food items. Therefore, infection occurs when live bacterial cells are ingested via food.
- **Vector:** A carrier of contamination.
- **Incubation period:** The time between the ingestion of foods and appearance of the first symptom of disease is called the Incubation Period.

## PROJECT BASED LEARNING

Students may be asked to prepare a detailed report on common food born diseases and the preventive measures for it.

## IMPORTANT QUESTIONS

Q. 1. Classify food borne diseases. What do you understand by Infections and Intoxications?

Q.2. Explain any three common diseases caused by food borne pathogens.

Q.3. What preventive measures can be taken for food borne diseases?

Chapter 32

# Food Additives

After reading this chapter, the student should be able to:

- Explain food additives
- Learn about different types of food additives
- *Explain various types of food additives.*

## INTRODUCTION

The World health organization (WHO), in 1965, had defined food additives as "A food additive is a substance or mixture of substances, other than the basic food staff, which is present in food area result of any aspect of production, processing, storage or packaging. The term does not include chance contamination"

It is clear from the above definition that food additives are substances which are added to the food intentionally. Therefore, it is expected that the food producers must use additives which are safe for human consumption. Food additives are added to the food by the food manufacturers for the following reasons:-

1. **Flavour**-Food Additive is added to make the food flavourful. It gives the consumers a wide choice to select the flavour of their choice in the same food items.
2. **Colour**-Food additives make the food look more colourful and attractive
3. **Texture**-Food additives ensure a smooth attractive texture of the food
4. **Safety**-Food additives help to retard the growth of microorganisms in the food making it safe for consumption
5. **Preservation**-Addition of Food additives increases the shelf life of the food
6. **Nutrition**-Addition of food additives helps to get the nutrients lost during processing.

It helps in reducing the loss of nutrients during processing and storage.

Most of the food that we eat now-a-days is processed to some extent. Therefore addition of food additives becomes more of a necessity.

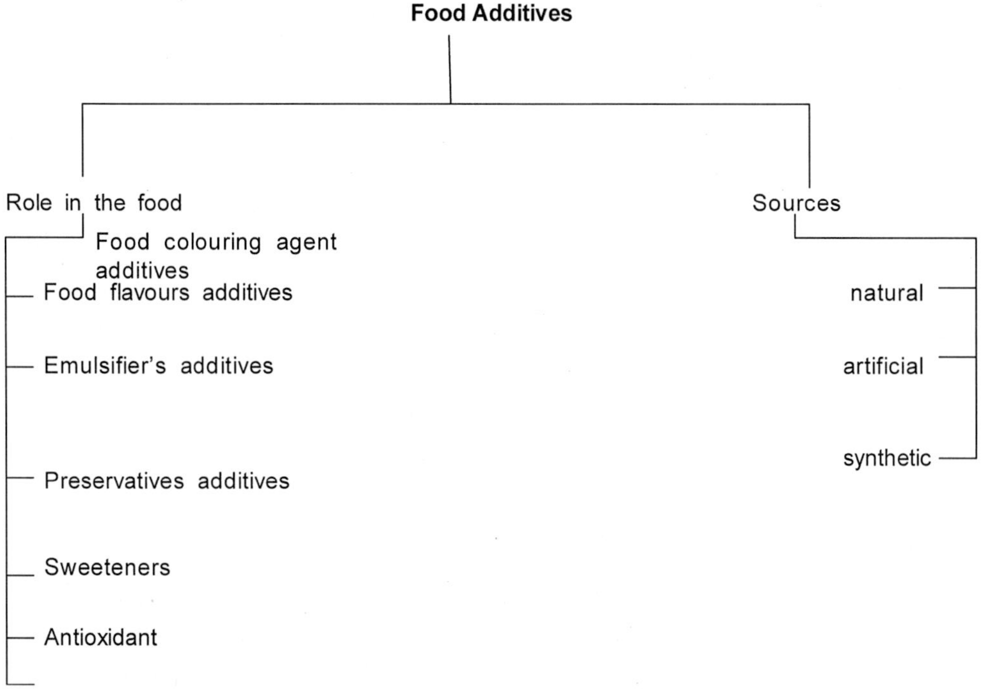


## TYPES OF FOOD ADDITIVES

There are various types of food additives used by the food manufacturers. They can be broadly divided on the basis of their—

a. Role it plays in the food and

b. Source e.g.-natural, synthetic and artificial.

We will discuss about the various food additives here:-

### Preservatives

Preservatives are those food additives which are added to the food to prevent or slow down the growth of pathogens in or on the food. The growth of microorganisms is the food results in food spoilage and food poisoning which leads to wastage, diseases and revenue loss. Therefore preservatives play an important role in increasing the shelf-life of the food. Chemical preservatives are those food additives which are purposefully added to stop deterioration of food. Use of nitrates in food reduces the growth of botulism. Benzoates, Sodium/calcium propionates are used extensively for the prevention of microbial attacks.

### Anti-Oxidants

Foods such as fats get rancid because the fatty acids present in it gets oxidised. The oxygen present in the atmosphere reacts with fatty acids and bring about rancidity in fats which makes it unfit for consumption. Addition of antioxidants helps in stopping this chemical changes in fats. The antioxidants added in various food items include:

Butter—Fumeric acid

Cheese—-Fumeric acid

Fruit and Fruit products: L - ascorbic acid-Vitamin C. It prevents browning reactions.

Oils-BHA or butylated hydroxyl anisole, BHT or butylated hydroxyl toluene

However, to use antioxidants in the oils and fats it should be soluble in it, should be stable when heated , should not alter colour and flavours and should not have any toxic effects on the food

### Sweeteners

The artificial sweeteners added to the food as food additives do not add any calories to the food. Sorbitol, Mannitol and Xylitol are used in confectionery food items.

The other artificial sweeteners such as saccharin, aspartame are used in beverages, in small quantities.

### Food Colours

Food colours are food additives added to the food by food manufacturers to improve the eye-appeal. Colour plays an important role in making the food attractive. In the catering industry, there are two types of colours used by the manufacturers-

i) Synthetic/artificial colouring agents

ii) Natural colouring agents, such as, the green pigment is extracted from spinach or caramel colour is made from heating sugar.

However, whichever colour is used by the food manufacturer, it should be legally approved and not toxic in nature. It should not be unstable when subjected to heat. It should blend with the food easily and be easily available in the market at a reasonable price. Natural colours when compared with the synthetic one are less stable, more expensive, and less versatile but it is safer.

We get purple and red colours from beetroot. The name of the pigment here is Betalin.

Green leaves and plants, we get green colours. The pigment here is Chlorophyll.

Yellow and orange colours are extracted from Turmeric. The pigment is Curcumin.

Caramel colours are made from sugar.

The synthetic/artificial colouring agents, which are permitted-

Blue: Brilliant Blue FCF

Yellow: Sunset Yellow FCF

Red: Erythrosine

Green: Green FCF.

## FLAVOURING AGENTS

The flavouring agents or flavour enhancers are of different types-

- Aromatic flavouring agents: These flavouring agents have a predominant flavour. These are extracted from various plants such as ginger, nutmeg etc.
- Natural flavouring agents: We get these from aromatics to enhance the natural flavour of the food e.g. Orange oil.
- Synthetic flavouring agents: These are synthesised compounds but has flavours just like the natural one e.g. Vanillin, which is exactly like vanilla.
- Artificial and Natural flavouring combo: These are used with natural flavours to enhance the natural flavours.
- Treated flavours: The heat treatment of offal and corn syrup produces 'roast meat' flavours.

## EMULSIONS

The word "emulsion" has been derived from the Latin word "to milk", the reason being milk is an emulsion of fat and water.

An **emulsion** can be described as a mixture of two or more liquids that are un-mixable. Emulsions are part of a more general class of two-phase systems of matter termed as Colloids. But in culinary world the term Emulsion is used as both phases, dispersed and continuous, are liquids. Therefore, in an emulsion, one liquid or the dispersed phase dispersed in the another phase or the continuous phase.

Emulsion in the food production can take two different forms:

- Fat dispersed into water and
- Water dispersed into fat.

Common fat in water emulsifications include hollandaise, mayonnaise, aioli, milk, cream, and pan sauces.

Other examples include Mayonnaise Sauce, Vinaigrette Sauce etc.

To get a stable emulsion (both in a short and long term perspective) it is of great importance to add an emulsifier. An emulsifier is a surface-active molecule that allows the two phases to homogenize. Surface-active molecules are mostly amphiphilic i.e. they have both hydrophobic and hydrophilic parts, which allow the two liquids to blend together.

## KEY TERMS:

- WHO: World health organization
- Food Additive: The World health organization (WHO), in 1965, had defined food additives as "A food additive is a substance or mixture of substances, other than the basic food staff, which is present in food area result of any aspect of production, processing, storage or packaging. The term does not

include chance contamination''. It is clear from the above definition that food additives are substances which are added to the food intentionally. Therefore, it is expected that the food producers must use additives which are safe for human consumption.

- Preservatives: Preservatives are those food additives which are added to the food to prevent or slow down the growth of pathogens in or on the food. The growth of microorganisms is the food results in food spoilage and food poisoning which leads to wastage, diseases and revenue loss. Therefore preservatives play an important role in increasing the shelf-life of the food. Chemical preservatives are those food additives which are purposefully added to stop deterioration of food. Use of nitrates in food reduces the growth of botulism. Benzoates, Sodium/calcium propionates are used extensively for the prevention of microbial attacks.
- Anti-Oxidants: Foods such as fats get rancid because the fatty acids present in it gets oxidised. The oxygen present in the atmosphere reacts with fatty acids and bring about rancidity in fats which makes it unfit for consumption. Addition of antioxidants helps in stopping this chemical changes in fats.
- Emulsions: The word "emulsion" has been derived from the Latin word "to milk", the reason being milk is an emulsion of fat and water. An **emulsion** can be described as a mixture of two or more liquids that are un-mixable. Emulsions are part of a more general class of two-phase systems of matter termed as Colloids. But in culinary world the term Emulsion is used as both phases, dispersed and continuous, are liquids. Therefore, in an emulsion, one liquid or the dispersed phase dispersed in the another phase or the continuous phase.
- Amphiphilic: Amphiphilic i.e. they have both hydrophobic and hydrophilic parts, which allow the two liquids to blend together.

## PBL:

- Students may be asked to visit the super market and find out the various types of food additives available.

## IMPORTANT QUESTIONS:

Q.1. What is Food Additive? Briefly explain each type of food additives.

Chapter 33

# Food Contaminants and Adultarants

After reading this chapter, the student will be able to:

- Explain food standards,
- Learn about various types of food contaminants,
- Know various common adulterants of food ( pesticide residues, bacterial toxins, Mycotoxins, seafood toxins, metallic contaminants, residue from packaging materials)
- *Understand methods of their detection ( basic principle )*

## FOOD STANDARDS

The Food Standard Agency of U.K. has given the following definition-"Food Standard is a set of criteria that a food must meet if it is to be suitable for human consumption, such as source, composition, appearances, freshness, permissible additives and maximum bacterial control".

**FSSAI or Food Safety and Standards Authority of India** is an autonomous body established under the Ministry of Health & Family Welfare, Government of India. FSSAI is responsible for protecting and promoting public health through the regulation and supervision of food safety.

Therefore, a food standard may be termed as a document which states the requirements, food specification, guidelines or characteristics that can be used consistently to ensure that the food materials, products, processes and services meet their ultimate purposes. This document acts as a guideline or benchmark for the food manufacturers to produce food items which will satisfy the food quality and safety requirements, reduce wastage, maintain and improve quality of food. These food standards are decided by a regulatory authority. It is the duty of the government to ensure the guidelines laid down are practiced by the regional and international food manufacturers.

**The food standards may be divided in the following ways-**

a) **Process Standards**: As is obvious from the term itself, the process standard gives the guidelines about how a food item should be produced.

b) **Product Standards**; - The product standards as the name suggests gives the guidelines about the features and characteristics of the food items should be.

c) **Information Standards**: The information standards gives the guidelines about the information provided none the labels. These deals with what all should be communicated about the product to the prospective consumers.

**The standards are classified further into the following two categories—-**

1) **Compulsory/Mandatory Standards:** This is the minimum standard a food product must have to ensure quality and safety. It is the duty of the government, international organisation and private companies to enforce the compulsory/ mandatory standards so that quality and safety of the food product is maintained.

2) **Voluntary Standards**: These are additional standards followed by food manufacturers other than the Compulsory/Mandatory Standards to get an upper-hand over their competitors.

Usefulness of Food Standards:

The food standards is important for the following reasons—

a) Food standard ensures consumer's safety by ensuring quality.

b) It earns the confidence, reliability and good will of the buyers on the system and the companies.

c) It helps to bridge the gap of communication between manufacturers and consumers through information provided on the label about the food product.

d) It helps the consumers to select and chose the right kind of product they are paying for.

e) It helps to maintain proper and approved food safety and quality.

f) It helps the food manufacturers to provide better products than their competitors. This competition helps the consumers in the long run.

## CODEX

Codex Alimentary Commission is a joint committee on food standards for international business. Codex is responsible for scientific research and tasting of foods. It sets standards for minimum level of pesticide residues, provides guidelines for food contaminants, sets standard for all the processed, semi-processed and raw foods etc.

## INTERNATIONAL ORGANISATION FOR STANDARDS (ISO)

ISO or the International Organisation for Standards is the largest global organisation, which sets standards for quality managements, food safety managements, Lab management etc. The ISO 22000 is used for Food Safety Management Standards. It helps to maintain international standards for global trade of food products. It ensures-

- Customer satisfaction
- Quality management

- Global food standards
- Continuous improvements in food quality and safety
- Free and fair trade
- Implementation of food traceability system
- Identify and control food safety hazards
- Adhere to trade specification etc.

## TYPES OF FOOD CONTAMINANTS

Contaminants may be defined as any biological or chemical agent, foreign matter or any other substances that may compromise food quality, safety and suitability for human consumption.

Therefore, contamination may be defined as the addition, intentional or accidental, of a contaminant in the food meant for human consumption. Thus contamination of food may occur from air, soil, water, animal, human, insects, pests etc.

Here, we will discuss about some of the contaminants--

### Pesticide Residues

Pesticide may be defined as a substance which is used on the crops to destroy the organisms which may damage the crops. There are various types of pesticides such as insecticides, fungicides, herbicides and nematocide (a substance that kills nematode worms). Pesticide Residues may be defined as the pesticides that remain on or in the food after they are used on the food crops. When these crops are harvested and sold in the markets, general population at large may get affected if the crops are not thoroughly cleaned before use for consumption. The derivatives of Chlorinated pesticides have a harmful effect on the humans. The foods that get affected by pesticide residues include meat, poultry, fish, vegetable oils, fruits and vegetables, nuts etc. Many of the pesticide residues are found to Lipophillic and can bio-accumulate in the body. Washing fruits and vegetables before using for cooking or eating raw will clean the pesticide residues and other contaminants such as soil. Children are more susceptible to pesticide residues. Neurotoxin and other chemicals that originate from pesticide residues are harmful for human brain and nervous system. Longer ingestion of pesticide residue in tiny amounts may also create problems.

The highly toxic compounds which pose greater threats are Arsenic, Mercury, Barium and Lead.

#### *Bacterial Toxin*

Bacterial toxins may be defined as toxic substances that are produced by their activities and released to target other bacteria and host cells. Bacterial toxins are -

##### *Exotoxins*

Exotoxins are those toxins which are separated from the cells producing it. Exotoxin producing bacteria are

Clostridium Tetani—-Causes Tetanus

Clostridium Perfringens- Causes Gangrene

Clostridium Botulinum—Causes botulism

Vibrio cholera——-Causes Cholera

*Enterotoxins*

Enterotoxins are exototoxins which causes diarrhoea and food intoxication. The bacteria which produces this type of toxins are V. cholera, Enterotoxigenic E. Coli , C. Perfringens etc.

Toxoid is a modified Exotoxin.

Exotoxin has two main characteristics-

I) Toxicity and

II) Antigenenicity

## Endotoxin:

Endotoxins are part of cell-wall of Gram-negative bacteria. The typical symptoms of endotoxin in humans are fever, Hypotension, shock, Hypoglycemia, Disseminated Intervascular Coagulation (DTC) etc.

The differences between Endotoxins and Exotoxins are

| Sl. No. | ENDOTOXINS | EXOTOXINS |
|---|---|---|
| 01 | Endotoxins are part of cell-walls of Gram-negative bacteria. It is released when the bacteria die or grow. | Exotoxins are excreted by living cells. |
| 02 | Formed by Gram-negative bacteria | It is formed by both the Gram-negative and Gram-positive bacteria. |
| 03 | The toxicity is caused by Lipid A | The toxicity is caused by Polypeptides. |
| 04 | The toxicity can be classified as moderate | The Exotoxins are highly toxic. |
| 05 | The toxin remains stable in heat application. | Toxicity is destroyed by the application of heat above $60^0$C. |
| 07 | Endotoxin cannot be converted to Toxoid | It can be converted to Toxoid. Toxoids are used for immunization. |
| 08 | One of the obvious symptoms is fever in the host. | Usually no fever in the host. |

## Mycotoxins

The word mycotoxin has been derived from the Greek word, Mykes means Fungus and Toxikon means Poison. Mycotoxins are toxic secondary metabolite produce by fungus, which can lead to diseases and death in human if ingested through contaminated food.

Mycotoxicosis is a disease which is caused due to natural toxin produced by fungus.

The major group of mycotoxins are Aflotoxin (It is produced by A. flavus and A. parasiticus. It is associated with commodities such as peanuts, spices, maize etc.),Ochratoxin, Citrinin, luteoskyrin, Patulin, Fusaricem etc.

The health effects include weak immune system, death, allergy etc. The effect depends on age, sex, diet, etc. it can be transmitted via ingestion, skin contact, inhalation. Though the health effect of Mycotoxins in human is not yet clear but their effects on animals are justifiable. The recent research has found its relation to carcinogenic property.

## Seafood toxins

Sea food toxins cause seafood intoxication, which a food borne disease is caused by the ingestion of shellfish that contain toxins. Marine bio toxins are algae metabolites which accumulate in shellfish make them unfit for human consumption. Bivalve shellfish such as mussels, scallops, oysters and clams pass a lot of water through their bodies and can ingest toxic algae of certain Dinoflagellate species. But the shellfish do not get affected by those toxins. However when human consume these toxic seafood, get poisoned. These toxins do not get destroyed by cooking. These toxins are saxitoxins, tetrodotoxins, Dioton toxins, dinoflagallate toxins etc. Symptoms include nausea, rumbles in lips, fingertips and tongue, vomiting, facial flushing, itching etc.

Some of the sea food poisoning are:

- Paralytic shellfish poisoning(PSP)
- Ciguatera poisoning
- Scombroid poisoning (SP)

PSP and SP are very common seafood poisoning. There is no antidote to deal with seafood poisoning which makes it great risk for safety. One of the best ways to reduce toxin in seafood is to keep shellfish in clean water.

## Metallic contaminants

Food may get contaminated by toxic metals such as lead, mercury, arsenic, cadmium, etc. through water, soil, temperature, etc. Many times the metal fumes in the atmosphere come down on soil and water which in turn contaminates cereals on the field and the lakes, ponds, and rivers. Fish may consume this contaminated water along with food. When humans eat this fish they get poisoned.

### *Lead*

lead contaminates the food from soil, cereals and fish; lead in human body can affect the central nervous system (CNS) and gastro intestinal system.

### *Cooper*

Higher dose of cooper creates problem to humans. Cooper contaminates the food through utensils etc.

### *Arsenic*

The biggest source of arsenic contamination is shellfish and vegetables. Long time consumption of contaminated water can cause dermatitis, cancer, memory loss, malfunction of reproductive system and cardiovascular diseases.

### *Mercury*

It gets its route to human body through swordfish and other sea water fish. It can affect the gastrointestinal system, immune system, respiratory system, eyes etc.

### *Cadmium*

It can enter human body through ground water, industrial process etc. It can damage GI system and kidney

### *Nickel*

It comes to the human food through environment contamination. It can cause allergy, growth problem, reproductive problem etc.

## Differences between metals added to food as food additive and metallic contaminants

| Metal as food additives | Metallic contaminants |
|---|---|
| • Added intentionally on purpose. | • Enters through contaminants |
| • It performs special functions in food items. | • No or little function in food. |
| • It is safe and tested by approved authorities before being used. | • Safety is checked by authorities to reduce long time excessive dose from food and other resources. |
| • The allowed concentration of metal is sufficient for the technological purpose. | • As low as reasonably achievable. |

Industrial discharge, vehicle fumes, natural erosion from soil, fertilizers, Lead water pipes, cigarettes smoking, leaded petrol, leaded food etc. produces metallic contaminants which then contaminates cereals, water, atmosphere, fish, and shellfish etc. Dental filing contains mercury.

## Residues from packaging materials

Packaging may become a dangerous source of contamination such as recycled paperboards, plastic foil etc. It may be thin coating of food grade wax or multilayered system of paper-plastic-metallic component-adhesive. Packaging material becomes a source of contamination when it leaches undesirable compounds into the food. These compounds may be toxins. It can also change the flavour, colour of product. The various inks and dyes applied to the finished packaging can also contaminate solvents derived from these sources are major contaminants. The contaminants for packaging into food depends on factors such as packaging material, food materials, temperature, storage time, size of the packaging (smaller packaging will have longer surface volume ratio). Chemical diffusion may contaminate the food by inks, adhesives. Glass-packaged oily food may get contaminated by migration of plasticizers. Non-inert materials e.g. paper, board, plastic, can have direct effect. A special case of contamination is "Off-set migration" where the printed, outside layer of packaging transfers chemicals to food inside.

## COMMON ADULTERANTS IN FOODS AND BASIC METHOD OF THEIR DETECTION

Food adulteration may be defined as intentionally substituting part of food items with some inferior substances. Therefore, an adulterant is such inferior quality substances which have bees intentionally added to the food by substituting or removing some valuable ingredients. Such adulterants obviously makes the food-

- Inferior in quality
- Unsafe for consumption
- Not of the nature and quality that the consumer paid for.

The manufacturers adulterate the foods to earn more money. But by doing that the food gets contaminated and becomes unsafe for consumption.

Some common adulterants in foods and how to detect them are discussed below-

a) **Tea**: Generally adulterated by tea coloured leaves, used tea leaves and iron fillings. Method of detection:

   i) If we rub the tea leaves on a white paper and the paper gets coloured then there is artificial colour in it.

   ii) If we put some tea leaves powder on a damp blotting paper and it gets orange, red or yellow colour then it definitely has been coloured artificially.

   iii) If we put a magnet in the tea leaves, it will attract the iron fillings

b) **Coffee**: It is adulterated with Chicory

   *Method of detection*

   If we put the coffee powder gently on the water in a pan, the coffee powder will float but chicory will settle at the bottom and leave colour also.

c) **Sugar and Salt powder**: usually adulterated with chalk powder.

   *Method of detection:*

   If we dissolve sugar/salt in a glass of water, after some time sugar/salt will get dissolved but chalk powder will settle down at the bottom.

d) **Ice-cream**: common adulterant is washing powder.

*Method of detection:*

If we put some lemon juice on it, bubbles will appear if it is adulterated with washing powder.

e) **Red Chilli Powder**: Common adulterant is brick powder.

*Method of detection:*

If we put the red chilli powder in a glass of water the chilli powder will settle down slowly whereas the brick powder will settle faster.

f) **Pulses ( such as moong dal, channa dal etc.)**: Common adulterant is Metanil Yellow or Lead Chromate.

*Method of detection:*

If we put a few drops of HCl in the pulses, the pink colour will prove the addition/presence of Metanil Yellow or Lead Chromate.

g) **Green vegetables** (such as green peas, green chilli etc.): Common adulterant is Malachite green.

*Method of detection*:

If we put some of the grren vegetables on the damp blotting paper, colour will come out.

h) **Wheat flour**: Common adulterant is Barn and Chalk powder.

*Method of detection of Barn*: If we put some flour on a glass of water the barn will float on the water surface.

*Method of detection of chalk powder*: If we put dil. HCl and shake, the effervescence will indicate the presence of chalk powder.

i) **Paneer, milk, khoya**: Common adulterant is Starch.

*Method of detection*: -Add water and boil. Cool down. Add a few drops of Iodine solutions. If it turns blue, then it was adulterated with starch.

j) **Ghee or butter**: Common adulterant is Vanaspathi.

*Method of detection:*

Take ghee or butter and add conc. HCl of equal quantity.

Add a pinch of cane sugar in it,

Shake well.

Crimson red colour will appear at the bottom in a few minutes.

k) **Honey**: Common adulterant is water.

*Method of detection*: -

Dip a piece of cotton ball in honey and burn it on a candle flame.

If water is added to it then it will not burn or burn with a cracking sound.

l) **Turmeric powder**: Common adulterant is Metanil Yellow.

*Method of detection*:

Put a few drops of turmeric powder in water.

Add a few drops of HCl in it (never add water in the acid).

If violet colour comes out, then it was adulterated with Metanil Yellow.

## KEY TERMS

- **Food Standard:** The Food Standard Agency of U.K. has given the following definition-"Food Standard is a set of criteria that a food must meet if it is to be suitable for human consumption, such as source, composition, appearances, freshness, permissible additives and maximum bacterial control".
- **FSSAI :** Food Safety and Standards Authority of India.
- **Mycotoxins**:-The word mycotoxin has been derived from the Greek word, Mykes means Fungus and Toxikon means Poison. Mycotoxins are toxic secondary metabolite produce by fungus, which can lead to diseases and death in human if ingested through contaminated food.
- **Mycotoxicosis:** It is a disease which is caused due to natural toxin produced by fungus.
- **Endotoxin:** Endotoxins are part of cell-wall of Gram-negative bacteria.
- ***Bacterial Toxin***: Bacterial toxins may be defined as toxic substances that are produced by their activities and released to target other bacteria and host cells. Bacterial toxins are -

  **Exotoxins**: Exotoxins are those toxins which are separated from the cells producing it.
- ***Pesticide Residues***: -Pesticide may be defined as a substance which is used on the crops to destroy the organisms which may damage the crops.
- **Contaminants:** Contaminants may be defined as any biological or chemical agent, foreign matter or any other substances that may compromise food quality, safety and suitability for human consumption.
- **Contamination:** Contamination may be defined as the addition, intentional or accidental, of a contaminant in the food meant for human consumption. Thus contamination of food may occur from air, soil, water, animal, human, insects, pests etc.
- **Codex:** Codex Alimentary Commission is a joint committee on food standards for international business. Codex is responsible for scientific research and tasting of foods. It sets standards for minimum level of pesticide residues, provides guidelines for food contaminants, sets standard for all the processed, semi-processed and raw foods etc.
- **International Organisation for Standards (ISO):** ISO or the International Organisation for Standards is the largest global organisation, which sets

standards for quality managements, food safety managements, Lab management etc. The ISO 22000 is used for Food Safety Management Standards. It helps to maintain international standards for global trade of food products.

- **Process Standards**: As is obvious from the term itself, the process standard gives the guidelines about how a food item should be produced.
- **Product Standards**; - The product standards as the name suggests gives the guidelines about the features and characteristics of the food items should be.
- **Information Standards**: The information standards gives the guidelines about the information provided none the labels. These deals with what all should be communicated about the product to the prospective consumers.
- **Compulsory/Mandatory Standards:** This is the minimum standard a food product must have to ensure quality and safety. It is the duty of the government, international organisation and private companies to enforce the compulsory/ mandatory standards so that quality and safety of the food product is maintained.
- **Voluntary Standards**: These are additional standards followed by food manufacturers other than the Compulsory/Mandatory Standards to get an upper-hand over their competitors.

## PROJECT BASED LEARNING OR PBL:

- Students may be asked to check adulterants in some of the common food items used on daily basis

## IMPORTANT QUESTIONS:

Q.1.What do you understand by Food Standards?

Q.2. Explain various types of Food Contaminants.

Q.3. Explain various common adulterants in food.

Q.4. Explain how will you detect common adulterants in at least five common food items.

Chapter 34

# Quality Management

After reading this chapter the student will be able to: -

- Learn about TQM
- Know about GMP
- Understand about Risk Assessment
- Learn the relevance of microbiological standard for food safety
- *Understand HACCP (basic principle and implementation)*

## TQM OR TOTAL QUALITY MANAGEMENT

TQM or Total Quality Management may be defined as an on-going effort by the management and staff members of an organization earn customer loyalty and customer satisfaction. A satisfied customer will come in again and again. He will also praise about the organization to his or her friends and relatives and help bring in more and more new potential clients. On the other hand an unsatisfied customer will spoil the business. One of the most important factor in building loyal customers and satisfied customers is to ensure consistently good quality of the products. Quality may be defined as a standard which decides the superiority or inferiority of a product/service. Therefore, quality of a product/service is an attribute which sets a company apart from its competitors. Quality plays an important role in the business. The marketing personnel of an organization emphasize on the quality of their product/service to the potential clients to win over their competitors.

## USEFULNESS OF TQM:

1) Quality management helps to maintain highest quality of the products and services. This quality of the product/services can be determined on the basis of durability, reliability and performances.

2) Total quality management is important for the satisfaction of the customers which in turn helps to create loyalty. This customer loyalty brings the customers back to the organization no matter what. This possible if the quality is consistently of higher grade.

3) The TQM tools help in designing and creating a product/service of an organization which is based on the needs and wants of the customers. As the 'needs and wants' of the customers are fulfilled, they automatically feel satisfied with the products/services.

4) The TQM helps to increase the revenue and productivity for an organization. If the customers are loyal and satisfied, automatically, there will be more business and more revenue earning. This in turn will ensure satisfied staff and better work culture.

5) The TQM helps an organization to reduce waste and manage inventory better. It enables employees to work closely with suppliers and incorporate "Just in Time" Philosophy.

## FOLLOWING ARE THE TQM TOOLS

A) **Check List -** . Check lists are a long list of identified problems which need to be addressed Check lists are useful in collecting data and information easily .Check list also helps employees to identify problems which prevent an organization to deliver quality products..

B) **Pareto Chart -** The credit for Pareto Chart goes to Italian Economist - Wilfredo Pareto. Pareto Chart helps employees to identify the problems, prioritize them and also determine their frequency in the system..

C) **The Cause and Effect Diagram/**Fishbone Chart: - Cause and Effect Diagram records causes of a particular and specific problem .The cause and effect diagram plays a crucial role in identifying the root cause of a particular problem and also potential factors which give rise to a common problem at the workplace.

D) **Histogram -** Histogram, introduced by Karl Pearson is nothing but a graphical representation showing intensity of a particular problem. Histogram helps identify the cause of problems in the system by the shape as well as width of the distribution.

E) **Scatter Diagram -** Scatter Diagram is a quality management tool which helps to analyze relationship between two variables. In a scatter chart, data is represented as points, where each point denotes a value on the horizontal axis and vertical axis.

F) **Graphs -** Graphs are the simplest and most commonly used quality management tools. Graphs help to identify whether processes and systems are as per the expected level or not and if not also record the level of deviation from the standard specifications.

**Total Quality management can be divided into four categories**:

1) Plan
2) Do
3) Check
4) Act

These four categories are also referred to as **PDCA cycle**.

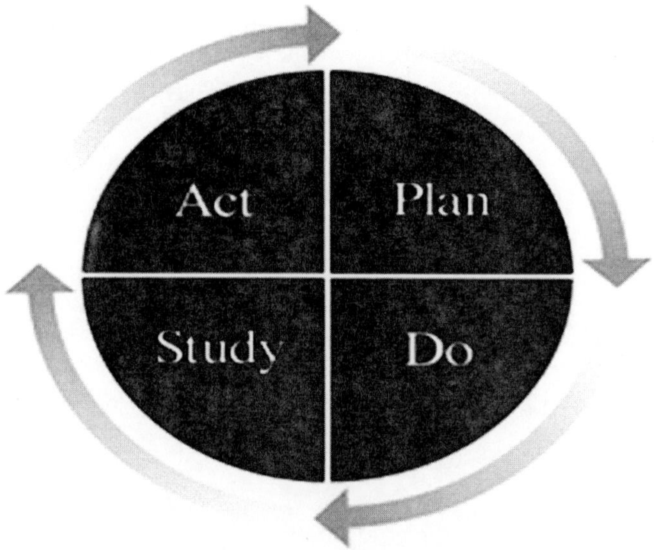


(Source: https://www.deming.org/theman/theories/pdsacycle)

The Relevance and importance of TQM in the food industry:

- Healthy Foods: The new generation consumers want healthy, nutrient-loaded and economical foods. TQM is absolutely necessary for any food manufacturing company to meet the demands of the customers.
- International-quality-oriented food market: The widely-travelled and quality-conscious customers want international quality-oriented, tasty and safe foods.
- Stiff Competition: The competition with the global market requires stringent quality management in every stage of food production. To survive in such competitive market the safety, quality, acceptability and price are important factors. Practicing TQM can only ensure it.
- Higher national and international standards for food safety and public health of animal welfare and animal food production.
- Demand for environment-friendly operations.
- Rise in ready-to-eat food items. This has increased the demand for food scientists, consultants; nutritionist and quality controllers.TQM has become an absolute necessary to produce such food items.
- The countries which have implemented stringent quality management rulesof food safety have found a decline in food-borne diseases.

## GMP OR GOOD MANUFACTURING PRACTICES

GMP or Good Manufacturing Practices may be defined as the essential practices followed during the operations of a food business which ensures safe production of food. GMP is an essential and integral part of Hazard Analysis and Critical Control Point or HACCP food system in food industry. Therefore, a lot of emphasis is given in following Good Manufacturing Practices in all food laws and regulations and customer certification standards. Good Manufacturing Practices are recommended by the agencies that control the licensing for the manufacture and sale of food. These must be followed to get the authorization certificate from these agencies. The guidelines laid down by these agencies for GMP of food manufacturing industries are only to ensure that the products are of superior quality and safe for human consumptions. These guidelines provide minimum requirements that an organization must follow.

## Basic GMP and the Food Industry

In order to follow the Good Manufacturing Practices, the food manufacturer will have to follow certain basic minimum operational requirements and procedures. These are:

- The correct construction and layout of the food premises.
- The correct condition of the external and internal environment of the food premises.
- Proper maintenance of all the equipments and utensils used in the premises.
- The use of approved and suitable chemicals in and around the food premises e.g. cleaning chemicals, pesticides, lubricants for machineries etc.
- Proper segregation, identification and storage of waste materials by the food business.
- Proper cleaning of the food premises, equipments and utensils, floors, walls, ceilings etc.
- An efficient and effective pest control being implemented in and around the food premises.
- Complete absence of foreign materials e.g. wood, glass, metal, paper, pests and insects, plastics, strings etc. in the finished products.
- For effective GMP, the food business must document all the procedures and maintain all relevant records about how GMP have been followed.
- The food business must undertake its own internal GMP inspections.

All these are minimum requirements to produce safe foods for the consumers. Other than these there are GMPs for written particularly for bakery and confectionery foods, pickled foods, fish, sea fish, bottled water etc.

## Importance of GMP

The importance of GMP cannot be overemphasized.

It is important to produce safe foods.

It helps the food business operators to discharge their legal and moral responsibilities towards the society.

The food business reputation can be built or spoilt on the basis of their sincerity towards the implementation of GMP.

The food business might have to pay heavily if the GMP is not properly followed.

The employees trained in practices of GMP in the organization turn out to be more efficient, reliable and disciplined.

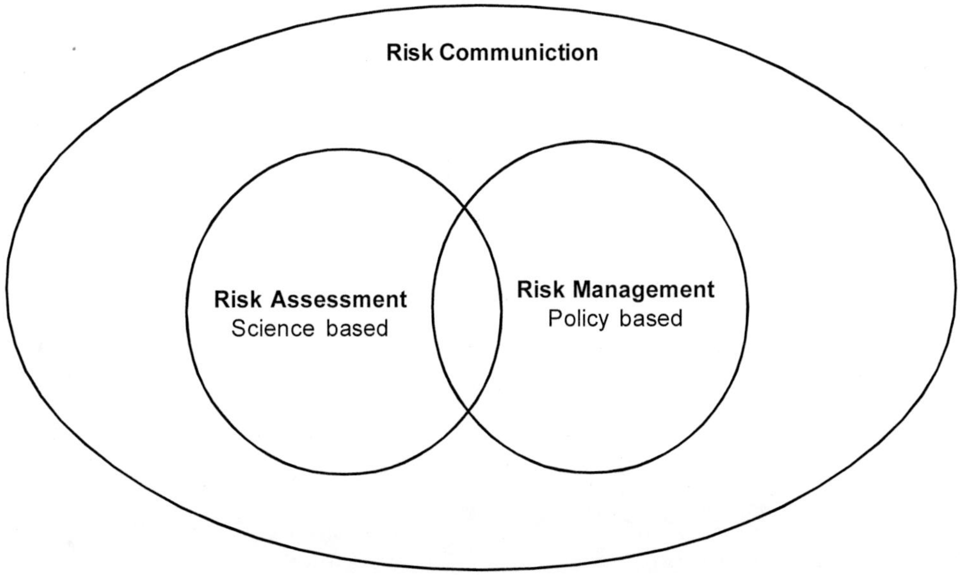


**Diagram: Risk Analysis paradigm**

## RELEVANCE OF MICROBIOLOGICAL STANDARDS FOR FOOD SAFETY

Microbiological testing is carried out to estimate the food safety and quality for the following reasons:

a) To develop process control

b) For monitoring and verification of process control

c) To investigate the causes of loss of control and

d) To directly assess food quality and safety.

In all the above cases the testing is carried out to determine the microbiological standard of the food or the acceptability of the process used to produce it. Microbes include:- bacteria, viruses, yeasts, moulds, and algae; parasitic protozoa; their toxins/ metabolites

The microbiological safety of foods is principally assured by

- Control at the source,
- Product design

- Process control, and
- The application of Good Hygienic Practices during production, processing (including labeling), handling, distribution, storage, sale, preparation and use, in conjunction with the application of the HACCP system.

This preventive approach offers more control than microbiological testing because the effectiveness of microbiological examination to assess the safety of foods is limited.

## Microbiological Criterion

A microbiological criterion for food defines the acceptability of a product or a food lot, based on the absence or presence, or number of microorganisms including parasites, and/or quantity of their toxins/metabolites, per unit(s) of mass, volume, area or lot.

To fulfill the purposes of a microbiological criterion, consideration should be given to:

- The evidence of actual or potential hazards to health;
- The microbiological status of the raw material(s);
- The effect of processing on the microbiological status of the food;
- The likelihood and consequences of microbial contamination and/or growth during subsequent handling, storage and use;
- The category(s) of consumers concerned;
- The cost/benefit ratio associated with the application of the criterion; and
- The intended use of the food.

## Microbiological methods

Whenever possible, only methods for which the reliability (accuracy, reproducibility, inter- and intra-laboratory variation) has been statistically established in comparative or collaborative studies in several laboratories should be used.The microbiological methods specified should be reasonable with regard to complexity, availability of media, equipment etc., ease of interpretation, time required and costs.

## Microbiological limits

Limits used in criteria should be based on microbiological data appropriate to the food and should be applicable to a variety of similar products. They should therefore be based on data gathered at various production establishments operating under Good Hygienic Practices and applying the HACCP system.

Microbiological limits should take into consideration the risk associated with the microorganisms, and the conditions under which the food is expected to be handled and consumed. Microbiological limits should also take account of the likelihood of uneven distribution of microorganisms in the food and the inherent variability of the analytical procedure.

## HACCP (HAZARD ANALYSIS AND CRITICAL CONTROL POINT)

The **HACCP** system, which is science based and systematic, identifies specific hazards and measure for their control to ensure the safety of food. HACCP is a tool to assess hazards and establish control systems that focus on prevention rather than relying mainly on end-product testing. Any **HACCP** system is capable of accommodating changes, such as advance in equipment design, processing procedures or technological developments.

**HACCP** can be applied throughout the food chain from primary production to final consumption and its implementation should be guided by scientific evidence of risks to human health. As well as enhancing food safety, implementation of **HACCP** can provide other significant benefits. In addition, the application of **HACCP** systems can be aid inspection by regulatory authorities and promote international trade by increasing confidence in food safety.

### HACCP plan

A document prepared in accordance with the principles of HACCP to ensure control of hazards which are significant for food safety in the segment of the food chain under consideration.

### Hazard

A biological, chemical or physical agent in, or condition of, food with the potential to cause an adverse health effect.

### Hazard analysis

The process of collecting and evaluating information on hazards and conditions leading to their presence to decide which are significant for food safety and therefore should be addressed in the HACCP plan.

## PRINCIPLES OF THE HACCP SYSTEM

The HACCP system consists of the following seven principles:

### Principle 1

Conduct a hazard analysis.

### Principle 2

Determine the Critical Control Point (CCP).

### Principle 3

Establish critical limit(s).

### Principle 4

Establish a system to monitor control of the CCP.

### Principle 5

Establish the corrective action to be taken when monitoring indicates that a particular CCP is not under control.

### Principle 6

Establish procedures for verification to confirm that the HACCP system is working effectively.

### Principle 7

Establish documentation concerning all procedures and record appropriate to these principle and their application.

## APPILCATIONS OF HACCP

The application of HACCP principles consists of the following tasks as identified in the logic Sequence for Application of HACCP.

### Assemble HACCP team

The food operation should ensure that the appropriate product specific knowledge and expertise is available for the development of an effective HACCP plan.

### Describe product

A full description of the product should be drawn, including relevant safety information such as: composition, physical/chemical structure, microbial/static treatment, packaging, durability and storage condition and method of distribution.

### Identify intended use

The intended use should be based on the expected uses of the product by the end user or consumer.

### Construct flow diagram

The flow diagram should be constructed by the HACCP team.

### On-site confirmation of flow diagram

Steps must be taken to confirm the processing information against the flow diagram during all stages and hour of operation and amend the flow diagram where batter.

### List all potential hazards associated with each step, conduct a hazard analysis, and consider any measure to control identified hazards

The HACCP team should list all of the hazards that may be reasonably expected to occur at each step according to the to the scope from primary production, processing, production, processing, manufacturing, and distribution until the point of consumption.

### Determine critical control

There may be more than one CCP at which control is applied to address the same hazard.

### Establish critical limits from each CCP

Critical limits must be specified and validated for each Critical Control Point.

### Establish a monitoring system for each CCP

Monitoring is the scheduled measurement or observation of a CCP relative to its critical limits.

### Establish corrective action

Specific corrective actions must be developed for each CCP in the HACCP system in order to deal with deviation when they colour.

### Establish verification procedures

Establish procedures for verification.

### Establish Documentation and Record Keeping

Efficient and accurate record keeping is essential to the application of a HACCP system.

## TRAINING

Training of the staff in HACCP is very important. Working instructions and procedures must be developed to for training. Coordination and cooperation amongst the industry, consumers, producers and other stakeholders are essential.

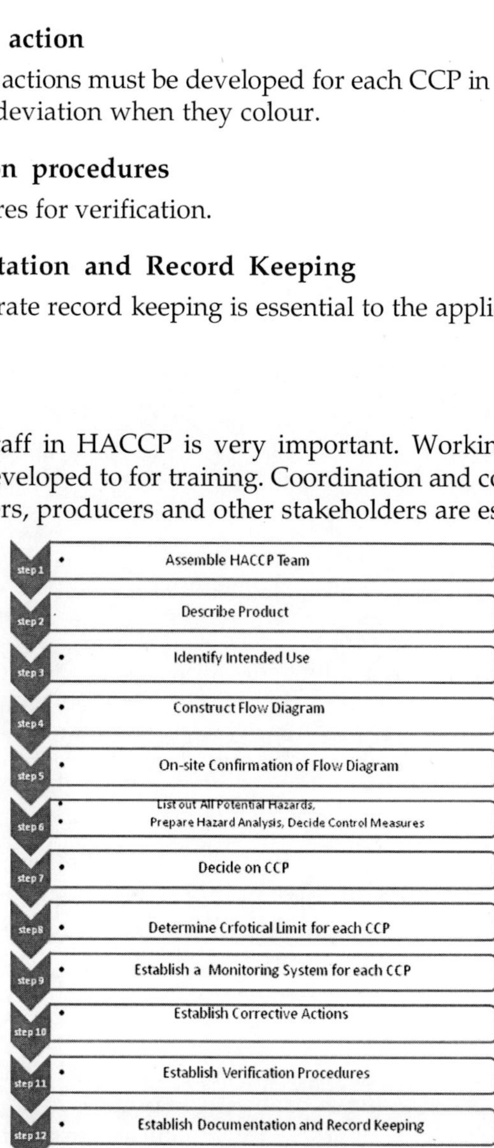


**Diagram: Logical Sequence for the Application of HACCP**

## DEFINITIONS

- **Control (verb):** To take all necessary actions to ensure and maintain compliance with criteria established in the HACCP plan.
- **Control (noun):** The state wherein correct procedures are being followed and criteria are being met.
- **Control measure:** Any action and activity that can be used to prevent and eliminate a food safety hazard or reduce it to an acceptable level.
- **Corrective action:** Any action to be taken when the results of monitoring at the CCP indicate a loss of control.
- **Critical Control Point (CCP):** A step at which control can be applied and is essential to prevent and eliminate a food safety hazard or reduce it to an acceptable level.
- **Critical limit:** A criterion which separates acceptability from unacceptability from unacceptability.
- **Deviation:** Failure to meet a critical limit.
- **Flow diagram:** A systematic representation of the sequence of steps and operation used in the production or manufacture of a particular food items.
- **HACCP:** A system which identifies, evaluates, and control hazards which are significant of food safety.
- **HACCP plan:** A document prepared in accordance with the principles of HACCP to ensure control of hazards which are significant for food safety in the segment of the food chain under consideration.
- **Hazard:** A biological, chemical or physical agent in, or condition of, food with the potential to cause an adverse health effect.
- **Hazard analysis:** The process of collecting and evaluating information on hazards and conditions leading to their presence to decide which are significant for food safety and therefore should be addressed in the HACCP plan.
- **Microbiological Criterion**: A microbiological criterion for food defines the acceptability of a product or a food lot, based on the absence or presence, or number of microorganisms including parasites, and/or quantity of their toxins/ metabolites, per unit(s) of mass, volume, area or lot.
- **GMP or Good Manufacturing**: - GMP or Good Manufacturing Practices may be defined as the essential practices followed during the operations of a food business which ensures safe production of food. GMP is an essential and integral part of Hazard Analysis and Critical Control Point or HACCP food system in food industry.
- **TQM or Total Quality Management:** TQM or Total Quality Management may be defined as an on-going effort by the management and staff members of an organization earn customer loyalty and customer satisfaction.

## IMPORTANT QUESTIONS:

Q.1. Explain the following terms:-

a) TQM

b) GMP

c) Risk Assessments

d) HACCP

Q.2. How microbiological standard is relevant to food safety?

Q. 3. State the basic principles of HACCP. How will you implement these?

Chapter 35

# Food Laws and Regulations

After reading this chapter the student will be able to:

- Explain PFA, ECA (FPO, MPO etc.)
- Know about CAC, ISO
- Learn about WTO
- Understand Consumer Protection Act or CPA

## PREVENTION OF FOOD ADULTERATION ACT (PFA)

The prevention of food adulteration act was enacted in 1954 (37 of 1954) to strengthen the system for preventing adulteration in articles of food. The rules framed under the act are known as the "Prevention of Food Adulteration Rules, 1955".

The act is being enforced since 1st June 1955.

The objective of this act was to

- Ensure that the food articles sold to the customers are pure and wholesome.
- It is also intended to prevent frauds or deception and encourage fair trade practices.
- The act prohibits the manufacture, sale and distribution of not only adulterated foods but also food contaminated with toxicants and misbranded foods.

All the food products manufactured in India or imported and sold in the country have to meet the requirements prescribed under PFA act, 1954. The PFA rules, 1955 are amended from time to time. As per notification GSR (365) E dated 7.6.2005, the same are called the prevention of food adulteration (Fourth Amendment) rules, 2005.The administration is through a three tier system

(a) Government Of India

(b) State /Union Territory Governments (UTs)

(c) Local Bodies

According to Prevention of Food Adulteration Act an article of food shall be deemed to be adulterated: --

1. If the article sold by a vendor is not of the nature, substance or quality demanded by purchaser and is to his prejudice, or is not of the nature, substance of quality which it purports or is represented to be.
2. If the article contains any other substance with affects, or if the article is so processed as to affect injuriously the nature as substance or quality thereof.
3. if any inferior or cheaper substance has been substituted wholly or in part for the article so as to affect injuriously the nature as substance or quality thereof.
4. If any constituent of the article has been wholly or in part abstracted so as to affect injuriously the nature, substance or quality thereof.
5. If the article had been prepared, packed or kept under unsanitary conditions whereby it has become contaminated or injurious to health.
6. If the article consists wholly or in part of any filthy, putrid disgusting, rotten, decomposed, or diseased animal or vegetable substance or is insect-infested or otherwise unfit for the human consumption.
7. If the article is obtained from a diseased animal.
8. If the article contains any poisonous or any ingredient which renders its contents injurious to health.
9. If the container of the article is composed, whether wholly or in part of any poisonous or deleterious substance which renders its contents injurious to health.
10. If any colouring matter other than that prescribed in respect thereof and in amounts not within the prescribed limits of variability is present in the article.
11. If the article contains any prohibited preservative in excess of the prescribed limits.
12. If the quality or purity of the article falls below the prescribed standards or its constituents are present in quantities which are in excess of the prescribed limits of variability.

## ESSENTIAL COMMODITIES ACT

The essential commodities act is an act of parliament of India which was established to ensure the delivery of certain commodities or products, the supply of which if obstructed owing to hoarding or black-marketing would affect the normal life of the people. This includes foodstuffs, drugs, fuels (petroleum products) etc.

The essential commodities act was enacted in 1955 with an objective to regulate the manufacture, commerce, and distribution of essential commodities, including food. The act extends to the whole of India. A number of control orders have been formulated under the provisions of essential commodities act, 1955 and few orders are enlisted here:

(a) Fruit product order, 1955 (Ministry of food processing Industries),

(b) Milk and milk product order, 1992 (Ministry of Agriculture),

(c) Vegetable oils product (Regulation order 1988),

(d) Solvent extracted oil, De-oiled meal and edible flour (control order)

(e) Meat product order, 1973

(f) Edible oil packaging (Development and Regulation) order 1998.

However, excluding the fruit product order, 1995, the majority of the orders under the essential Commodities Act, 1955 have not prescribed specification of food products but specify the hygiene and food safety requirements. Specification of food articles formulated under these order are in the line with the standards laid down under the PFA Act and Rules. The details of fruit product order and milk and milk product order are given here.

## THE SALIENT FEATURES OF THE ESSENTIAL COMMODITIES ACT

The Salient Features of the Essential Commodities Act are: -

1. Use of non-standardised weights, measures is an offence under this act.
2. Every manufacturer, dealer and repairer of weights & measures is required to obtain licence.
3. Every licensee has to keep records of his business as per conditions of this licence.
4. All weights, measures, weighing and measuring instruments are required to be verified and stamped in requisite period.
5. Use or sale of non-verified and unstamped weights, measures is offence under this act.
6. Distribution of quantity less than the standard weights, measures to consumer or excess demand of quantity than the standard weights, measures is an offence under this act.
7. Use of fake weights and measures or elimination of the verification and stamping marks is offence under this act.
8. Sale or distribution of good by means of
9. Sale or distribution of goods by means of under standardized weights and measures is offence under this act.
10. Display of certificate of verification & stamping at prominent place is essential
11. Every package shall bear there on or a label securely affixed there to a declaration regarding manufacturer's packer's or importer's name, generic name of the product, number of content, net weight/measure, year and month of the manufacturing, packing or importing & sale price of the package i.e. maximum retail price (inclusive of all taxes). Sale of package commodity at higher price

than the declared price or elimination of such information or label on packing is offence under this act.

12. Manufacturer, packer or importers of the pre packed commodities are required to register as manufacturer, packer or importer.

The act is enforced by the ministry of consumer affairs, food and public distribution, government of India. The government of India is revising the various rules under the act from time to time.

## FRUIT PRODUCT ORDER (FPO)

- The Government of India promulgated a fruit products order in 1946. In 1955 the order was revised under the essential commodities act. This order is operated by the Food and nutrition board of the ministry of Food Processing industries.
- The Fruit Product Order (FPO) lays down statutory minimum standards in respect of the quality of various fruits and vegetable products and processing facilities at manufacture, storage and sale. The PFA and FPO are enforced by the Department of Health.
- The Agricultural marketing Advisor is authorized by taw to issue a license for manufacturing fruits and vegetable products, after due inspection of the factory for hygiene, sanitation and quality of formulation.
- Periodic inspection by Government inspectors in registered establishments is carried out to ensure conformity of standards by processors.
- Packaging fruits and vegetables of a standard below the minimum prescribed standards is an offence punishable by law.
- Manufacture of labelling of fruit and vegetable products can be carded out only after a valid license is issued by the licensing officer after himself satisfying with regard to the quality of product, sanitation, personnel, machinery and equipment, work area as required in the order.
- Licenser is empowered to put the FPO specification mark on the product.
- The labels on the final product are required by law to display the FPO license number. Fruit and vegetable products, not conforming to the FPO specifications are considered adulterated.
- The FPO specifications cover list of constituents, a method of presentation permissible colours in the preparation and also minimum quality requirement of the product. An expert committee known as the Central Food Product Advisory Committee deals with all matters relating to the FPO,
- The main objective of the PFA and FPO standard is to determine the minimum level of quality that can be attained, under the farming, manufacturing and retailing conditions in India.
- When qualities above the minimum are attained they are identified by other standards set up by the Government, through the Directorate of Marketing

Inspection, These cover definitions of quality for various agricultural products such as cereals, oils, butter: ghee, legumes etc.

- Depending on their quality the products are graded in four categories as ordinary, fair, good and special (4-1).
- The order lays down specifications and quality control requirements on production and marketing of the following food products.
- Fruit juice, pulp concentrate, squashes, cordials, crush, fruit syrups, nectar, aerated water containing fruit juice or pulp and read to serve beverages.
- Fruit nectar, canned mango pulp (natural and sweetened), and sweetened aerated beverages with no fruit juice or pulp or containing less than 10% fruit juice or pulp, jams and jellies, grape fruits etc.

Other than these specifications, the order also lays down specific requirements in regard to the following:

- Containers and labeling requirement
- Limits of poisonous metals in fruit products
- List of permissible harmless food colors
- Limits for permitted preservatives in fruit products
- Other permitted additives

## MILK AND MILK PRODUCTS ORDER (MMPO)

- The Milk and milk products order (MMPO) 1992 is exercised under the essential commodities Act and is regulated by the ministry of Agriculture through the department of Animal husbandry and Dairying and fisheries.
- According to this order, it is essential for a dairy plant to process more than 10,000 liters of milk per day or handle more than S00 tones of milk solids per annum.
- The production, collection, transportation, distribution and supply of milk and milk products are controlled by the Milk and Milk Products Order, 1992.
- The order sets sanitary requirements for dairies, machinery and premises and includes quality control, certification, packing. marking and labelling standards for milk and milk products. The standards specified in the order also apply to imported products.
- Every person the business of handling, processing or manufacturing milk or milk products should provide proper labelling based on the certification by a certified officer.

The label on the package of milk or milk products should contain -

(a) The name, trade name or description of the article contained in the package

(b) The name and business address the holder of registration certificate and number

(c) The net weight or number or volume of contents as may be the case

(d) The batch or code number, except in case of package less than 60g or 60ml.

(e) The day. month and year of manufacture of the packing milk and month and year of manufacture for packing of milk products

(f) The date of manufacture for packages containing sterilized milk and infant milk food

A holder of registration shall not pack milk or milk products other than those processed or manufactured by him or, those obtained from any other person holding registration certificate.

General conditions of sanitary and hygiene for dairy establishments: Every dairy establishment have the following:

- Facilities for hygienic handling and protection of non-packed raw material
- Appropriate protection from pests, rodents, insects and other vermin. They shall be systematically destroyed continuously
- Instruments and working equipment intended to come in direct contact with raw material will be made water tight and noncorrosive as they are intended for human consumption
- Appropriate facilities for cleaning and disinfecting of equipment and instruments especially cleaning in place (CIP) system
- An adequate waste disposal system which is hygienic and approved by the Pollution Control Board
- Supply of potable water or non-portable water is permitted if does not Indirectly risk contamination of the dairy products
- Appropriate number of changing rooms with smooth, waterproof, washable walls and floor
- Lockable room or secure place for storage of detergents, disinfectants and similar substances
- Room with adequate capacity for storing raw materials and dairy products.
- Working area should be maintained hygienically

The Meat Food Product Order

- Regulation for the production of meat products are covered by the Meat Food Product Order 1973.
- The Directorate of Marketing and Inspection at the Ministry of Agriculture is the regulatory for the order.
- The order deals with hygiene and sanitation requirements, packing and labeling provisions, permissible quantity of additives etc.

There are four stages of inspections:

1) Ante-mortem inspection of the animal before slaughter
2) Post-mortem inspection of the animal after slaughter
3) In-process inspection of meat, hygiene and sanitation of the work place
4) Sampling and analysis of meat products in the laboratory.

## CODEX ALIMENTARIUS COMMISSION

- Codex Alimentarius Commission was established in 1962. The Codex Alimentarius which means: 'Food law' or "Food code" In Latin. The Codex Alimentarius Commission develops food standards, guidelines and related texts such as codes of practice under the joint FAO/WHO food standards program. it is also called Codex harmonized international standards due to involvement of both FAO( Food and Agriculture Organization) and WHO (World Health Organization).
- The dual objectives of the Codex Alimentarius commission are to protect the health of consumers and to facilitate the international trade.
- It brings all together at the interested parties like scientists, technical experts, governments, consumers and industry representatives to help develop standards for food manufacturing and trade.
- These standard guidelines and recommendations are recognized worldwide for their vital role in protecting the consumers and facilitating international trade.
- The codex contract point in India Is the Directorate General of Health Services (DGHS) In the ministry of Heath; however the m try of food process industries is closely associated with the activities of Codex Alimentarius.

## SALIENT FEATURES OF CODEX ALIMENTARIUS:

- Protecting health of the consumers and ensuring fair trade practices
- Promoting coordination of all food standards work undertaken by international governmental and non- governmental organizations
- Determining priorities and initiating and guides the preparation of draft standards
- Finalizing the standards
- Amending published standards.
- Submission of proposal for a standard
- A decision by the commission or the executive committee
- Preparation of a proposed draft standard by subsidiary body
- Adoption of standard by the commission
- Addition of CODEX STANDARD in the Codex Alimentarius.

The codex secretariat is located at Rome and is financed jointly by the FAO and the WHO. At present there are 170 countries, Including India as Codex members and this covers 98 percent of the world's population. The codex commission meets every two years either in Rome or in Geneva.

Codex can be divided into three main groups

1. The commodity standards committee work vertically dealing with food products such as processed fruits and Vegetables, fats and oil, fresh fruit and vegetables, natural mineral water, cocoa products and chocolates, h and fishery products, sugar, milk, products, cereal and meat produces.
2. The general subject committees work horizontally on standards such veterinary drug residues, food additives and contaminants; pesticide residues, hygiene, labeling, Inspection and ration systems, analysis and sampling, nutrition and foods for special dietary uses.
3. The six regional coordinating committees are based In Africa, Asia, Europe, Latin, America, and Caribbean, North America and South West Pacific and the near East.

Codex decisions are not binding on its members not has any format legal statues, prior to the signing of the General Agreement on Tariff and trade, GATT In December 1894. Foods everywhere will ultimately be Influenced by codex. In many different dimensions- In safety standards, food additives, pesticide uses, labeling of pre-packed foods, international trade, competition and pricing be the food locally grown or imported from the other side of the world.

## ISO OR INTERNATIONAL ORGANIZATION FOR STANDARDS

Following facts need to be kept in mind about ISO or International Organisation for Standards:

- It was established on 23rd February 1947.
- It is responsible for setting international standards.
- It has official body who are representatives of various national standards organizations
- It promotes industrial and commercial standards all over the world.
- It has presence in 163 countries
- It is an independent, non-governmental organization
- It is the world's largest developer of international standards
- It provides common standards for various nations
- It has so set standards for more than twenty five thousand products which includes almost everything form manufactured products to healthcare, food safety, agriculture etc.
- ISO is not an acronym. The organization adopted the name ISO, which is derived from Greek word Isos, meaning Equal. This is because the name will

differ in different languages e.g. IOS in English or OIN in French etc. So, in all countries and in all language the short form of the name will be ISO.

## IMPORTANCE OF ISO:

1) It helps in setting standards for products/services that are safe, reliable and of good quality.
2) It helps in increasing productivity of an organization as the guidelines of standard minimize wastage and faulty products/services.
3) It helps in comparing products/services from different countries with the prescribed standards.
4) It helps in establishing fair trade practices
5) It helps manufacturers/service-providers to explore and venture into new markets.
6) It helps the consumers by providing safe, reliable standard products/services

which conform to the minimum international standards.

## WTO OR WORLD TRADE ORGANIZATION

WTO or World Trade Organization is an intergovernmental organization which controls global business. The WTO started on 1st January, 1995.

Following facts need to remembered about WTO:

- It is an intergovernmental organization
- It controls global business
- It started on 1st January 1995
- 123 nations are officially attached
- It is the largest global economic organization.

Following are some of the most important functions of WTO:

- It executes all the decisions as per agreements
- It provides a platform for negotiations amongst the member nations
- It helps in settling disputes
- It formulates national trade policies
- It helps in maintaining transparency in trade policies
- It provides technical cooperation and training to the member countries whenever needed.

The WTO agreement has an effect on the various food business such as Marine Product Processing Industry, Beverage Processing Industry, Meat Processing Industry, Dairy Processing Industry, Cereal-based Consumer Food Industry, Fruit and Vegetable Processing Industry and other key processing industries.

The WTO agreement which affect the Food Processing Industry are-

Agreement On Agriculture or AOA, Trade Related Investment Measures or RTIMs, Agreement on Technical Barriers to Trade or TBT etc.

## CONSUMER PROTECTION ACT

Following points need to be kept in mind about Consumer Protection Act:

- The Consumer Protection Act of the Parliament of India was enacted in1986.
- The act protects the interest of the consumers in India.
- The act helps the consumers a simpler and quicker redress of their grievances.
- It protects the consumers from deficiencies and defects in product/goods/services.
- It protects consumers from unfair trade practices.
- The consumer forum helps both producer and consumers from long process of litigations. Through 'informal adjudication', the consumer forum members bring both the parties to a common table and help to reach a compromise.
- The act is applicable to private, public and cooperative sectors.
- The act provides machinery (every district has at least one redress forum which is also called as Consumer Court) where the consumers can lodge their complaints. It helps consumer save huge court fees also.

However, one must remember that the consumer court files complaints only if the goods/services were intended for personal use and not for commercial use.

The basic rights of consumers are-

- Right to be safeguarded from hazardous goods and services.
- Right to know the weight/volume, price, ingredients, quality, quantity etc, of the goods/services.
- Right to consumer education
- Right to consumer grievance redressal.

## DEFINITIONS

- "Adulterant" means any material which is or could be employed for the purposes of adulteration.
- "Adulteration" it includes intentional addition, substitution or abstraction or substances which adversely affect the purity and quality of foods incidental contamination of foods with deleterious substance such as toxins and insecticides due to ignorance, negligence or lack of proper storage facilities.contamination of the foods with harmful insects, micro organism like bacteria, fungus, moulds etc during production, storage and handling.

- "Consumer" means persons and families purchasing and receiving food in order to meet their personal needs.
- "Contaminant" means any substance, not intentionally added to food, which is present in such food as a result of the production (including operations carried out in crop husbandry or veterinary medicine), manufacture, processing, preparation, treatment, packing, packaging, transport or handling such foods or as a result of environmental contamination, but does not include insect fragments, rodent hair and other extraneous matter.
- "Enforcement authority" means an authority prescribed by the act, rules, and regulation for the purpose of enforcement of this act.
- "Enforcement officer" means the officer by whom they are to be enforced and executed and includes food inspector and the state commissioner of food safety and authorised officer of the food authority.
- "Food authority" means any substances which is added to food for a technological purpose in the manufacture, processing, preparation or treatment of such food affects the characteristics of such foods, but does not include contaminants.
- "Food" (or "foodstuff") means any substance or product, whether processed, partially processed or unprocessed, consumed by humans and includes, drinking water, chewing gum and beverages.
- "Food authority" means the food safety and standards authority of India under section 4.
- "Food hygiene" means all the condition and measures necessary for the manufacture, processing, sale, storage and distribution of food designed to ensure safe and wholesome food for human consumption.
- "Food inspector" means an officer authorised by the state commissioner for food safety to enforce and execute rules and regulation, order and any other provision of this act relating to manufacture, distribution, sales of articles of food.
- "Food law" means the law acts, order, rules, regulation, notification and order governing food at every stage of its production, processing and distribution.
- "Food laboratory" means any laboratory or institute established by the central or the state governments or any other agency and accredited by national accreditation board for testing and calibration of testing laboratories (NABL) and recognised by food authority.
- "Genetically modified food" or GMF means the food, which is produced through techniques in which the genetic material has been altered.
- "Hazard "means a biological, chemical or physical agent in food with the potential to cause an adverse effect on the health of consumer.
- "Ingredient" means any substance, including a food additive used in a manufacture or preparation of food and present in the final product although in a modified form.

- "Irradiation" means any physical procedure, involving the intentional exposure of food to ionizing radiation.
- "Label" means any tag brand mark pictorial or other descriptive matter or display.

## IMPORTANT QUESTIONS:

Q.1. Briefly explain the following:

a) PFA

b) FPO

c) MPO

d) ISO

e) WTO

Q.2. Explain Consumer Protection Act.

Chapter 36

# Hygiene and Sanitation in Food Sector

## GENERAL PRINCIPLES OF FOOD HYGIENE

Food hygiene may be defined as all conditions and measures necessary to ensure the safety and suitability of food at all the stages of the food chain.

## CODEX GENERAL PRINCIPLES OF FOOD HYGIENE

### Primary production

a) Managing primary production in a way that ensures that food is safe and suitable for its intended use.

b) Reduction of likelihood of introducing a hazard which may adversely affect the safety of food, or its suitability for consumption, at later stages of food chain.

### Establishment: design and facilities

a) Premises, equipment and facilities should be located, designed and constructed according to the nature of operations and associated risks.

b) Control of hazards through good hygiene design and construction, appropriate location and provision of adequate facilities.

### Control of Operation

a) Production of food which is safe and suitable for human consumption.

b) Reduction of risk of unsafe food by taking preventive measures to assure the safety and suitability of food at an appropriate stage in the operation by controlling food hazards.

### Establishment: maintenance and sanitation

a) Establishment of effective systems

b) Facilitation of continuing effective control of food hazards, pests, and other agents likely to contaminate food.

### Establishment: Personal hygiene

a) Reduction of food contamination by people with direct or indirect contact with food.

b) Food contamination and illness transmission by people who do not maintain an appropriate degree of personal cleanliness, who have certain illness or conditions or who behave inappropriately.

### Transportation

a) Taking of necessary measures to prevent food contamination, damage and growth of pathogens.

b) Effective control measures during transport prevent food contamination and assure that the food reaches its destination in suitable condition for consumption.

### Production information and consumer awareness

a) Products should bear appropriate information.

b) Consumers should have enough knowledge to make informed choices.

c) Avoidance of mishandling of product at later stages in the food chain.

Training

a) Those engaged in food operations should be trained in food hygiene.

b) Training is fundamental in any food hygiene system.

c) Inadequate trained personnel poses a potential threat to the safety of food and its suitability for consumption.

### Codex General Principles of Food Hygiene Objectives

- Identifies principles of food hygiene applicable throughout the food chain.
- Recommends a HACCP -based approach to ensuring food safety.
- Provides Guidance on how to implement hygiene principles.
- Establishes a framework for specific hygiene codes.

HACCP may be defined as a system which identifies evaluates and controls hazards which are significant for food safety.

Food safety may be defined as an assurance that food will not cause harm to the consumer when it is prepared and/or eaten according to its intended use.

Food suitability may be defined as an assurance that food is acceptable for human consumption according to its intended use.

GHP or Good Hygiene Practices for Commodities, Equipments, Work Areas and Personnel

Good Hygiene Practices are the set of requirements to prevent contamination of food in order to provide safe food to the consumers. It refers to post harvest handling of produce to minimize contamination.

Contaminants are identified as being

- **Biological**: Biological contaminants include bacteria, viruses or parasites that are present in air, food, water, soil, animals or humans
- **Physical**: Physical contaminants include pebbles, stones, metal, glass, wood, insects, soil, dirt, jewelry, hair, fingernails etc. These contaminate the foods due to poor handling practices.
- **Chemical**: Chemical contaminants include chemicals used for cleaning and sanitizing food contact surfaces, pest control chemicals, paints and water treatment chemicals, pesticides, fertilizers, fungicides and also a group of some naturally occurring harmful chemicals like Mycotoxins.

A GHP food safety program reduces the risk of microbial contamination that can cause consumer illness from consumption of fresh fruits and vegetables

GHP is described and defined by the Codex Alimentarius Code of Principles of Food Hygiene. GHP regulations address issues related to

- public hygiene,
- verification and control of equipments and
- record-keeping,
- staff training

GHP food audits cover such areas of attention as:

- Food handling practices.
- Employee hygiene practices.
- Sanitation facilities.
- Pest control.
- Prevention of physical and chemical hazards.

Food Business Operators should apply the hygienic practices in order to:

- Ensure that food is safe and suitable for consumption; -
- To ensure that consumers have clear and easily understandable information, through labelling and other appropriate means,
- to enable them to protect their food from contamination and growth or survival of pathogens to create in food by storage, processing and preparation in an appropriate manner;

- Have confidence in food trading.

GHP for commodities, equipments, work area and personnel:

- Lot and batch identification on food packaging must be as per Codex standard and FSSA rules.
- Product information must bear adequate information to enable the next person in the food chain to handle, display, store prepare and use the product safely and correctly
- Labelling must be as per Food Safety & Standards Regulations, 2011.
- Labelling instructions must be adequate and informative about the nutrition value for consumer to make safe and healthy choices.

## GHP for Commodities

- All the fruits and vegetables must be cleaned in treated water to free them from soil, dust, pesticides etc.
- The raw commodities must be kept away from the cooked food items.
- While cleaning the commodities ensure to change the water. Otherwise the water will get contaminated and pass on the microbes from one to another commodities.
- The commodities must be of good quality. Sub-standard commodities must be discarded.
- Check the date of manufacturing, date of expiry etc. before use.
- Personnel should always wash the hands before preparing food. Washing hands is one of the best ways to prevent the spread of bacteria.

## GHP for personnel

- There must be adequate hand washing facilities. The staff must be trained to wash hands frequently.
- One must take bath twice a day-before the duty and after the duty hours.
- One must cut the nails short at all times.
- Staff suffering from any infectious diseases must not be allowed to come on duty.
- Eyes, teeth, mouth, foot and foot wear must be kept clean at all times. One must brush his teeth regularly before coming on duty.
- All staff should carry clean clothes when working with food. They must dress clean protective clothes before starting work and not to carry these clothes out of the food preparation area. Clothes are a source of contamination with bacteria in food preparation areas. Wearing of clean clothes helps in preventing it.
- Work clothes or uniforms should be long sleeve and have such colour to see stains.

- Recommended that staff carry duster or a clean cloth particularly when working with meat and eggs.
- Staff should keep hair tied back and take a cap or hair net when preparing food. If hair are not covered or tied back, most likely that they fall in food and that he / she can touch them by hands.
- Staff should not wear watch or jewelry when preparing food. These can collect and spread harmful bacteria.
- Activities such as smoking, chew the gum are prohibited in the work areas.
- After touching the face or nose, and coughing or sneezing, one must clean their hands. While coughing or sneezing one must cover his mouth with a handkerchief.
- Staff must be encouraged to take enough rest, exercise, recreation and balanced meals. Daily exercise and balanced diet is essential for good health.

## GHP for Equipments

- Effective cleaning is essential to eliminate harmful bacteria and to prevent them from being introduced into food.
- Follow the manufacturer's instructions on how to use cleaning chemicals. It is important to ensure that chemicals have been removed thoroughly before use.
- Ensure rinse, clean and rinse method.
- Clean work surfaces and equipment thoroughly between tasks.
- Wash and disinfect them after each preparation of raw meat or eggs. This helps prevent contamination and spreading of bacteria to other foods of the area or device.
- Regularly wash / wipe and disinfecting of all tools which often affect people, such as surfaces, sink, water taps, door handles, switch at the end of each day. It is important to keep these clean to prevent contamination and spread bacteria.
- Wash and disinfecting refrigerators should be done when there is not much food inside.
- Transfer food to another freezer or in a cold and safe place and keep it covered.
- Pay special attention to the frequency of cleaning of equipment parts or moving parts. Disassemble all the parts, scrap to free from food, rinse, clean and rinse again.
- Wash dishes, dishwasher parts, tools and parts disassemble if possible. If dishwasher is not available then, wash dishes, tools, etc. in hot soapy water.
- Remove the oil and any pieces of leftover food. Then enter them in the water that is clean and very hot. Wipe clean with any clean and dry cloth.

- Drying is essential to prevent rusting, electric shock and growth of microorganisms.
- The Dishwasher washes items completely in a very high temperature so this is the best way to clean tools and destroy bacteria (disinfection).

## GHP for Work Area

- All the work surfaces whether made of aluminum, wood or fiber must be cleaned thoroughly before and after use.
- The chopping boards must be cleaned before and after use. Colour codes for chopping boards should be used for meat, fish, vegetables etc.
- The floors must be cleaned with cleaning agents at regular intervals. Spot cleaning should be done as and when necessary. Floors in the busy areas must be scrubbed with hot water and detergent every day. The central kitchen, pantry, dining halls, toilets etc. are busy areas.
- Drains should be cleaned regularly to avoid stagnant water and blockage.
- Shelves, cupboards and windows should be dusted regularly. The shelves and cupboards must be emptied and thoroughly cleaned at least once a week.
- All furniture must be dusted and cleaned daily.
- The dust bins must be cleared at regular intervals. Dust bins must be emptied as and necessary.
- The walls must be kept clean at all times in the food preparation areas.
- Special care should be taken to clean the ceilings of the kitchen.
- Pest control measures must be carried out in and around the premises regularly. This will ensure that the food preparation area is free from pests, insects etc.
- Special care must be taken for the disposal of waste water and waste disposal.
- It is the responsibility of the food business operator to train and educate the staff for good hygiene practices so that the hygiene is taken as of prime importance. Every staff should be made responsible for utmost practice of hygiene and cleanliness in the work areas.
- The staff toilets must be well maintained and kept clean at all time. There should be adequate facilities for cleaning hands for the staff.

All consumers have the right to expect safe, hygienically prepared and good quality food. This is the reason that the handling of food requires care to prevent the hazards. Food borne illnesses can result from contamination due to improper practices like when there is

- Lack of environmental hygiene and poor sanitation
- Mixed and inappropriate transportation
- Poor storage

- Poor personal hygiene,
- Unsafe source of food

Food safety includes food handling, food preparation, food storage & food distribution according to the standardized procedures and guidelines as stated in compliance to Food Safety and Standards Regulations. It shall also be deemed to be the responsibility of the food business operator to ensure adherence to necessary requirements. Besides the steps outlined here, FBO or Food Business Operator must identify activities and take necessary steps to ensure food safety and also make sure that safety procedures are identified, implemented, maintained and reviewed periodically.

## CLEANING AND DISINFECTION

In food sectors, cleaning may be defined as a process by which food soil is removed by using right detergent chemical under recommended conditions. The cleaning staff should have the knowledge of different types of food soils and how to remove these. The right way of cleaning and disinfecting of food products contact surfaces is rinse, clean, rinse and sanitize.

## CLEANING METHODS:

There are mainly three types of cleaning methods used in the food sectors and various equipments can be classified according to the cleaning methods used for them.

- **Mechanical Cleaning Method**: Mechanical cleaning is also called 'clean in place' or CIP method. Mechanical Dishwashing is an example of mechanical cleaning method. Mechanical dishwashing method is used for cleaning and sanitizing of all types of plates, saucers, glasses, cutleries etc. detergents are mixed with hot water to make the cleaning effective. Dishwashing machines are available in two types i.e. Conveyor machines and stationary machines. This method needs no disassembly. The pipelines in milk plants are permanently fixed and need to be cleaned in place. Hot water is mixed with detergents and passed through the pipes, rinsed and then sanitized.
- **Clean Out of Place method or COP Method**: 'Cleaning out of place' method, as the name suggests , is a method of cleaning equipments by removing them from the area of operation and taking them to a designated cleaning station for cleaning purposes. Therefore, in this case, the apparatus need to be dismantled, take them to the central washing station by using an automated system ansd then reassemble.
- **Immersion Cleaning**: in this method of cleaning, the parts to be cleaned are immersed in the cleaning solution. It reduces the cycle time, reduces the detergent usage and also minimizes the water usage. it is a comparatively slow process though agitation of the solution will enhance cleaning quality as well as reduce the time.
- **Manual Cleaning Method**: Manual cleaning depends on the expertise of the people involved in the cleaning process. The two factors that increases or

decreases the effectiveness of the manual cleaning method are the concentration of detergent and the temperature of the washing solution.

To sterilize means to destroy and remove all living organisms.

To Disinfect means to inanimate objects and to destroy all the vegetative cells (not spores).

To Sanitize means to minimize microbes to levels that is safe from a public health viewpoint. The official definition (Association of Official Analytical Chemists) of sanitizing for food product contact surfaces is a process which reduces the contamination level by 99.999% (5 logs) in 30 sec. General types of sanitization include the following:

- Thermal Sanitization: This involves the use of hot water or steam for a specified temperature and contact time.
- Chemical Sanitization: This involves the use of an approved chemical sanitizer at a specified concentration and contact time.

## CLEANING AGENTS

Cleaning Agents may be defined as the substances used to get rid of dust, stains, foul smells and soils on surfaces. The cleaning agents may be liquids, powders, sprays or granules.

The purposes of using cleaning agents are-

- To improve safety and health
- To improve beauty
- To remove bad odour
- To prevent contamination and sterilize.

Common Cleaning Agents used in the hospitality industry are-

- Water is the cheapest, best and most commonly used cleaning agent. The advantage of the water is that it is a good solvent.
- Detergents
- Soaps
- Ammonia
- Citric acid
- Acetic acid
- Sodium Hypochlorite and Sodium Hydroxide
- Baking soda or Sodium bi-carbonate
- Tetrachloroethylene
- Chromic acid

- Salt water soap
- Acetone
- Xylene

## DISINFECTANTS

Disinfectants may be defined as antimicrobial agents which are used on the non-living objects to kill the flora of microorganisms living on the surface of the object. It is less effective than the sanitizers as it does not kill the spore-forming bacteria. Whereas, a sanitizer will destroy all types of bacteria. Therefore, sanitisers kill as well as disinfects. The disinfectant destroys the cell-walls of microorganisms or disrupts their metabolism process. In hospitality industries the disinfectants are mostly used in the kitchens and toilets.

### Properties of a good Disinfectant:

- It should give total microbe-free sterilization
- Should be non-toxic in nature
- Should be inexpensive
- Should not be corrosive to the objects
- Should have a good smell
- Should be easily available

### Types of Disinfectants

- Air Disinfectants: Air disinfectants may be defined as chemical substances that destroy the microbes suspended in the air. An air disinfectant spreads either as a vapour or as an aerosol in the air and kills infectious pathogens and improves the air quality. Various Glycols are good air disinfectants as they have low mammalian toxicity yet powerful antimicrobial.
- Alcohols: Alcohols and alcohol plus compounds are effective disinfectants. A mixture of ethanol and water or Isopropanol and water in 7:3 ratio can kill wide range of microorganisms. A mixture of 80% ethanol and 5% Isopropanol can inactivate Hepatitis C, Hepatitis B and HIV virus.
- Aldehydes: Aldehydes such as Formaldehydes can destroy a wide range of microbes. They are effective against fungi and spore-forming bacteria also.
- Oxidizing Agents: Chlorine and Oxygen are capable of oxidizing the cell membrane of the microbes thus lead to their death.
- Sodium hypochlorite is commonly used in drains and toilets as disinfectants. Calcium hypochlorite is used in swimming pool water for disinfection.
- Chloramines is very commonly used for drinking water treatment. Chlorine di-oxide is used in drinking water to prevent water borne diseases.

- Hydrogen Peroxide is a powerful disinfectant and is used to disinfect surfaces. Hydrogen peroxide vapour is used as air disinfectant.
- Iodine, Peracetic acid, KMNO4 are commonly used disinfectants.
- Phenolics: Phenolics are common disinfectants are widely used in handwashes, soaps, mouthwashes etc.

## SAFETY ASPECTS OF PROCESSING WATER

### Drinking Water Quality Standards

Drinking water may be defined as water required for the consumption of the mankind for the purposes of drinking and cooking from any source.

Drinking water quality standards refers to the quality parameters of water that is fit for human consumption for drinking. However there is no parameter for drinking water which is accepted by all the countries. Most of the developed countries have set their own standards applicable to a particular country. In Europe, the standard is set by European Drinking Water Directive or EDWD. In USA, this standard is established by United States Environmental Protection Agency or EPA under the Safe Drinking Water Act. The World Health Organization has published guidelines for drinking water, which is followed by the countries which do not have any legislative or administrative authority to set water quality standards.

In 1981, United Nations declared an International Drinking Water Supply and Sanitation decade. This declaration was made due to the report prepared by WHO and World Bank which stated that more than 1230 million people across the globe were dependant on unsafe drinking water supplies.

In 1983, BIS or Bureau of Indian Standards published the standard for drinking water in India. This was revised and specification of drinking water was taken from-

- EU Directives for the quality of drinking water for the human consumption
- EPA of US
- WHO Guidelines for Drinking Water Quality (GDWQ)
- Manual on Water Supply and Treatment, Ministry for Urban Developments, Delhi.

According to the BIS:

1) Undesirable Substances: Aluminum maximum 0.03mg/l, Barium maximum 0.7mg/l, Boron 0.5mg/l, Ammonia 0.5mg/l, Chloramine max. 4.0mg/l, Copper max 0.05mg/l, Fluoride max 1.0mg/l.
2) Toxic Substances: Cadmium max 0.003mg/l, Cyanide max 0.05mg/l, Lead max 0.01mg/l, Mercury max 0.001mg/l, Nickel max 0.02mg/l
3) Radioactive Substances: Alpha emitters max 0.01Bq/l, Beta emitters max 1.0Bq/l
4) Pesticide Residues: Pesticide Residues such as Atrazine, Aldrin/Dieldrin, Beta HCH Delta HCH etc. in water is on the rise. Limits and test methods are specified in the guidelines.

5) Microbial quality standards:

   a) No E. coli or Thermotolerant coliform bacteria should be found in 100ml of water sample meant for drinking of the humans.

   b) No E. coli or Thermotolerant coliform bacteria should be found in 100ml of water entering the distribution system.

   c) No E. coli or Thermotolerant coliform bacteria should be found in 100ml of treated water sample in the distribution system.

## WASTE WATER DISPOSAL

Waste Water may be defined as water that got un-hygienically affected, has poor quality and anthropogenic influence. Waste water in the hotels can be originated from kitchen, laundry, dish washing areas, bathrooms, sanitary sewers etc. The waste water is contaminated with human excreta, urine, solid waste and storm water. Sewage is a term that is used for any type of waste water. Sewerage is a term that is used to describe the physical infrastructure that carries sewage from its point of to the treatment plant or disposal. The waste water may be treated in an on-site waste water treatment plant. The treated water may be reused. The waste water carries heavy metals, gases, toxins, soluble organic particles, pathogens etc. There are various processes that can used to treat the waste water and the process adopted depends on the type and extent of pollutions. Waste water is treated in waste water treatment plants which includes chemical, biological and physical processes.

Sewage water should be disposed off in a public sewage system. The hotel must check up what is the approved way of disposing waste water from the local health authority. The hotels must ensure the following factors while disposing of the waste water:

- The waste water must be disposed of in a manner as approved by the local health authority.
- The waste water should not come in contact with raw or cooked food, utensils, work surface, equipments, treated water etc.
- The waste water should not come in contact with the drinking water inlets or reservoirs.
- There should not be pests, insects and rodents around the sewerage system.
- Wherever possible, the sewerage system should be built under ground.
- During outdoor catering operations, the manager must take special care about proper disposal of waste water.
- There should not be stagnation of waste water.
- There should not be leakages or breakages of waste water pipes.
- Sewerage water, if not disposed through underground to a public sewage system, then must be treated in a septic tank.

If the treated water is safe and free from pathogens, it may be reused wherever safe. It may be used for cooling towers or for wetlands, toilet flush and irrigation etc. The WHO has issued guidelines for safe use of waste water.

## WASTE DISPOSAL

Waste Disposal may be defined as a suitable and safe action needed to manage wastes from its point of origin till final disposal. This action in a hotel will typically include proper collection, safe transport and treatment and finally disposed/recycled as per the guidelines of regulatory authority.

In the hotels the solid wastes are thrown in the garbage bins. These bins should be cleaned, rinsed and disinfected after they are emptied. The wastes must be disposed in a manner that it does not pose a problem to health, environment and beauty. The refuse is collected in big plastic bags. After the collection, the garbage is disposed in the following manners; -

- Dumping: The solid wastes are dumped in the designated dumping ground. These are generally dumped in the low-lying grounds. It should be far away from the dwelling places as it pollutes the air and gets infested by pests.
- Burial: The dry waste is safely buried under the ground.
- Incineration: Dry garbage, harmful chemicals, rotten linen etc. are burnt in a safe place.
- Composting: Vegetable waste, dry plants, garbage etc. are used for composting. The manure such made is used in the gardens.
- Mechanical Disposer: Mechanical disposers are used for soft food wastes, cans, cartons etc. mechanical Disposer are of two types such as disintegrators and mechanical compactors. This is the safest, easiest and fastest way of waste disposal. It reduces the volume of the waste by one fifth.
- Vermiculture: Vermiculture may be defined as the cultivation of earthworms in order to use these earthworms to transform organic waste into fertilizer. The sewage and food waste is used for these purposes. The waste is used for rearing the earthworms. The excreta of earthworms is called Vermicompost.
- Recycling: Recyclable materials are glass, papers, cardboards, plastics, textiles etc. these are separated from other waste materials. Recycling is a process of converting waste materials into new usable items and objects. It is an alternative to conventional waste disposal.
- Biogas: Biogas refers to a mixture of different gases produced by the breakdown of sewage, vegetable waste, food waste etc. in the absence of oxygen. The advantages of biogas is that it is a non-polluting and renewable source of energy. It produces organic manure, a healthy process and lowers the greenhouse effect.
- Soak pits/Soak away/Leach pit: This is a covered, porous-walled chamber that allows the waste water for bathrooms, kitchen and wash up area to gradually soak into the ground.

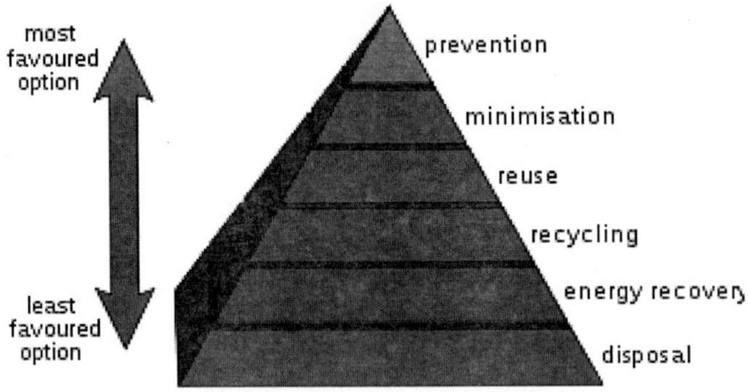


**Diagram (source Wikipedia): Principle of the waste hierarchy (refers to the "3 Rs" i.e. Reduce, Reuse, Recycle).**

## KEY TERMS

- Food Hygiene: Food hygiene may be defined as all conditions and measures necessary to ensure the safety and suitability of food at all the stages of the food chain.
- HACCP: HACCP may be defined as a system which identifies evaluates and controls hazards which are significant for food safety.
- Food Safety: Food safety may be defined as an assurance that food will not cause harm to the consumer when it is prepared and/or eaten according to its intended use.
- Food Suitability: Food suitability may be defined as an assurance that food is acceptable for human consumption according to its intended use.
- Good Hygiene Practices: Good Hygiene Practices are the set of requirements to prevent contamination of food in order to provide safe food to the consumers. It refers to post harvest handling of produce to minimize contamination.
- Cleaning: - In food sectors, cleaning may be defined as a process by which food soil is removed by using right detergent chemical under recommended conditions. The cleaning staff should have the knowledge of different types of food soils and how to remove these. The right way of cleaning and disinfecting of food products contact surfaces is rinse, clean, rinse and sanitize.
- Sterilize: To sterilize means to destroy and remove all living organisms.
- Disinfect: To Disinfect means to inanimate objects and to destroy all the vegetative cells (not spores).
- Sanitize: To Sanitize means to minimize microbes to levels that is safe from a public health viewpoint. The official definition (Association of Official Analytical Chemists) of sanitizing for food product contact surfaces is a process which reduces the contamination level by 99.999% (5 logs) in 30 sec. General types of sanitization include the following.

- Cleaning Agent: Cleaning Agents may be defined as the substances used to get rid of dust, stains, foul smells and soils on surfaces. The cleaning agents may be liquids, powders, sprays or granules.
- Disinfectant: Disinfectants may be defined as antimicrobial agents which are used on the non-living objects to kill the flora of microorganisms living on the surface of the object. It is less effective than the sanitizers as it does not kill the spore-forming bacteria. But a sanitizer will destroy all types of bacteria. Therefore, sanitisers kill as well as disinfects. The disinfectant destroys the cell-walls of microorganisms or disrupts their metabolism process. In hospitality industries the disinfectants are mostly used in the kitchens and toilets.
- Drinking water: Drinking water may be defined as water required for the consumption of the mankind for the purposes of drinking and cooking from any source.
- BIS: BIS or Bureau of Indian Standards
- Waste Water: Waste Water may be defined as water that got un-hygienically affected, has poor quality and anthropogenic influence.
- Waste Disposal: Waste Disposal may be defined as a suitable and safe action needed to manage wastes from its point of origin till final disposal. This action in a hotel will typically include proper collection, safe transport and treatment and finally disposed/recycled as per the guidelines of regulatory authority.

## IMPORTANT QUESTIONS:

Q.1. What do you understand by general principles of Food Hygiene?

Q.2. Explain the GHP for commodities and personnel.

Q.3. What are the cleaning methods used in the hospitality industry? Name some common cleaning agents.

Q.4. Write short notes on any two:

a) Waste water disposal

b) Waste disposal

c) Water quality standard

Chapter 37

# Recent Concerns

After reading this chapter the student will be able to; -

- Learn about Emerging pathogens
- Know about genetically modified foods
- Understand food labelling
- Learn newer trends in food packaging and technology
- *Explain BSE*

## EMERGING PATHOGENS

An emerging pathogen may be defined as the microbes of an infectious disease, the incidence of such infectious disease had increased for the last two decades or threaten to increase in future in a new or existing host population.

The examples of emerging pathogens are:

- *E. coli* O 157.H7,
- Hantavirus,
- HIV/AIDS,
- Severe Acute Respiratory syndrome (SARS),
- Cryptosporidiosis,
- MRSA
- H1N1 Influenza

WHO or World Health Organization had published a list of top five to ten emerging pathogens which can cause severe outbreak of epidemic in the near future. These are:

- Crimean Congo Haemorrhagic Fever
- Ebola virus
- Marburg

- Lassa fever
- MERS
- SARS
- Nipah and
- Rift Valley fever

The WHO has prepared blueprint for research and development of countermeasure for these diseases. There are other diseases which pose tremendous are risks Chickungunya, Zika, Tuberculosis etc.

The factors which contribute to the emergence of pathogens are:

- Climate change
- Unmindful deforestation
- Shift in food preparation styles
- Change in food distribution practices, globalization of food supply which transfers microorganisms.
- Increased travelling to different countries
- Change in food habits
- Genetic changes in pathogenic microorganisms

The emerging food borne diseases are:

- Hepatitis (by Hepatitis E virus)
- Intestinal Spirochetosis (by Brachyspira P)
- Gnathostomiasis (by Nematodes)

Possible ways to prevent these diseases:

- Educating the masses about emerging pathogens
- Changes in food production
- Proper handling and following GHP from farm to fork
- Intensive R & D in counter measures

## GENETICALLY MODIFIED FOODS

According to the World Health Organisation, "Genetically modified organisms or GMOs can be defined as organisms ( i.e. plants, animals or microorganisms) in which the genetic material (DNA) has been altered in a way that does not occur naturally by mating and/or natural recombination. The technology is often called 'modern biotechnology' or 'gene technology', sometimes also 'recombined DNA technology' or 'genetic technology'. Foods produced from or by using GM organisms are often refered to as GM foods or Genetically Modified Foods or GM Foods or Genetically Engineered Foods or Bio-engineered Foods. These are the foods produced from organisms that have had changes introduced into their DNA using the methods of genetic engineering.

**Advantages of GM foods are:**

- It gives better taste
- It has better nutrition and quality
- Higher revenue earning for the farmers
- It is virus and insect resistant
- It has herbicide tolerance
- It provides a solution to world hunger through higher productivity.

However GM food consumption may pose some health risks as has been identified through animal studies. These risks are:

- Infertility
- Early aging symptoms
- Weaker immune system
- Functional alteration of liver, kidney, gut and spleen
- Altered genes associated with cholesterol synthesis, insulin regulation, protein formation etc.
- There are many unknown facts about long-term effects of GM crops.

Some of the Genetically Modified Foods are:

- Papaya was genetically modified to resist the Ringspot virus
- Corn used for food and for ethyl alcohol has been genetically modified to resist Herbicides and to destroy certain insects. It is widely used for corn chips, Tortillas, Taco shells etc.
- Soybeans have been genetically modified to resist Herbicides and produce healthier oils.
- Some derivative products such as Starch sugars, lecithin etc.
- Genetically modified beetroots and sugarcanes are used to extract sugar
- Cooking oils, vegetable oils, corn oils, canola etc. is directly sold to consumers and are used to prepare foods.
- Animal feeds are produced from GM crops.
- GM fish such as Salmon.
- Regulation: The government of every country has their own regulations of GMO development.

## FOOD LABELLING

Food Labelling may be defined as a written communication of all the information that a potential need to know about the product on sale besides ensuring safety standards set by the regulatory body. An effective, elaborate and comprehensive label creates a good impression in the mind of the potential customer about the product.

## Importance of Food Labelling

- It acts as a link between the manufacturer and the distributor
- It acts as an important link between the manufacturer and the potential consumer
- It helps the manufacturer to create an impression on the customer
- It helps the buyer to compare the same product marketed by different manufacturers
- It helps the customers to buy the product of their need/choice
- The customer feels safe to buy a product.

The food items which are packafged must have a label in accordance to the Food Safety and Standards (Packaging and Labelling) Regulations, 2011, notified by Food Safety and Standards Authority of India (FASSAI). The packaged foods which are going to exported must have a label as per the food laws & regulations applicable to the country which is importing it.

In order to safe guard the interest of the consumer, the Food Safety and Standards (Packaging and Labeling) Regulations, 2011, provides that every packaged food article has to be labeled and it shall provide the following information:: -

1. The name of Food
2. List of Ingredients,
3. Nutritional Information,
4. Declaration regarding Veg or non-veg,
5. Declaration regarding Food Additives,
6. Name and complete address of the manufacturer or packer
7. Net Quantity,
8. Code No,/Lot No./Batch No.,
9. Date of manufacture or packing,
10. Best Before and Use By Date,
11. Country of Origin for imported food and
12. Instructions for use

In addition to the above information the manufacturer or the packer has to also ensure that the label complies with the general requirements of labeling prescribed under the regulations I.e. the label should not become separated from the container, contents on the label shall be correct, clear and readily legible and shall be in English or Hindi language, etc.

It is very easy to notice the defect in labeling through visual inspection and there is no need to send the sample for analysis and no analysis report is required to identify the labeling defects. If the food product is not labeled in accordance to the regulations or it does not provide the required complete information or the food product is promoted for sale with false, misleading or deceptive claims then it is considered as misbranded food and attracts the penalties as given below-

## OFFENCES & PENALTIES

1. Misbranded Food Up to 3lakh rupee
2. Misleading advertisement Up to 10lakh rupees

The consumer can notice the labeling defect easily through visual inspection and that may create suspicion about the quality of the product also in the mind of the consumer.

If during food inspection the regulator notices any labeling defect then it creates doubt in the mind of the regulator about the quality of the food product also and invariably the sample of such food product is taken and sent for analysis for the check of its quality. If the sample is found confirming to standards, the prosecution is launched for misbranding. The Food Business Operator should understand the importance of correct labeling and if the label declaration is incorrect and not in accordance to the regulations then the food business operator have to face the punishments as per the laws and regulations.

## NEWER TRENDS IN FOOD PACKAGING AND TECHNOLOGY

There have been a lot of changes in the way food used to be packed. The technology has invented newer and better way of packaging.

The changes in food packaging have taken place for the following reasons:

- Demand for more convenient packing
- Longer shelf life
- More demand for ready to eat, tasty, colourful and flavourful foods
- Higher safety and better quality
- Changed life style with less time for cooking.

All the above reasons have contributed towards a great change in the way foods are packed these days. Bio-active packaging which involve intentional interaction with the food or its surroundings and influence on consumer's health has been a major breakthrough in the field of packaging technology.

The newer and innovative food packaging techniques provide the following advantages:

- Active packaging
- Intelligent packaging

- Increased shelf life
- Better quality control
- Providing indication
- Better freshness of food products
- Hindering of oxidation and respiratory process
- Prevents microbial growth
- Prevents/absorbs moisture
- Preservative releaser
- Use of $CO_2$ scavenger/emitters
- Ethylene scavengers
- Aroma emitters
- Time-temperature sensors
- Ripeness indicators
- Bio-sensors
- Sustained release of antioxidants during storage
- Increased safety

## Active Packaging

Active packaging caters to the demand for environment-friendly packaging material. The materials used in active packaging are natural, recyclable and bio-degradable. It increases the shelf life and safety of the food by changing the condition of the foods. It has very little environmental effect and gets easily degraded. The most recent active packaging even contains some additives which has anti-microbial effect.

## Intelligent/Smart Packaging

Intelligent packaging or Smart packaging may be defined as packaging with involvement of intentional association between food and its package or between food and its surroundings by which the quality, characteristics and safety is increased. The principal purposes of intelligent packaging are-

- To regulate internal and external conditions of the packaging
- To check the quality of food product by the use of indicators for the safety of packaged food .

Therefore, Intelligent packaging or Smart packaging has the following novel technological advancements-

### *Time-temperature regulator*

This type of food packaging monitors the actual shelf life and optimum storage conditions of the foods. It helps by informing the exact temperature and number of days a highly perishable item such as meat and fish can be stored.

*Ripeness regulator*

This type of packaging, as the name suggests, helps in regulating the ripeness thereby helps in maintaining food safety and quality.

*Bio-sensors*

A biosensor is a chemical sensor that uses specific biochemical reactions to detect chemical, thermal or optical signals of the foods in the package.

*RFID or Radio Frequency Identification*

It helps the food manufacturer and the distributors to have full control by continuous visibility of their supply chain.

*Edible coating*

Edible films and coatings offer huge future potential to satisfy the consumer desire for environment friendly and natural foods. They do not completely replace traditional food packaging materials but provide extra functionalities to the food.

In both Active and Intelligent Packaging the following aspects must be kept in mind to ensure the food safety and quality:

- Labeling: Proper labeling should be done in order to prevent misuse and misunderstanding by the consumers.
- The migration of active and intelligent substances with respect to their toxicity should comply with food legislation.

## KEY TERMS

- Emerging Pathogen: An emerging pathogen may be defined as the microbes of an infectious disease, the incidence of such infectious disease had increased for the last two decades or threaten to increase in future in a new or existing host population.
- The examples of emerging pathogens are:
- E. coli O 157.H7, Hantavirus, HIV/AIDS, Severe Acute Respiratory syndrome (SARS),
- Cryptosporidiosis, MRSA, H1N1 Influenza.
- Genetically Modified Foods: According to the World Health Organisation, "Genetically modified organisms or GMOs can be defined as organisms ( i.e. plants, animals or microorganisms) in which the genetic material (DNA) has been altered in a way that does not occur naturally by mating and/or natural recombination. The technology is often called 'modern biotechnology' or 'gene technology', sometimes also 'recombined DNA technology' or 'genetic technology'. Foods produced from or by using GM organisms are often referred to as GM foods or Genetically Modified Foods or GM Foods or Genetically Engineered Foods or Bio-engineered Foods. These are the foods produced from

organisms that have had changes introduced into their DNA using the methods of genetic engineering.

- GMO: Genetically Modified Organism
- Food Labelling: Food Labelling may be defined as a written communication of all the information that a potential need to know about the product on sale besides ensuring safety standards set by the regulatory body. An effective, elaborate and comprehensive label creates a good impression in the mind of the potential customer about the product.
- Active Packaging: Active packaging caters to the demand for environment-friendly packaging material. The materials used in active packaging are natural, recyclable and bio-degradable. It increases the shelf life and safety of the food by changing the condition of the foods. It has very little environmental effect and gets easily degraded. The most recent active packaging even contains some additives which has anti-microbial effect.
- Intelligent/Smart Packaging: Intelligent packaging or Smart packaging may be defined as packaging with involvement of intentional association between food and its package or between food and its surroundings by which the quality, characteristics and safety is increased.

## IMPORTANT QUESTIONS

Q.1. Explain Emerging Pathogens

Q.2. What do you understand by Genetically Modified Foods?

Q.3. write short notes on

a) Food labelling

b) Newer trends in packaging

c) BSE

Chapter 38

# Glossary

**Adulterant** means any material which is or could be employed for the purposes of adulteration.

**Adulteration** it includes intentional addition ,substitution or abstraction or substances which adversely affect the purity and quality of foods incidental contamination of foods with deleterious substance such as toxins and insecticides due to ignorance ,negligence or lack of proper storage facilities .contamination of the foods with harmful insects, micro organism like bacteria ,fungus, moulds etc during production, storage and handling.

**Consumer** means persons and families purchasing and receiving food in order to meet their personal needs.

**Contaminant** means any substance ,not intentionally added to food ,which is present in such food as a result of the production (including operations carried out in crop husbandry or veterinary medicine),manufacture ,processing ,preparation , treatment, ,packing, packaging, , transport or handling such foods or as a result of environmental contamination ,but does not include insect fragments ,rodent hair and other extraneous matter .

**Enforcement authority** means an authority prescribed by the act, rules, and regulation for the purpose of enforcement of this act.

**Enforcement officer** means the officer by whom they are to be enforced and executed and includes food inspector and the state commissioner of food safety and authorised officer of the food authority.

**Food (or "foodstuff"**) means any substance or product , whether processed , partially processed or unprocessed , consumed by humans and includes , drinking water, chewing gum and beverages .

**Food authority** means any substances which is added to food for a technological purpose in the manufacture , processing , preparation or treatment of such food affects the characteristics of such foods, but does not include contaminants .

**Food hygiene** means all the condition and measures necessary for the manufacture, processing, sale, storage and distribution of food designed to ensure safe and wholesome food for human consumption.

**Food inspector** means an officer authorised by the state commissioner for food safety to enforce and execute rules and regulation, order and any other provision of this act relating to manufacture, distribution, sales of articles of food.

**Food laboratory** means any laboratory or institute established by the central or the state governments or any other agency and accredited by national accreditation board for testing and calibration of testing laboratories (NABL) and recognised by food authority.

**Food law** means the law acts, order, rules, regulation , notification and order governing food at every stage of its production ,processing and distribution .

**Genetically modified food** or GMF means the food ,which is produced through techniques in which the genetic material has been altered

**Hazard** means a biological, chemical or physical agent in food with the potential to cause an adverse effect on the health of consumer.

**Ingredien**t means any substance, including a food additive used in a manufacture or preparation of food and present in the final product although in a modified form .

**Irradiation** means any physical procedure, involving the intentional exposure of food to ionizing radiation.

**Label** means any tag brand mark pictorial or other descriptive matter or display.

Active Packaging: Active packaging caters to the demand for environment-friendly packaging material. The materials used in active packaging are natural, recyclable and bio-degradable. It increases the shelf life and safety of the food by changing the condition of the foods. It has very little environmental effect and gets easily degraded. The most recent active packaging even contains some additives which has anti-microbial effect.

**Ale**: Ale is a fermented beverage made from malted barley.

Amphiphilic: Amphiphilic i.e. they have both hydrophobic and hydrophilic parts, which allow the two liquids to blend together.

**Anti-biotic**: - The word antibiotic has been derived from the Greek word Antiviotika. It is also called antibacterials. It either kills or inhibits the growth of bacteria. The term antibiotic means 'opposing life'. In 1928, Sir Alexander Fleming identified Penicillium , a molecule produced by certain molds that kills or stops the growth of certain kinds of bacteria. Penicillin is produced by fungi in the genus Penicillium. The production of the active compounds is carried out using fermentation. Producing antibiotics can be done by three methods e.g. natural fermentation, semi-synthetic and synthetic. Industrial microbiology can be used to produce antibiotics via the process of fermentation, where the source microorganism is grown in large containers.

Anti-Oxidants: Foods such as fats get rancid because the fatty acids present in it gets oxidised. The oxygen present in the atmosphere reacts with fatty acids and bring about rancidity in fats which makes it unfit for consumption. Addition of antioxidants helps in stopping this chemical changes in fats.

**Bacilli**: These are in the shapes of rods and tubes. The Bacilli can change into **spores**. These spores protect them from unfavourable conditions such as heat and cold. They remain inactive and do not grow at this stage. When in **spores** they cannot be destroyed by heat and cold which otherwise will kill them. This spore formation helps Clostridium Botulinum withstand severe conditions. When the condition becomes congenial again they become active and starts reproducing.

***Bacterial Toxin***: Bacterial toxins may be defined as toxic substances that are produced by their activities and released to target other bacteria and host cells. Bacterial toxins are -

**Exotoxins**: Exotoxins are those toxins which are separated from the cells producing it.

Bacteriophages: Viruses that attack bacteria are called Bacteriophages

Baking: -Baking is a heat treatment process used to hinder spoilage of food. The temperature, generally, do not exceed 100°C. The baking of breads, cakes etc. use this heat treatment method. Ropiness in bread is caused by the bacteria which do not get killed by the heat-treatment.

**Beer:** Beer is an alcoholic beverage manufactured by a long process in which the sugar in Wort is converted by yeasts to alcohol and carbon dioxide. The strain of yeasts used is Saccharomyces Carlbergensis.

**Binary Fission**: Binary Fission is a type of reproduction by which a cell divides into two cells and then into four and so on.

**BIS**: BIS or Bureau of Indian Standards

$$C_{12}H_{22}O_{11} + H_2O \text{——} 2C_6H_{12}O_6$$

$$C_6H_{12}O_6 \xrightarrow[\text{Heterolactic bacteria}]{\text{By the action of}} CH_3CHOHCOOH + C_2H_5OH + CO_2$$

$$C_6H_{12}O_6 \xrightarrow[\text{Heterolactic bacteria e.g. Lactobacilli}]{\text{By the action of}} CH_3CHOHCOOH$$

$$C_6H_{12}O_6 \xrightarrow{\text{By the action of Yeast}} 2C_2H_5OH + 2CO_2$$

**Canning**: Canning may defined as a method of preservation of food in an air-tight containers which is subjected to heat treatment to destroy the spoilage microbes.

**Capsule:** The capsule is a jelly-like layer that protects the bacteria during unfavourable conditions such as heat and cold. This acts as a thick protective layer.

Chemical spoilage: The Chemical type of spoilage includes chemical toxicity, enzyme spoilage, rancidity, non-enzyme browning etc.

**Cider**: Fermented beverages made from apples.

**Class I Preservative**: No legal restrictions are imposed on the use of Class I Preservatives. The Class I Preservatives include the items such as sugar, salt, glucose, fructose, alcohol, spices, vinegar, honey, wood smoke ( wood smoke is used for giving flavour to the food as well as preservation). The addition of either sugar or salt dehydrates the food, thus the growth of microorganisms is prevented due to lack of moisture content.

**Class II Preservatives**: The use of Class II Preservatives is restricted by law. The Class II Preservatives are chemicals added to some of the foods in a definite quantity to prevent the growth of microorganisms. Whenever these are used, it must be mentioned on the label. This preservative includes the salt of fumaric acid, sulphurous acid, propionic acid, acetic acid, benzoic acid etc. These preservatives are commonly used in Tomato sauce ( Benzoic acid and its salts), meat items (nitrates and nitrites of sodium and potassium). Sorbic acid and its salts are used for the preservation of various fruit juices, jams, sauces, margarine etc.

**Cleaning Agent**: Cleaning Agents may be defined as the substances used to get rid of dust, stains, foul smells and soils on surfaces. The cleaning agents may be liquids, powders, sprays or granules.

**Cleaning**: In food sectors, cleaning may be defined as a process by which food soil is removed by using right detergent chemical under recommended conditions. The cleaning staff should have the knowledge of different types of food soils and how to remove these. The right way of cleaning and disinfecting of food products contact surfaces is rinse, clean, rinse and sanitize.

**Cocci:** These are round-shaped bacteria.

**Codex:** Codex Alimentary Commission is a joint committee on food standards for international business. Codex is responsible for scientific research and tasting of foods. It sets standards for minimum level of pesticide residues, provides guidelines for food contaminants, sets standard for all the processed, semi-processed and raw foods etc.

**Cold Storage***:* In the catering industry all perishable food items such as eggs, meats, vegetables, fruits are stored in cold storage before use in the kitchen. The temperature is above freezing point and thus the growth and activities of spoilage microbes are arrested.

**Compulsory/Mandatory Standards:** This is the minimum standard a food product must have to ensure quality and safety. It is the duty of the government, international organisation and private companies to enforce the compulsory/ mandatory standards so that quality and safety of the food product is maintained.

**Contaminants:** Contaminants may be defined as any biological or chemical agent, foreign matter or any other substances that may compromise food quality, safety and suitability for human consumption.

**Contamination:** Contamination may be defined as the addition, intentional or accidental, of a contaminant in the food meant for human consumption. Thus contamination of food may occur from air, soil, water, animal, human, insects, pests etc.

**Control (noun):** The state wherein correct procedures are being followed and criteria are being met.

**Control (verb):** To take all necessary actions to ensure and maintain compliance with criteria established in the HACCP plan.

**Control measure:** Any action and activity that can be used to prevent and eliminate a food safety hazard or reduce it to an acceptable level.

Cook Chill: This is another method of preservation in which cooked food is subjected to rapid chilling and then stored at a temperature ranging between $0^0$C to $03^0$ C. in this method food is cooked first to kill the flora of vegetative bacteria present in the food. Food must be reheated at above $70^0$ C, served and consumed within an hour otherwise discarded.

Cook Freeze: As the name suggests, the food is cooked and then subjected to blast freezing at around $-20^0$C, and subsequently, stored at the same temperature. Food must be reheated at 75°C, served, consumed or discarded.

**Corrective action:** Any action to be taken when the results of monitoring at the CCP indicate a loss of control.

**Critical Control Point (CCP):** A step at which control can be applied and is essential to prevent and eliminate a food safety hazard or reduce it to an acceptable level.

**Critical limit:** A criterion which separates acceptability from unacceptability from unacceptability.

Cryptosporidiosis, MRSA, H1N1 Influenza.

**Deviation:** Failure to meet a critical limit.

Disinfect: To Disinfect means to inanimate objects and to destroy all the vegetative cells (not spores).

Disinfectant: Disinfectants may be defined as antimicrobial agents which are used on the non-living objects to kill the flora of microorganisms living on the surface of the object. It is less effective than the sanitizers as it does not kill the spore-forming bacteria. But a sanitizer will destroy all types of bacteria. Therefore, sanitisers kill as well as disinfects. The disinfectant destroys the cell-walls of microorganisms or disrupts their metabolism process. In hospitality industries the disinfectants are mostly used in the kitchens and toilets.

**DNA**: Deoxyribonucleic acid.

**Drinking water**: Drinking water may be defined as water required for the consumption of the mankind for the purposes of drinking and cooking from any source.

**E. coli** O 157.H7, Hantavirus, HIV/AIDS, Severe Acute Respiratory syndrome (SARS),

**Emerging Pathogen**: An emerging pathogen may be defined as the microbes of an infectious disease, the incidence of such infectious disease had increased for the last two decades or threaten to increase in future in a new or existing host population.

**Emulsions**: The word "emulsion" has been derived from the Latin word "to milk", the reason being milk is an emulsion of fat and water. An **emulsion** can be described as a mixture of two or more liquids that are un-mixable. Emulsions are part of a more general class of two-phase systems of matter termed as Colloids. But in culinary world the term Emulsion is used as both phases, dispersed and continuous, are liquids. Therefore, in an emulsion, one liquid or the dispersed phase dispersed in the another phase or the continuous phase.

**Endotoxin:** Endotoxins are part of cell-wall of Gram-negative bacteria.

**FERMENTATION**: Fermentation may be defined as a process in which a substance goes through chemical breakdown by the action of microorganisms (e.g. bacteria, fungi, yeast etc.), also produces heat and gases. Therefore, fermentation is a metabolic process in which yeasts and bacteria consumes sugar in the absence of oxygen and produces alcohol or organic acids and gases. So, this is an energy-releasing metabolic process that takes place under anaerobic conditions. But if the sugars are available, the presence or absence of oxygen has little effect. A chemical representation of fermentation is given below in which glucose is broken down by the action of yeasts to produce Ethyl alcohol or Ethanol—

**Flagella:** This is like a thread which is found on the outer surface of bacteria that helps bacteria in movement.

**Flow diagram:** A systematic representation of the sequence of steps and operation used in the production or manufacture of a particular food items.

**Food Additive**: The World health organization (WHO), in 1965, had defined food additives as "A food additive is a substance or mixture of substances, other than the basic food staff, which is present in food area result of any aspect of production, processing, storage or packaging. The term does not include chance contamination". It is clear from the above definition that food additives are substances which are added to the food intentionally. Therefore, it is expected that the food producers must use additives which are safe for human consumption.

**Food Hygiene:** Food hygiene may be defined as all conditions and measures necessary to ensure the safety and suitability of food at all the stages of the food chain.

**FOOD LABELLING:** Food Labelling may be defined as a written communication of all the information that a potential need to know about the product on sale besides ensuring safety standards set by the regulatory body. An effective, elaborate and comprehensive label creates a good impression in the mind of the potential customer about the product.

**Food Safety**: Food safety may be defined as an assurance that food will not cause harm to the consumer when it is prepared and/or eaten according to its intended use.

**Food spoilage**: Food spoilage may be defined as a process in which food deteriorates to the point in which it is no longer safe or becomes unfit for human consumption.

**Food Standard:** The Food Standard Agency of U.K. has given the following definition- "Food Standard is a set of criteria that a food must meet if it is to be suitable for human consumption, such as source, composition, appearances, freshness, permissible additives and maximum bacterial control".

**Food Suitability:** Food suitability may be defined as an assurance that food is acceptable for human consumption according to its intended use.

**Frozen Storage/ Freezing**: By this method the growth and activities of spoilage microorganisms are completely stopped and the food enzyme reactions are hampered. However, it is recommended to blanch the vegetables, whenever possible, before freezing to get better results.

**Frying:** The outer part of the food gets hotter whereas the inner part of the food gets cooked at a temperature below $100^0$ C.

**FSSAI :** Food Safety and Standards Authority of India.

**Fungi**: Fungus is the plural form of fungi

**Genetically Modified Foods**: According to the World Health Organisation, "Genetically modified organisms or GMOs can be defined as organisms ( i.e. plants, animals or microorganisms) in which the genetic material (DNA) has been altered in a way that does not occur naturally by mating and/or natural recombination. The technology is often called 'modern biotechnology' or 'gene technology', sometimes also 'recombined DNA technology' or 'genetic technology'. Foods produced from or by using GM organisms are often referred to as GM foods or Genetically Modified Foods or GM Foods or Genetically Engineered Foods or Bio-engineered Foods. These are the foods produced from organisms that have had changes introduced into their DNA using the methods of genetic engineering.

**Ginger Beer**: Less alcoholic, made from fermentation ginger and sugar solution.

**GMO**: Genetically Modified Organism

**GMP or Good Manufacturing**: - GMP or Good Manufacturing Practices may be defined as the essential practices followed during the operations of a food business which ensures safe production of food. GMP is an essential and integral part of Hazard Analysis and Critical Control Point or HACCP food system in food industry.

**Good Hygiene Practices**: Good Hygiene Practices are the set of requirements to prevent contamination of food in order to provide safe food to the consumers. It refers to post harvest handling of produce to minimize contamination.

**HACCP plan:** A document prepared in accordance with the principles of HACCP to ensure control of hazards which are significant for food safety in the segment of the food chain under consideration.

**HACCP:** A system which identifies, evaluates, and control hazards which are significant of food safety.

**Hazard analysis:** The process of collecting and evaluating information on hazards and conditions leading to their presence to decide which are significant for food safety and therefore should be addressed in the HACCP plan.

**Hazard:** A biological, chemical or physical agent in, or condition of, food with the potential to cause an adverse health effect.

**Hetero-lactic-Fermentation:** Hetero-lactic Fermentation are the fermentations in which some lactate is metabolized further and results in Ethyl alcohol, carbon-di-oxide, Acetate or other metabolic products. Therefore, some bacteria produce a mixture of acid plus neutral products and are termed as Hetero-lactic Fermentation. Chemical representation would be—

Homo-lactic Fermentation: ***Homo-lactic Fermentations*** (producing only lactic acid) is the simplest type of fermentation. Some bacteria produce only lactic acid during fermentation, so is termed as Homo-lactic Fermentation.

In case of yogurts and cheese, lactose is fermented into glucose first.

**Incubation period:** The time between the ingestion of foods and appearance of the first symptom of disease is called the Incubation Period.

*Infections* will refer to food borne diseases caused by the entrance of microorganisms into the body through the ingestion of contaminated food items. Therefore, infection occurs when live bacterial cells are ingested via food.

**Information Standards**: The information standards gives the guidelines about the information provided none the labels. These deals with what all should be communicated about the product to the prospective consumers.

Intelligent/Smart Packaging: Intelligent packaging or Smart packaging may be defined as packaging with involvement of intentional association between food and its package or between food and its surroundings by which the quality, characteristics and safety is increased.

**International Organisation for Standards (ISO):** ISO or the International Organisation for Standards is the largest global organisation, which sets standards for quality managements, food safety managements, Lab management etc. The ISO 22000 is used for Food Safety Management Standards. It helps to maintain international standards for global trade of food products.

**Intoxications** are the food borne diseases caused by the presence of toxins in the food items. The toxicants may come from some plants or animals or from a toxic metabolic product excreted by a microorganism.

IRRADIATION: Irradiation is a process by which an item is exposed to radiation.

**LTH**: LTH method or Low Temperature Holding method, food is subjected to low temperature for a longer period of time.

**Microbial spoilage**: The microbial spoilage is due to the growth of microorganism in or on the food items.

**Microbiological Criterion**: A microbiological criterion for food defines the acceptability of a product or a food lot, based on the absence or presence, or number of microorganisms including parasites, and/or quantity of their toxins/metabolites, per unit(s) of mass, volume, area or lot.

**Microorganism/microbe**: A microorganism or microbe is a microscopic organism, which may be single-celled or multi-cellular. The study of microorganism is called Microbiology. It was Antonie Van Leeuwenhoke , who discovered microorganism in 1670. Louis Pasteur found out, that it was microorganisms which are responsible for the spoilage of food. Mr. Robert Koch, latter, found out that microorganisms are responsible for causing diseases also. Microorganisms include Bacteria, virus, protozoa, Algae, Fungi etc. it does not include some other microscopic organisms such as Eelworm and Rotifiers.

Mycology: Study of fungi is called mycology

**Mycotoxicosis:** It is a disease which is caused due to natural toxin produced by fungus.

**Mycotoxins**:-The word mycotoxin has been derived from the Greek word, Mykes means Fungus and Toxikon means Poison. Mycotoxins are toxic secondary metabolite produce by fungus, which can lead to diseases and death in human if ingested through contaminated food.

Non-Perishable Food items :- These are the food items which has a much longer shelf life such as rice, atta, sugar, etc.

Parasitology: Parasitology is the study of parasites.

Pasteurization: Pasteurisation may be defined as a heat treatment method by which the microorganisms present can be partly destroyed by heating at below 100°C. pasteurization process is best employed when the food contains lesser number of heat-resistant microbes and the food is also subjected to another preservative process e.g. Chilling.

Perishable or Highly Perishable Food items: All the foods that get spoiled fast are included in this category. Examples include fish, meat, poultry, milk, eggs, majority of the fruits and vegetables.

***Pesticide Residues***: -Pesticide may be defined as a substance which is used on the crops to destroy the organisms which may damage the crops.

Physical spoilage: The Physical spoilage includes the damage of the outer surface and dryness of the food item.

Preservatives: Preservatives are those food additives which are added to the food to prevent or slow down the growth of pathogens in or on the food. The growth of microorganisms is the food results in food spoilage and food poisoning which leads to wastage, diseases and revenue loss. Therefore preservatives play an important role in increasing the shelf-life of the food. Chemical preservatives are those food additives which are purposefully added to stop deterioration of food. Use of nitrates in food reduces the growth of botulism. Benzoates, Sodium/ calcium propionates are used extensively for the prevention of microbial attacks.

**Process Standards**: As is obvious from the term itself, the process standard gives the guidelines about how a food item should be produced.

**Product Standards**; - The product standards as the name suggests gives the guidelines about the features and characteristics of the food items should be.

**Pulque**: American alcoholic beverage just like beer, produced by natural fermentation by yeast of Agave juice.

**RNA**: Ribonucleic acid. RNA translates genetic information from DNA into proteins.

Roasting*:* Another heat treatment method to prevent spoilage of food. The temperature used is about $60^0$ C to $80^0$ C.

**Sake**: Sake is a Japanese yellow rice wine or beer.

Sanitize: To Sanitize means to minimize microbes to levels that is safe from a public health viewpoint. The official definition (Association of Official Analytical Chemists) of sanitizing for food product contact surfaces is a process which reduces the contamination level by 99.999% (5 logs) in 30 sec. General types of sanitization include the following.

Semi-Perishable Food Items: This group includes all the food items which have comparatively longer shelf life if they are stored properly. This group includes potatoes, onion, apples, etc.

Simmering*:* This is a cooking method in which food is cooked by gentle heat. The temperature is below $100^0$ C.

**Spirilla:** These bacteria are spiral in shape. These bacteria are not harmful to humans.

**Sterilize**: To sterilize means to destroy and remove all living organisms.

The examples of emerging pathogens are:

The HTST method: HTST or High Temperature Short Time method. As the name suggests, food is subjected to high temperature for a shorter period of time.

**TQM or Total Quality Management:** TQM or Total Quality Management may be defined as an on-going effort by the management and staff members of an organization earn customer loyalty and customer satisfaction.

UHTS: The UHTS or Ultra High Temperature Sterilization method, foods are subjected at above $135^0$ C for only 02 seconds.

**Vector:** A carrier of contamination.

**Virion**: A single virus is called a Virion.

**Virology**: The study of virus is called Virology.

**Voluntary Standards**: These are additional standards followed by food manufacturers other than the Compulsory/Mandatory Standards to get an upper-hand over their competitors.

**Waste Disposal**: Waste Disposal may be defined as a suitable and safe action needed to manage wastes from its point of origin till final disposal. This action in a hotel will typically include proper collection, safe transport and treatment and finally disposed/recycled as per the guidelines of regulatory authority.

**Waste Water**: Waste Water may be defined as water that got un-hygienically affected, has poor quality and anthropogenic influence.

**WHO**: World health organization

**Wines**: Wines are alcoholic beverages produced by the fermentation of freshly gathered grape's juice, at the place of their origin, according to the local tradition and custom. Nothing artificial is added to it. The fermentation starts by the addition of yeasts. Wines are also produced by fermenting juice of Rhubarb, berries, dandelions etc.

Chapter 39

# Question Bank

NATIONAL COUNCIL FOR HOTEL MANAGEMENT AND CATERING TECHNOLOGY, NOIDA

ACADEMIC YEAR-2016-2017

COURSE: 3RD SEMESTER OF 3-YEAR B. SC. IN H &HA

SUBJECT: FOOD SAFETY AND QUALITY

TIME ALLOWED: 2Hrs. Max. Marks: 50

**(Marks allotted to each question are given in brackets)**

Q1. Define Food Contaminants. Discuss the various types of food contaminants.

Or

Define food adulteration. Discuss the simple tests used for detection of commonly used adulterants in foods. (10)

Q2. Enlist different national and international food laws and regulations. Discuss FSSA, 2006, in details.

Or

Enlist the general principles of food hygiene. Discuss the GHP for various Commodities and equipment used in kitchen (10)

Q3. What do you understand by HACCP? Discuss the principles of HACCP

Or

What is HACCP? Discuss the potential benefits of implementation of principles of HACCP by a catering establishment ( 10 )

Q4. Write short notes on any two ( 2x5=10 )

(a) Genetically modified tools

(b) Characteristics of a food label

(c) Types of a food storage

(d) Food hazards

Q5. Discuss the role of micro-organisms in the fermentation of foods.

Or

List the measures to be adopted to prevent food borne diseases ( 5 )

Q6. What do you understand by food additives? Discuss the role of food preservatives in the preparation of food.

Or

Discuss any five methods of food preservation ( 5 )

## NATIONAL COUNCIL FOR HOTEL MANAGEMENT AND CATERING TECHNOLOGY, NOIDA

### ACADEMIC YEAR-2016-2017

### COURSE: 4TH SEMESTER OF 3-YEAR B.SC. IN H & HA

### SUBJECT: Food Safety and Quality

TIME ALLOWED: 2Hrs. Max. Marks: 50

**(Marks allotted to each question are given in brackets)**

Q1. Explain the principles of HACCP and discuss its importance in the food sector.

OR

Discuss Quality assurance system comprising TQM, JIT, KAIZEN & Quality Cycle. (10)

Q.2. Discuss the importance of FSSAI and food industries.

OR

Discuss various methods of food preservation in detail. (10)

Q.3. State the factors for the growth and multiplication of microorganisms and classify them based on these factors. (5)

Q.4. Define "food Additives". Discuss different food additives used. (5)

Q.5. Explain the following terms:

a) CAC b) CPA c) ISO d) MPO e) FPO (5x1=5)

Q.6. Chefs depend on microorganisms. Discuss with examples. (5)

Q.7. Food borne illness is caused due to lack of knowledge of food hygiene, kitchen hygiene and personal hygiene. Discuss in brief. (10)

## NATIONAL COUNCIL FOR HOTEL MANAGEMENT AND CATERING TECHNOLOGY, NOIDA

### ACADEMIC YEAR-2015-2016

### COURSE: 4TH SEMESTER OF 3-YEAR B. SC. IN H &HA

### SUBJECT: Food Safety and Quality

TIME ALLOWED: 2Hrs. Max. Marks: 50

**(Marks allotted to each question are given in brackets)**

Q.1. List and discuss the various factors responsible for growth of bacteria. Also explain the growth curve of bacteria. (10)

Q.2. Define Food Additives. Classify and explain various food additives being used in the hotel kitchen.

OR

Discuss in details the various methods of food preservation. (10)

Q.3. What do you mean by food adulteration? Enlist various food adulterants.

OR

Discuss beneficial role of microorganisms in food industry. (5)

Q.4. Write short notes on any two:

(a) Essential Commodities Act (b) AGMARK (c) FPO (2x2.5=5)

Q.5. Why personal hygiene is important in food sector? (5)

Q.6. Discuss HACCP and its principles. (5)

Q.7. What are the various cleaning agents used in the hotel industry? (5)

Q.8. What is GMF and BSE?

OR

Discuss various food borne diseases. (5)

## NATIONAL COUNCIL FOR HOTEL MANAGEMENT AND CATERING TECHNOLOGY, NOIDA

### ACADEMIC YEAR-2016-2017

### COURSE: 3RD SEMESTER OF 3-YEAR B. SC. IN H &HA

### SUBJECT: FOOD SAFETY AND QUALITY

TIME ALLOWED: 2Hrs. Max. Marks: 50

**(Marks allotted to each question are given in brackets)**

Q.1. (a) What is a food label and its requirement?

(b) List the hygiene control measures during the processing of food. (5+5=10)

Q.2. Define the following terms (any two):

Risk analysis

3E's of food safety

Food additives (2.5+2.5=5)

Q.3. Describe the role of international standards in meeting the emerging challenges of global food trade. (5)

Q.4. How does consumer protection act protect the rights of the consumer?

OR

Describe the functions of colouring agents flavouring substances and leavening agents in food processing citing suitable examples. (5)

Q.5. Explain the causes and symptoms of food infections of bacterial origin.

OR

Define fermentation and give examples of fermented food. (5)

Q.6. Explain growth curve of micro-organisms.

OR

Describe the morphological characteristics of different micro-organisms found in food. (5)

Q.7. (a) Explain risk analysis with its components.

(b) List points to improve the quality of risky street vended food. (5)

Q.8. State True or False:

Cooking destroys vegetative cells and spores of pathogen.

Danger zone temperature ranges from 25°C- 40°C.

Anaerobes can grow in absence of free oxygen.

Saccharomyces cerevisiae is used for fermentation of bread dough.

The toxin produced by clostridium botulinum is one of the most toxic substances known.

Gelatine, a food additive is an antioxidant.

Alcoholic beverages are adulterated with methanol and mineral oil.

Appearance of bluish black colour on addition of iodine solution to milk

Indicates that the sample is pure.

Food safety and standards act, 2006 has replaced PFA Act, 1954.

The GM foods do not pose any potential risk to human health or for the Environment. (10×1=10)

## NATIONAL COUNCIL FOR HOTEL MANAGEMENT AND CATERING TECHNOLOGY, NOIDA

### ACADEMIC YEAR-2013-2014

### COURSE: 3RD SEMESTER OF 3-YEAR B. SC. IN H &HA

### SUBJECT: FOOD SAFETY AND QUALITY

TIME ALLOWED: 2Hrs. Max. Marks: 50

**(Marks allotted to each question are given in brackets)**

Q.1. Discuss the various factors affecting the growth of micro-organisms along with the Growth Curve. (10)

Q.2. Explain the principles of HACCP and discuss its importance in food sector. (10)

Q.3. What is food contamination and its various sources? Discuss in detail.

OR

Discuss the various methods of food preservation in detail. (10)

Q.4. (a) Explain the following terms:

i) GAP

ii) GMP

iii) PFA

iv) WHO

v) FPO

(b) Differentiate between food additives and adulterants. Give example of each.

(5+5=10)

Q.5. Discuss food packaging along with classifying packaging materials.

OR

Discuss the role of codex alimentarius and WHO in food industry. (10)

## NATIONAL COUNCIL FOR HOTEL MANAGEMENT AND CATERING TECHNOLOGY, NOIDA

### ACADEMIC YEAR-2012-2013

### COURSE: 3RD SEMESTER OF 3-YEAR B. SC. IN H &HA

### SUBJECT: Food Safety and Quality

TIME ALLOWED: 2Hrs. Max. Marks: 50

**(Marks allotted to each question are given in brackets)**

Q.1. Explain the growth of bacteria. Discuss the factors affecting the growth of Bacteria in food. (10)

Q.2. List and explain the various methods of food preservation. (10)

Q.3. Explain the basic principles of food preservation.

OR

What is contamination? Explain the different sources of food contamination. (5)

Q.4. What is fermentation? Describe the different types of fermentation.

OR

What is foods borne diseases? Explain the different agents responsible for food Borne diseases. (5)

Q.5. Write the benefits of HACCP to the society. (5)

Q.6. Explain the various types of cleaning agents used in food sector.

OR

What are food additives? List types of additives with examples. (5)

Q.7. Explain the risk analysis with its components. What are the steps followed to Identify the risk assessment in food sector? (5)

Q.8. Expand and write short notes on: (5)

(a) PFA

(b) FSSA

(c) MAP

(d) BSE

(e) GMP

**SUBJECT CODE:BHM207 EXAM DATE :24.04.2015**

**NATIONAL COUNCIL FOR HOTEL MANAGEMENT AND CATERING TECHNOLOGY,NOIDA**

**ACADEMIC YEAR 2014-2015**

**COURSE : 4TH SEMESTER OF 3-YEAR B.SC IN H&HA**

**SUBJECT : FOOD SAFETY & QUALITY**

TIME ALLOWED : 02 Hours MAX. MARKS: 50

**(Marks allotted to each question are given in brackets)**

Q1. Define "food additives" .Explain different food additives used in food preparation in form of Sweeteners, antioxidants, preservation, colours and flavours. (2+8=10)

Q2 Food borne illness is caused due to lack of knowledge about food hygiene, kitchen hygiene and personal hygiene. Discuss in brief. (10)

Q3 Write short notes on: (5x1=5)

(a)PFA

(b) FSSA

(c) FSSAI

(d) CAC

(e) WTO

Q4 Discuss factors favourable for the growth and multiplication of microorganisms.

OR

State and explain the beneficial and harmful effects of micro-organisms with example. (5)

Q5 TQM is a quality assurance system. State its element and applications. (5)

Q6 List basic components of food labelling.

OR

What are the basic principles of HACCP. (5)

State the sources of contaminations. (2+3=5)

Q7 (a) Explain risk analysis with its components

(b) List points to improve the quality of risky street vended food. (2+3=5)

Q8 Fill in the blanks:

GHP stands for __________

__________ is the toxin present in CL. Botulinum.

__________ is the heat resistant pathogen present in milk.

MPO stands for __________ in national food legislation.

_________ is the common adulterant in milk. (5x1=5)

## SUBJECT CODE: BHM207

## NATIONAL COUNCIL FOR HOTEL MANAGEMENT AND CATERING TECHNOLOGY, NOIDA

## ACADEMIC YEAR-2014-2015

## COURSE: 3RD SEMESTER OF 3 YEAR B.S IN H&HA

**SUBJECT: Food Safety & Quality**

TIME ALLOWED: 02 Hours MAX.MARKS:50

**(MARKS ALLOTED TO EACH QUESTION ARE GIVEN IN BRACKETS)**

1. (a) What favourable conditions are necessary for growth of micro-organisms?

   (b) List and explain various principles of food preservation. (5+5=10)

2. What are the common borne infections?

   OR

   Explain the importance of food safety to hospitality industry. (10)

3. Write short notes on any two:

   (a) Food poisoning (b) Food additives (c) HACCP (2*2½=5)

4. Explain briefly (5x1=5)

   (a) TQM

   (b) GMP

   (c) Genetically modified foods

   (d) Food label ling

   (e) ISO

5. Explain various cleaning and disinfection methods along with agents commonly used in hospitality industry.

   OR

   Briefly state how waste water and waste disposal is treated in hotels. (5)

6. Briefly explain the micro-organisms role in hotel industry.

   OR

   Differentiate between food infection and food intoxication (5)

7. State the methods of detection of various adulterants found in the following:

   (a) Maize fibre in saffron

   (b) Dried papaya seeds in peppercorns

   (c) Saw dust in chilli powder

(d) Chicory in coffee

(e) Horse dung powder in coriander (5x1=5)

8. Expand the following (any five): (5x1=5)

(a) PFA

(b) MPO

(c) BIS

(d) WHO

(e) FPO

(f) BSE

**Q/NOV/ODD/14-15/01 PAGE 1OF1**

**NATIONAL COUNCIL FOR HOTEL MANAGEMENT AND CATERING TECHNOLOGY, NOIDA**

**ACADEMIC YEAR 2013-2014**

**COURSE : 4TH SEMESTER OF 3-YEAR B.SC. IN H&HA**

**2nd year of 3 year B. Sc in H&HA**

**SUBJECT : Food Safety &quality**

TIME ALLOWED : 02 Hours MAX MARKS 50

**( Marks allotted to each question are given in bracket )**

1.(a) discuss the method of preservation (ANY TWO) (5+5=10)

(b) Define Food adulteration with examples.

2. Elaborate on essential Commodity Act and Consumer Protection Act. (10)
3. Write short notes on any two : (2*2.5=5)

   (a)Waste disposable

   (b) Food additives

   (c) GMP

   (d) ISO
4. Discuss the new trends in food packaging.

   or

   List mandatory of food label (5)
5. HACCP is an essential form of Quality Assurance. Discuss

   or

   Chefs are dependent on microorganisms. Discuss with examples. (5)

   6. What are the 3E's of food safety?

   Or

   Which is the common food borne microorganism? (5)
7. What are the causes of spoilage of canned foods and eggs ? (5)
8. Discuss any two food borne diseases and also its preventive measure. (5)

Chapter 40

# Abbreviations Used in this Book

AGMARK: -Agricultural Produce (Grading and Marketing) Act. **AG** for Agricultural And **Mark** for Marketing.

BHA: Butylated Hydroxy Anisole

BIS: Bureau of Indian Standards

BSE: Bovine Spongiform Encephalopathy

CCP: Critical Control Point

CJD: Creutzfeldt-Jakib Disease

EEC: Enteropathogenic Escherichia coli

FAO: Food and Agriculture Organisation

FDA: Food and Drug Administration

FIFO: First In First Out

FPO: Fruit Products Order

FSSAI: Food Safety and Standards Authority of India

GAP: Good Agricultural Practice

GHP:-Good Hygiene Practice

GMO: Genetically Modified Organisms

GMP: Good Manufacturing Practices

HACCP: Hazard Analysis Critical Control Point

ISO: International Organisation for Standardisation

LTH: Low Holding Time

MMPO: Milk and Milk Products Order

PDCA: Plan-Do-Check-Act

PFA: Prevention of Food Adulteration Act

Ppm: Parts per million

RFID: Radio Frequency Identification

RH: Relative Humidity

SRM: Sanitation Risk Management

TQM: Total Quality Management

UHTS: Ultra High Temperature Sterilization

UV: Ultra Violet

WHO: World Health Organisation

# Bibliography


*Applied Science for FOOD Studies*, V.L.Brownsell, C.J.Griffith, Eleri Jones, Longman Scientific & Technical, England.

*CRC Handbook Series in Nutrition and Food*, Miloslav Recheigh, CRC Press Inc. Ohio

*Food Microbiology* by William C, Frazier and Denis C. Westhoff, fourth edition, Tata Mcgraw-Hill Publishing Company.

*Nutrition an inquiry into the issues*, P.J. Long/ Barbara Shannon, Prentice-Hall, Inc. New Jersey.

*Nutrition for the Foodservice Professional*, K.E.Drummonel, Van Nostrand. Reinhold.

*Nutrition science and application*, Leri A. Smolin & Mary B. Grosvenor, Saunder College Publishing, New York.

*Quantity Food Production*, Planning and Management. John B. Knight, Lendal H. Kotschevar. CBI Publishing Company Inc. Massachusetts.

*Robinson's Basic Nutrition and Diet Therap*y, Eighth edition, E.S. Weigley, D.H. Muller, C.H. Robinson. Merrill, New Jersey.

*Understanding Nutrition*, eighth edition, E.N. Whitney, S.R. Rolfes, West Wadshorth an International Publishing Company.

*WHO Technical reports*

*Wikipedia*, Encyclopedia and other free electronic references (websites)

# NHTET Practice Paper

1. Why the body needs nutrients?

Ans. Body needs nutrients for proper growth, optimum energy, maintenance and repair.

2. If a person consumes diet high in saturated fats, which disease he is most likely to get?

Ans. Cardiovascular disease.

3. Which vitamin we get from citrus fruits?

Ans. Vitamin C.

4. What the 'milk, cheese and yogurt group' are required for?

Ans. To build strong bones, muscles and teeth.

5. Which vitamin is known as Sunshine Vitamin?

Ans. Vitamin D.

6. Which vitamin provides us with strong immune system and connective tissues?

Ans. Vitamin C.

7. Name a good dietary source of omega-3 fatty acid.

Ans. Fish.

8. Deficiency which vitamin causes spina bifida?

Ans. Folate.

9. Which vitamin is required for healthy vision?

Ans. Vitamin A.

10. The deficiency of which nutrient our body can easily tolerate.

Ans. Lipids.

11. The AGMARK standard is set by which organisation?

Ans. Directorate of Marketing and Inspection, GOI.

12. Amongst vitamin A, K, C and D, which one gets destroyed by heat?

Ans. Vitamin A.

13. Name a food item which is a rich source of vitamin B.

Ans. Fish, meat, dairy, eggs.

14. Amongst cellulose, Pectin, Lignin and Agar, which is not a component of dietary fibre?

Ans. Cellulose is a dietary fibre.

15. What is 'cold sterilization'?

Ans. Ionising Radiation.

16. What is most heat resistant, anaerobic, spore forming pathogen that can grow in low acid canned food?

Ans. Clostridium Botulium.

17. Which of the following describes fermentation?

a. Anaerobic degradation of carbohydrates

b. Putrefaction of protein.

c. Hydrolysis of carbohydrates

d. Denaturation of proteins.

Ans. A (anaerobic degradation of carbohydrates).

18. What is the term that describes all of chemical reactions occurring inside organisms?

Ans. Metabolism

19. What is a food called that has ability to cause a sharp rise in blood glucose?

Ans. Glycemic effect/Hyperglycaemia/hypoglycaemia/glycaemia food.

20. What is the ideal temperature for pathogens to flourish?

Ans. 40°F to 140°F or 5°C to 60°C (Danger Zone)

21. How is Margarine different from butter?

Ans. Butter is dairy based, made from milk, rose water & less fat and calories. Margarine is oil based with 80% Veg. Oil.

22. What is absorbed by large intestine?

Ans. Water

23. What is Benedict Solution?

Ans. A blue solution with Sodium Carbonate, Sodium Cifnate & $CuSO_4$.

24. Which nutrient does not get absorbed or digested but is required by body implant?

Ans. Fibre

25. When iodine is added to starch, what colour is formed?

Ans. Blue-black colour.

26. What are body's primary sources of energy?

Ans. Carbohydrates.

27. The 'Energy Currency of Cells' is?

Ans. ATP or Adenosine Triphosphate.

28. Fatty Fish are good source of?

Ans. Omega-3 fatty acids and proteins.

29. How a potassium-rich diet helps us?

Ans. It helps us to control blood pressure.

30. Name some food items rich in Potassium.

Ans. Banana (420mg), one cup yogurt (530mg), Orange juice (1 cup 500mg), Broccoli (460 mg 1 cup).

31. How much fibre is required for us every day?

Ans. 21 grams to 35 grams.

32. Name the live bacteria and yeasts that are good for health, especially for digestive system.

Ans. Probiotics.

33. 'When starch is heated with water, it absorbs water, swells and forms a paste and then stiffens forming a gel'——-What this process is known as?

Ans. Gelatinization.

34. What is the term used to describe the re-crystallization of the gelatinized starch?

Ans. Retrogradation.

35. Which penetrometer is used to determine the stiffnes of carbohydrate gels?

Ans. The Bloom Gelometer.

36. 'Dextrines are polysaccharides'—-True or False?

Ans. True.

37. When dry heat is applied to bread it gets brown, as in the case of toasts—Why?

Ans. The starch in bread gets converted into dextrin, which is brown in colour.

38. What is the leakage of liquid from a gel known as?

Ans. Synersis.

39. What is Autoxidation?

Ans. It is the oxidation that occurs in the presence of open atmospheric air or in the presence of oxygen and forms peroxides and hydroperocides.

40. "Higher the concentration of fat, higher will be the shortening power"—-true or false?

Ans. True.

41. What is objective of refining fats and oils?

Ans. To prevent degradation, to eliminate undesirable components, elimination of undesirable products to preserve vitamins, reduce losses etc.

42. What are proteins made by?

Ans. Amino Acids.

43. "Proteins are primary components of Enzymes, Antibodies, Hormones and Blood"_ true or false?

Ans. True.

44. Name the bond by which amino acids are joined?

Ans. Peptide Bonds.

45. What is the term used to describe the mixture of two or more liquids that are immiscible?

Ans. Emulsion.

46. What is TVP?

Ans. Textured Vegetable Protein or Protein Analogs (these are produced by plant protein)

47. What is native protein?

Ans. Native protein are the protein found in the in the cells an din its fluids of the living tissues of plants and animals.

48. What is mean by BV or Biological value?

Ans. BV is proportion of nitrogen absorbed that is retained by the body for the growth and maintenance. This helps us to determine Protein Quality.

49. What is Sterilization?

Ans. Cold sterilization or Ionizing Radiation is the modern innovation which kills all the disease-causing microbes without raising temperature.

50. Who invented canning?

Ans. Canning was invented by Nicolas Appert.

51. At what temperature the disease causing micro-organisms become inactive?

Ans. At -10° C.

52. What is the temperature of the domestic freezers?

Ans. -18°C

53. At what temperature the enzyme activity of stored food is stopped and the food quality is retained?

Ans. At -18°C.

52. What is the temperature maintained by commercial freezers?

Ans. Commercial freezers stone food at -29°C.

53. What is Food Additive?

Ans. Food additive may be defined as chemical substances intentionally added to food to increase food quality.

54. Which preservatives include all those substances, the additions of which are not governed by law?

Ans. Class I preservatives.

55. Name some class I preservatives.

Ans. Honey, sugar salt, spices, alcohol, vinegar etc.

56. Name some nutrients which are destroyed during processing of food.

Ans. Vitamin B, Thiamine, Nicotinic Acids, Minerals, Iron, calcium.

57. What is primary use of Antioxidants?

Ans. It stops oxidation of fats and delays the process of oxidative rancidity.

58. What is Humectants?

Ans. Humectants are food additives which reduce the effect of humidity on food by absorbing moisture for e.g. Baking powder.

59. Name some artificial sweeteners.

Ans. Aspartane, Saccharine, isomalt, Xylitol etc.

60. What are MAP and CAP?

Ans. MAP— Modified Atmosphere Packaging

CAP—Controlled Atmosphere Packaging.

62. Name the equipment used for measuring viscosity of liquid items?

Ans. Viscometer.

63. What is Bancroft Rule?

Ans. Bancroft rule states that "the phase in which an emulsifier is more soluble constitutes the continuous phase"

64. What is an Emulsifier?

Ans. An emulsifier is a substance that stabilizes an emulsion.

65. What is Food Theology?

Ans. It is the study of consistency and flow of food under tightly specified condition.

66. What is sol?

Ans. It may be defined as colloidal suspension of very small particles in a continuous liquid medium.

67. "Gelatin is a sol when hot and a gel when cool"- true or false?

Ans. True

68. What is a gel?

Ans. It is a solid jelly like material that can have properties ranging from soft and weak to hard and tough.

69. What is True Solution?

Ans. In true solution the size of particles are up to 1 mill- micron.

70. What is Browning?

Ans. It is the process of food turning brown because of the chemical reaction between an amino acid and reducing sugar at an elevated temperature (sugar-protein reaction).It is a non enzymatic browning.

71. At what temperature caramelisation takes place?

Ans. At 163 to 170 degree Celsius.

72. What is SDA?

Ans. Specific Dynamic Action or SDA refers to that amount of the energy expenditure of the body which needs energy for digestion, ingestion, absorption, transportation, utilization, storage and exertion. The other term used for calorigenic effect of food or thermic effect of food or diet induced thermo genesis.

73. Can vitamins-A be synthesised by our body?

Ans. No it is essential nutrient for vision but our body cannot synthesize it.

74. Can Lecithin be synthesized by our body?

Ans. Yes.

75. Does water provide energy?

Ans. No

76. How much calories are provided by carbohydrates?

Ans. Carbohydrates provides 04K calories or 16.7K joules per gram.

77. How much calories are provided by fats?

Ans. Fats provides 09 kilo calories or 37.6 kilo joule/gm.

78. How much calories are provided by proteins?

Ans. Proteins provide 04 k calories or 16.7 k joule per gram.

79. What is Basal Metabolism?

Ans. Basal Metabolism is a term used for mountainous of vital body functions such as respiration, blood circulation, kidney functions, beating of heart, regulating body temperature etc.

80. How much energy is used- required for basal metabolism or involuntary activities of our body?

Ans. Nearly 60%-75% of total energy requirement.

81. What is BMR or BEE?

Ans. The BMR (Basal Metabolic Rate) or BEE (Basal Energy Expenditure) is defined as - "Measure of the minimum amount of energy that an awake, resting body requires to maintain the basic life sustaining, vital functions" e.g. Blood circulation, Breathing, Heartbeat, kidney functions, maintaining body temperature and maintaining muscles.

82. What is Energy Balance?

Ans. When the amount of energy consumed by the body through diet equals to the amount of energy expanded by the body, the state is called energy balance.

83. If the body-weight is 10% to 20% above the desirable weight then what the condition will be termed as?

Ans. Over-weight.

84. If someone's body-weight is more than 20% above the desirable weight then what the condition will be termed as?

Ans. Obese.

85. What is Crude Fibres?

Ans. Crude Fibre is a fibre that remains after a food has been treated with acids and base.

86. Name some food source of insoluble fibre?

Ans. Wheat-bran, rye bran, broccoli etc.

87. Name some food sources of soluble dietary fibre?

Ans. Oat-bran, apple, beans etc

88. Name a poly-saccharides found in animals?

Ans. Glycogen.

89. Name the poly-saccharides found in plants?

Ans. Starches and fibres,

90. What is VLDL?

Ans. Very Low Density Lipoprotein. It consist of mainly tri-glycerides.

91. What is LDL?

Ans. Low Density Lipoproteins. Synthesized by liver. Main carrier of cholesterol.

92. What is HDL?

Ans. High Density Lipoprotein. High in protein, commonly known as good cholesterol.

93. Name some food items which have no cholesterol.

Ans. Egg white & all plant food.

94. What is USFA?

Ans. Unsaturated Fatty Acids.

95. What is MUFA?

Ans. Mono-saturated fatty acids.

96. What is Complete Protein?

Ans. Complete proteins are those proteins which provide all the essential amino acids in the right amount and right proportion as needed by a body such as milk, eggs, cheese, curd, fish, meat, poultry etc.

97. Name the water-soluble vitamins.

Ans. Vitamin B & Vitamin C

98. Name the fat-soluble vitamins.

Ans. Vitamins A, D, E, K.

99. Which Vitamin is also called Thymine?

Ans. Vitamin $B_1$

100. Which vitamin is also called Riboflavin?

Ans. Vitamin $B_2$ (Riboflavin)

101. Which Vitamin is also known as Niacin?

Ans. Vitamin $B_{3.}$

102. What is Cynocobalamin?

Ans. It is vitamin $B_{12}$ . It is man-made. Vitamin $B_{12}$ contains approximately 4%-5% cobalt

103. What is the daily requirement of Minor Minerals (or Trace Minerals or Micro Minerals) in our body per day?

Ans. The daily requirement of Minor minerals is less than 100 mg. per day.

104. Name some minor Minerals.

Ans. Iron, Zinc, Copper, Magnesium, Iodine and Selenium.

105. What is minor Mineral/Trace Mineral/Micro Minerals?

Ans. These are the essential mineral nutrients found in the human body in amount less than 05g( or present in the body in amounts less than 0.01% of body weight.

106. Name the proteins in the body where most of the body's iron is found.

Ans. Haemoglobin in the RBC and myoglobin in the muscle cells.

107. Name the disease caused by the deficiency of iron.

Ans. Anaemia.

108. Name one disease caused by the deficiency of iodine.

Ans. Goitre.

109. What is water balance?

Ans. Water balance may be defined as the equalisation between water intake and water output of the body.

110. What is ORT?

Ans. Oral Rehydration Therapy.

111. What is water Intoxication?

Ans. Water intoxication results in excess intake of water.

112. Name the three Basic Food Groups.

Ans. Energy providing, Body-building and Protective Food Groups.

113. What is Kempner's Rice Diet?

Ans. Kempner, in 1948, had given a strict rice fruit sugar diet (2000Kcal) for individuals having high BP.

114. What is Prebiotics?

Ans. Prebiotics are non-digestible substances that help the growth of bacteria and fungi, which are beneficial to the host.

115. What is Antioxidants?

Ans. It is a molecule that stops the oxidation of other molecules. An antioxidant such as Thiols or Ascorbic acid stops the chain reaction of oxidation which damage cells by producing for radicals, vitamin A, vitamin etc.

116. What is Neutraceutical?

Ans. A Neutraceutical is a pharmaceutical-grade and standard nutrients. These are products extracted from food sources that are purported to provide extra benefit for health.

117. What is Megavitamin Therapy ?

Ans. Megavitamin Therapy is one use of large amount of vitamins, much more than RDA to prevent or treat diseases. It is mainly used in alternative medicine.

119. "Bacteria belong to Prokaryotic cells"_ True or False?

Ans. True. Prokaryotic cells do not contain nucleous.

120. "Bacteria unicellular plants contain chlorophyll, _ true or false?

Ans. Bacteria belong to unicellular plants but do not contain chlorophyll.

121. What is Binary Fission?

Ans. Binary Fission is a type of reproduction by which a cell divide into two cells and then into four cells and so on.

122. "Virus can be crystallised and stored" _ true or false?

Ans. True.

123. A single virus is called?

Ans. Virion.

124. What are Endoparasites and Ectoparasites?

Ans. Endoparasites remain inside a host's body. Ectoparasites line on a Host's body surface to feed.

125. What is Prokaryotic cells?

Ans. It does not have a well defined nucleous with nuclear membrane. The only organelle is Ribosome.

126. What is Eukaryotic cell?

Ans. It has a well defined nucleous and membrane bound cell organelles.

127. What helps bacteria to move?

Ans. Flagella.

128. What is bacteria phases?

Ans. These are viruses that attack bacteria.

129. What are HTST method, LTH and VHTS method?

Ans. HTST method or High Temperature Short Time Method. LTH method or Low Temperature method. UHTS or Ultra High Temperature Sterilization method.

130. What is Canning?

Ans. Canning may be defined as method of preservation of food in an air tight container which is subjected to heat treatment to destroy the spoilage microbes.

131. What is Irradiation?

Ans. Irradiation is a process by which an item is exposed to radiation.

132. What is cold sterilization or Ionizing Radiation?

Ans. It has been observed that "high frequency with shorter wavelength radiation" are effective in destroying microorganisms in the food and also food temperature remain normal.

133. What is Homo-lactic Fermentation?

Ans. Some bacteria produce only lactic acid during fermentation, so it is termed as Homo-Lactic Fermentation.

134. What is Hetero-lactic Fermentation?

Ans. In this case some lactate is metabolized further and result in ethyl alcohol, $CO_2$, Acetate or other metabolic products. This fermentation produce a mixture of acid plus neutral products and are termed as Hetero-Lactic Fermentation.

135. What is Sauerkraut?

Ans. It is obtained by the process of fermentation of shredded cabbage. The salt content is restricted from 2-3% by weight. The microorganisms used in ENTEROBACTOR.

136. What is FSSAI?

Ans. Food Safety and Standards Authority of India

137. What is CODEX?

Ans. Codex Alimentary Commission is a joint committee on food standards for international business. CODEX is responsible for International reserved and tasting of foods.

138. What is ISO?

Ans. ISO or the International Organisation for standards is the largest global organisation, which sets standards for quality management, food safety management, lab management etc.

139. Which ISO number is used for Food Safety Management Standard?

Ans. ISO 22,000.

140. PSP and SP are seafood poisoning. Give the full forms.

Ans. Paralytic Shellfish Poisoning and Scombroid Poisoning.

141. What is TQM?

Ans. TQM or Total Quality Management is an on going effort by the management and staff members od an organisation to earn customer loyalty and customer satisfaction.

142. What is Pareto Chart?

Ans. It is a tool of TQM. Pareto Chart helps employees to identify the problems, prioritize them and also determine their frequency in the system.

143. What is Histogram?

Ans. It is a tool of TQM. It is graphical representation showing intensity of particular problem. It helps to identify the cause of problems in the system by the shape and width of the distribution.

144. What are the four categories, TQM can be divided?

Ans. The Four categories are Plan, Do, Check and Act.

145. What is GMP?

Ans. GMP is good Manufacturing Practices.

147. What is HACCP?

Ans. HACCP is Hazard Analysis and Critical Control Point.

148. What is FPO?

Ans. Fruit Products Order.

149. What is WTO?

Ans. World Trade Organisation.

150. What is TBT?

Ans. Technical Barriers to Trade.

151. What is RTIMs?

Ans. Trade Related Investment Measures.

152. What is AOA?

Ans. Agreement on Agriculture.

153. What is GHP?

Ans. Good Hygiene Practices.

154. What is BIS?

Ans. Bureau of Indian Standards.

155. What is GMF?

Ans. Genetically Modified Foods.

156. What is GEF?

Ans. GEF or Genetically Engineered Food.

157. What is BEF?

Ans. BEF or BIO-Engineered Food.

158. What is RFID?

Ans. RIFD stands for Radio Frequency Identification.

# Index

## FOOD SCIENCE

## NUTRITION

## FOOD SAFETY AND QUALITY